From Eternity to Eternity

From Eternity to Eternity

Memoirs of a Korean Buddhist Nun

Bulpil Sunim

Translated by
Eunsu Cho, with Soojin Oh

Cover photograph by Minsook Kim

Published by State University of New York Press, Albany

Korean edition first published in 2012 by Gimm-Young Publishers, Inc.
© Bulpil Sunim, 2012

© 2024 State University of New York

For information, contact State University of New York Press, Albany, NY
www.sunypress.edu

Library of Congress Cataloging-in-Publication Data

Names: Bulpil Sunim, author. | Cho, Eunsu, translator. | Oh, Soojin, translator.
Title: From eternity to eternity: memoirs of a Korean Buddhist / Bulpil Sunim and
    Eunsu Cho with Soojin Oh.
Description: Albany : State University of New York Press, [2024] | Includes
    bibliographical references and index.
Identifiers: ISBN 9798855800425 (hardcover : alk. paper) | ISBN 9798855800432
    (ebook) | ISBN 9798855800418 (pbk. : alk. paper)
Further information is available at the Library of Congress.

Dedicated to the memory of
Seongcheol Keun Sunim

Heading Alone toward the Truth of Immortality

彌天大業紅爐雪跨海雄基赫日露
誰人甘死片時夢超然獨步萬古眞

Unimaginably great achievements are but snowflakes melting on a fire,
Foundations spanning entire oceans are but dewdrops disappearing in
    sunlight.
Who doesn't live but a dream in this fleeting, illusory world before dying?
I walk aloof and alone toward the eternal truth.

> —Seongcheol Sunim, when entering the
> monastery 1936 at twenty-five years of age[1]

Contents

viii ✿ Contents

Illustrations

Translator's Acknowledgments

My personal and academic interest in Buddhist nuns came unexpectedly into my life quite late. The field of gender studies and the topic of women in Buddhism were rather new to me, as my main training and research was on the theoretical analysis of ancient Buddhist philosophical writings produced in India, China, and Korea. However, when I began teaching Korean Buddhism at the University of Michigan, my undergraduate students made me wake up to the fact that philosophy is simply one of many facets of religion, and that people are more interested in how Buddhism functions in people's lives. This was Buddhism as a living tradition, not a text or scroll from antiquity. The scope of my understanding of Buddhism expanded tremendously through my teaching, in many ways. Then, after a complex series of causes and conditions, I came to publish an edited volume on Korean Buddhist nuns and laywomen. I am always grateful, academically and personally, for all the surrounding events that led me to that moment.

Through these years of researching Korean Buddhist nuns, I am continuously overwhelmed by the existential dimension of the lives of these religious women, their relentless pursuit of the meaning of life and what lies beyond it, and also shocked by the extreme dearth of extant publications of their writings or records of their lives. In that sense, it was a great relief to find *Women in Korean Zen: Lives and Practices* by Martine Batchelor, the story of a young French woman living in Korean nunneries for ten years in the 1970s, as it was almost the only readable source of information on the daily lives of Korean Buddhist nuns. It also contained a valuable biography of Seongyeong Sunim, an elder nun and a lifelong Zen practitioner, and became one of the first such works to reveal the monastic lives of Korean Buddhist nuns who lived throughout the twentieth century, decades before Korea became the country that we know today. It was my great fortune, with the encouragement of Martine, to have an opportunity to translate this book into Korean.

Bulpil Sunim's memoir was originally published in Korea in 2012 and was an instant success, becoming a top-twenty seller within two weeks of publication. Korea's largest newspapers wrote reviews and it earned major publication awards. This success was partly due to the reputation of her father, Seongcheol Sunim, the mysterious and charismatic monk who was probably the most outstanding figure in the last fifty years of Korean Buddhist history, but her writing was of great merit in itself. Readers are drawn to the heart and courage of this female practitioner; her genuine sense of dedication and religious resolution, sprinkled with her unique humor and levity, make us both cry in sympathy and laugh with joy at her cheerful and innocent mind.

I am very grateful for the generous financial support of the White Lotus Foundation of Buddhist Culture and Wontaek Sunim, the Chair of the Board, in completing this project. I am also deeply appreciative of the assistance provided by the Literature Translation Institute of Korea for Joe Choe's initial translation. I would also like to take this opportunity to thank my daughters, Soojin and Catherine, for being an invaluable part of this endeavor. From the moment they joined the project, they were able to revitalize my halting first steps, as they brought a new vigor and a different writing style to the table. In the end, this work became a project that united my family, bringing me a humbling sense of great fortune.

I am grateful for Lunah Kim, who produced the map of notable places in the book and helped with the cover design. I owe thanks to the Yale University Council on East Asian Studies and Department of Religious Studies, which invited me to New Haven as a visiting professor in 2023–2024, during which time I was able to stay in the States and focus on completion of this manuscript, for which I am immensely grateful.

For all of this, I would like to express my deep gratitude and respect for Bulpil Sunim, who has encouraged me to work hard and to not give up. When I visited her to ask questions about the text, she had a great feast prepared just for me. She once mentioned to me her old age, something I realized to be her indirect way of telling me that time moves quickly, and we don't know what may come to us in each new moment. How imminent life is! Along the way I have also become inclined to adopt parts of her lifestyle. I've even started performing 108 prostrations every day upon her suggestion. My children joked to me last winter, "Mom, we'll be alright if you become a nun." No way! I don't intend to, but in their eyes, I must seem like I'm moving closer to a certain direction. This journey of translation was a long one, but I have learned and earned a lot through this path, and that's another reason why I feel so lucky to have met Bulpil Sunim and her book in this life. I hope this book can do for its readers what it has done for me—expanding the horizon of life, ever widening.

Translator's Introduction

The Women's Buddhist Tradition in Korea

Korea is one of the only places in the world where the traditional style of Buddhist monastic training continues to be authentically preserved and practiced in its original form. Contrary to the common perception that Korean Buddhist history up until the very recent present simply equals the history of monks, the history of nuns is visible in historical records and biographical excerpts, and we can see, albeit fragmentarily, that Korean nuns have maintained a tradition of religious practice and commitment to the Dharma from the very inception of Buddhism in Korea. This is important not simply for Korean Buddhist history, but for Buddhist history more broadly, and for women's roles in all histories.

Stretching back 1,600 years, Korean nuns hold a prominent place in the history of world religion. When the monks' order was formed upon the transmission of Buddhism to Korea, a nuns' order was established almost simultaneously. It is well known that nuns traveled to Japan during Korea's Baekje dynasty (18 BCE–660 CE) and played a decisive role in the establishment of a nuns' order there. At present, Korea is one of the few countries in the world to maintain a bhiksuni (Sk. *bhikṣuṇī*, Pali. *bhikkhuni*, Kr. *biguni*; fully ordained nunhood) order, and Korean nuns have built a thriving monastic community that has not only survived near-obliteration during the Joseon dynasty (1392–1897) and afterward but now flourishes in the present, reflected in the order's continuing growth, its social activism, and its meditation programs. The combination of longevity and dynamism make the Korean bhiksuni order one of the most vibrant female monastic communities in the modern world, Buddhist or otherwise.

This memoir by Bulpil Sunim (1937–) is a vivid firsthand description of one very significant life within this order and her experiences
as a Korean female Buddhist nun and meditation practitioner. Born the
daughter of the late Seongcheol Sunim (Sŏngchŏl, SongChol, Song-chol,
1912–1993), a monk who indelibly defined modern Korean Buddhism,
she is herself a senior Buddhist nun and a leading figure and teacher of
Korean Seon (Ch. Chan, J. Zen, McCune-Reischauer Kr. romanization
system, Sŏn) meditation, philosophy, and practice, the three pillars form-
ing the basis of modern Korean Buddhism. Arguably the most important
female Buddhist figure in contemporary Korean Buddhism, Bulpil Sunim
currently teaches Seon practice at Seongnamsa (Seongnam Monastery),
the most prestigious Seon training center in Korea.

Her autobiography, one of the first of its kind in Korean Buddhist
literature, bears important significance for understanding the contemporary
Korean Buddhist world. The stories within present a picture of traditional
female Korean Seon practice, offering a candid portrayal of a woman's
experience of meditation, its aims and its impact on her life. Inside her
telling are rare glimpses into the often private and overlooked history and
lifestyles of Korean Buddhist nuns. As a journal of seventy-five years of
life, from her birth in 1937 to this book's publication in Korean in 2012,
her autobiography has us follow her path to enlightenment—from early
childhood memories, middle and high school, and then to various episodes
before and after her ordination. Within her one story are multiple tales
of her family, the many friends and companions whom she met along
the path, and of course her father. Finally culminating in her gaining
the renown of being Korea's greatest female Seon practitioner, it is the
intimate record of an incredibly well-led life.

Through its rich detail of the daily life of such an exceptional person, this memoir accessibly introduces Korean Buddhist practice without
simplifying it. It provides a window into the intricacies of the practice
and the lives of the many renowned teachers Bulpil Sunim has encountered on her path. While Robert Buswell's *The Zen Monastic Experience*
(1992) gives a detailed description of monastic life from the perspective
of a nonnative practitioner and ethnographer, this book presents a fresh
and down-to-earth portrayal of Korean monastic culture from a native
practitioner, steeped in its tradition. To the practitioners seeking answers
to the questions commonly asked about the nature of Seon and enlightenment, this book offers them, not from a man's perspective as is so often
the case, but in a woman's voice.

Another intriguing feature of this autobiography is its exploration of the thoughts and teachings of the late Seongcheol Keun Sunim from the unique perspective of his daughter. Bulpil Sunim dives into a remarkable tale that captures their complicated relationship, both as her father but more importantly as her teacher on the path. As she writes, "I was the one closest to Keun Sunim, yet at the same time I needed to be the one furthest removed." We learn that he left his family and his home to pursue the path to "eternal happiness" when Bulpil Sunim was still in the womb. When meeting her father at his hermitage for the first time when she was thirteen years old, instead of being welcomed as his daughter, his only words to her were "Go away!" In that moment, she made the decision to completely surrender her longing for him, her ideas of family, and her ties to him as a father. Standing atop a cliff at the hermitage site overlooking the sea in Busan, she threw her yearning for her father into the ocean. The author reflects today, "It was because my father was heartless that I was able to leave behind my attachment to him."

On their second meeting, he posed an important question to Bulpil:

"So, what is it that you live for?"

"I live for happiness."

"Oh yeah? Well, there's an eternal happiness and a temporary happiness. Which kind of happiness are you trying to live for?"

This conversation was a crucial moment in her life. When she heard the words "eternal happiness," her hatred toward her father melted as if it were a warm spring day. She writes, "My life's path was decided for me the moment he mentioned the idea of eternal happiness. . . . From then on, the name Seongcheol no longer meant 'my father' but instead a true teacher, the one who set me on the path to becoming an eternal being of great freedom."

By this time, Seongcheol was a near-mythological patriarch of the Jogye Order of Korean Buddhism and widely considered a living Buddha. He found renown for his central role in reforming Korean Buddhism in the post–World War II era. It was then, after the end of Japanese rule of Korea in 1945 and the Korean War (1950–1953), that Seongcheol led the revitalization of the tradition together with like-minded monks at Bongamsa in Mungyeong. They vowed to shake off the forcibly imposed legacies of Japanese influence and reestablish the Korean tradition of Seon practice.

Even though he officially held the title of supreme patriarch of the Korean Jogye Order from 1981 to 1991, shortly before his death, Seongcheol led a notoriously mysterious and private life. He rarely made public appearances and spent most of his time secluded in meditation at the hermitage of Baengnyeonam in the monastery of Haeinsa. His death in 1993 was followed by the largest funeral for a monk ever seen in Korean history, with over three hundred thousand mourners flocking to the remote monastery to pay their respects. His Dharma sermons have been collected, some even translated into English, but much of his life, teachings, and legacy still remains shrouded in mystery. Bulpil Sunim's description of her unique relationship with Seongcheol offers the public a rare and personal glimpse of the man and his teachings. The inner aspects of his extremely ascetic lifestyle and meditation training are now revealed for the first time to the outside world.

Another important figure in Bulpil's life is her vocation master Inhong Sunim (1908–1997), a nun widely considered to have cemented the foundations of nunhood in modern Korean Buddhism. The influence of Inhong Sunim on Bulpil's practice and outlook on life is no less than that of her father, Seongcheol Sunim. When they first met, Inhong Sunim was already a prominent nun whose leadership and dedication to practice were well recognized by all the preeminent sunims in Korea.

Korean Buddhism as an institution stood on shaky ground in the 1950s, despite its long and rich history in the country. Having been suppressed by various means with fluctuating intensity during the five hundred years of the Joseon dynasty, Buddhism and Buddhist monks were often held in low regard as a result of the government's anti-Buddhist policies. The situation was even worse for nuns. During the colonial period of 1910–1945, records are limited, but we know that nuns were trying to continue their meditation practice tradition and there were emerging Buddhist nun lecturers who taught scriptures, as well. However their presence was not noticed, as those people mentioned in the official histories of Korean Buddhism are all men. In the rapid modernization that followed the liberation from Japanese rule in 1945, Christianity and other religions showed remarkable growth through aggressive proselytization and flexible adaptation to the times. Meanwhile, Korean Buddhism had lost much of its material foundation and human talent. The traditions of teaching were fading away, qualified teachers were difficult to find, the physical spaces to practice were in shambles, and avenues of financial support dried up.

Facing the reality that these larger threats to Korean Buddhism had even more dire consequences for the Buddhist nuns' order, Inhong Sunim believed that these problems could only be solved through ferocious practice. She believed that the most important thing to do to raise the prestige of Korean nuns was to establish a rigorous practice regimen and strict training rules. It was only after this success that the wider society would be forced to accept and respect their existence. Through her efforts laying the groundwork for what has since become one of the largest communities of Buddhist nuns in the world, she succeeded in restoring the monastic spirit and noble practice traditions of the countless generations of Korean women who sought refuge in the Dharma. As implied by her nickname, the "Tiger of Gajisan," she was incredibly exacting toward her disciples. She emphasized such practices as *hwadu* meditation, prostrations, prayer and chanting, strict adherence to temple regulations, maintaining a communal environment, and physical labor. She also practiced under the guidance of masters such as Seongcheol Sunim, establishing this as a custom at her temple, Seongnamsa. She also took her Seon practice community to try to see Seongcheol after every three-month summer and winter retreat. At the time, Seongcheol had set out a barbed wire fence around his house and had severed all communication with the outside world. When these nuns would come to see him as a group, he would ask them a few questions and inevitably begin shouting, insulting, and scolding them, only to finally throw them out. Nevertheless, the fact that Inhong Sunim and her nuns kept doing so for ten years demonstrates her intent: to set the bar of practice ever higher and harness the emotions of fiery indignation at their treatment to fuel their desire to practice harder. Bulpil Sunim states, "Teaching lectures and offering alms is Dharma, but receiving scorn and getting thrown out is also Dharma. Only one who has been rebuked and thrown out knows the great strength that can be gained from it."

Though the rules were strict and you were expected to devote yourself completely, as a result, Seongnamsa began to flourish as it gained a reputation for being a place where you would learn to practice properly. This unwavering and uncompromising mission enforced by exacting teachers such as Inhong Sunim was the reason Korean Buddhism, and particularly the community of Buddhist nuns, returned to a position of respect and legitimacy while growing dramatically in the 1960s and '70s. Since then, Korean Buddhism has produced many female luminaries: not just accomplished practitioners such as Bulpil, but administrators of the Buddhist Order, scholars who went on to receive doctorates, social activists, and social welfare experts. Consequently, Buddhist nuns have become synonymous with model practitioners who are above reproach in their practice and strict adherence to the monastic code. This achievement owes a great debt to Inhong Sunim, the woman at the forefront of these changes.

The second half of the book is thus full of Bulpil's reminiscences and tributes to her vocation master. We see the many sights she saw traveling as Inhong's attendant, hear recollections of the friendships between her teacher and other elder nuns, and learn the story of the time she accidentally dyed her teacher's robes jet black instead of gray, and how her teacher wore the robes happily regardless. Through Bulpil's telling, we meet the one who taught her, right or wrong, to always examine people's hearts before anything else.

Seongcheol once asked Bulpil, "What kind of master do you want to be?" She replied, "I want to become a master who lives hidden away." These words describe her entire life as a nun. Just as she proclaimed, Bulpil has steadfastly shied away from public activities, focusing only on her personal meditative practice. Despite being widely known as the most spiritually accomplished nun in all of Korean Buddhism, and having taught Seon at Seongnamsa for nearly her entire life as a nun, she has never once served as an abbess of a temple or accepted a position in the administration of the Jogye Order.

Despite her avoidance of monastic administration, Bulpil Sunim is revered for her fierce dedication to practice. She took part in and led several *gyeolsa*, where a group of monastics make a pact to perform long, intensive practice together in pursuit of a certain goal. Their methods of practice were primarily *hwadu* meditation, with twice-daily 300-prostration repentance prayers and recitation of the *Surangama Sutra* dharani, while maintaining ascetic practices such as sleeping less than four hours and only eating two meals a day, with breakfast strictly consisting only of gruel. During certain stretches of intensive practice, she would refuse to even lie down or rest against anything to avoid any interruption of her contemplation of the *hwadu*. When she felt sleepy at night, she would meditate while walking in the mountains for five hours straight. It was after a three-year *gyeolsa* that Bulpil witnessed an incredible sight in a dream: "a brilliant light, as if from a great fire, shining in the mountain facing the meditation hall of Simgeomdang. . . . It may have been a dream, but my *hwadu* was so vibrant." Her incredible modesty and unwillingness to boast about her achievements prevents her from elaborating further, but this moment gives us a momentary glimpse into her spiritual attainment.

When her father passed away in 1993, it was said that all the mountains and rivers wept at his funeral, and over three hundred thousand mourners gathered from across the nation to Haeinsa on the mountain of Gayasan to witness his cremation. Yet Bulpil was not able to attend. As the news of his death brought new public attention to the existence of his daughter, she decided it would be best for his reputation if she kept her distance. Watching over the cremation from far away at the hermitage of Geumganggul, her own residence, she performed nine prostrations toward him: a promise to one day meet him again as an enlightened being of eternal freedom.

In 1997, she watched over Inhong Sunim's passing at Seongnamsa as well, where they received their teacher's final missive: to come together as a community and take good care of the temple. Bulpil continues working to fulfill her teacher's last wish: she spends the summer and winter retreats teaching meditation at Seongnamsa and in the offseason she resides at Geumganggul. (She embarked on the construction project to build Geumganggul, her own hermitage, beginning in 1976, which was finished in 1989 after thirteen years, near Haeinsa, for which she received a stern letter from Seongcheol scolding her for breaking her promise to live as a hidden nun. However, he came for the completion ceremony and gave a blessing.) Today, the author is an established Seon master whose disciples number over one hundred. She presently spends most of her time guiding her students in practice, shaping them into true practitioners.

Map of Notable Locations

Chronology

(*Note*: Ages in Korea are considered to be one at birth to account for time in the womb. The ages in this text have been left according to the original Korean age system.)

1937: Birth in the village of Mukgokri, Sancheong, near the city of Jinju (Seongcheol was born in 1912).

1945 (age nine): Older sister Dogyeong dies at age fourteen.

1948 (age twelve): Moves to Seoul, transfers to Hyehwa Elementary in fifth grade.

1949 (age thirteen): Sixth grade at Hyehwa Elementary. Meets Seongcheol Sunim for the first time when she visited him at the monastery of Myogwaneumsa, Busan, together with her uncle and Myoeom Sunim, only to be harshly rebuffed by his: "Get out! Go!" Seongcheol was then engaged in practice with Hyanggok Sunim.

1950 (age fourteen): Korean War breaks out, Seoul falls to North Korean troops in one day. People's courts and public executions are held. Flees Seoul with her mother after the Han River Bridge is blown up, making a 480-km. journey fraught with danger to Jinju, her hometown.

1951 (age fifteen): Returns to Seoul to study, only to be told to return to Jinju by her grandfather because of the worsening war. Transfers to Jinju Middle School.

1953 (age seventeen): Enrolls at Jinju School of Education.

1954 (age eighteen): Meets Seongcheol for the second time at the hermitage of Cheonjegul at the monastery of Anjeongsa in the city of Tongyeong (his age forty-three). She decides to "pursue eternal happiness" instead of "temporary happiness" and receives her *hwadu*.

1956 (age twenty): Graduates from Jinju School of Education. Seeks out Seongcheol at the hermitage of Seongjeonam in the monastery of Pagyesa along with Okja; receives Dharma notebook from Seongcheol.

1956 summer (age twenty): Begins the life of a postulant at the monastery of Cheongnyangsa, Hapcheon.

1956 fall (age twenty): Visits the hermitage of Yunpilam in Mungyeong and meets with Weolhye Sunim, a senior nun. Witnesses her passing and is strongly moved by her humble funeral.

1956 winter (age twenty): First winter retreat at the monastery of Hongjesa on the mountain of Taebaeksan with Okja and their teacher Inhong Sunim.

1957 summer (age twenty-one): Summer retreat at the hermitage of Myojeokam. Visits Seongcheol in retreat at the hermitage of Seongjeonam in Daegu. Receives the Dharma name "Bulpil."

1957 fall (age twenty-one): Receives sramaneri (novice nun) precepts in an ordination ceremony at Seongnamsa, formally entering the path of nunhood.

1961 March (age twenty-four): Receives bhiksuni (full-fledged nunhood) precepts at the Diamond Ordination platform at the monastery of Tongdosa.

1969–1972: Completes a three-year intensive meditation pact at the monastery of Seongnamsa, then enters a hundred-day no-sleep practice.

1976: Starts construction on the hermitage of Geumganggul, her own temple, near the monastery of Haeinsa, which continues for the next thirteen years.

1993: Seongcheol Sunim passes away.

1997: Her teacher and vocation master, Inhong Sunim, passes away.

2011: Finishes construction of the monastery of Geoboesa at the birth site of her father in Jinju.

Author's Preface

Where Am I Going?

I ponder as I walk down a forest path in Ongnyudong in autumn.

"Where am I going?"

The clear and cold water of the valley gurgles leisurely by, as white clouds rest high atop the mountain of Gajisan. I enter the meditation hall to briefly escape the heat, and I worry. If Seongcheol Sunim were here, what would he say about publishing this book? I remember something he said before he reached Nirvana.

"When I'm gone, you think you'll meet someone like me ever again?"

As I remember all the connections I've had with people, now faded away like shadows, even though I wrote throughout the winter retreat, until my fingers had callused over, I worry that I haven't been able to write what's truly deep inside my heart.

Seongcheol Sunim. The one who guided me to the path of becoming an eternal being of great freedom, moving from eternity to eternity.

Although I was born into this earthly world as Keun Sunim's daughter, not even once have I been able to call him father. From the moment I first saw him when I was eighteen years old at Cheonjegul in Anjeongsa, he was simply a teacher to me, not a father. Nevertheless, it seems as if people around me always saw me as Keun Sunim's daughter.

I was the one closest to Keun Sunim, yet at the same time I needed to be the one furthest removed. For this reason, I did not attend his funeral ceremony and cremation rite. It was only in the late afternoon of the day of his cremation that, on a mountain ridge above Geumganggul,[1] I looked upon the dying funeral pyre and was able to offer him my prostrations. I bowed nine times—three times each for the past, present, and future—as a way of promising to meet again.

I had turned down several proposals to write a book because, as a Seon [Zen] nun who has lived her entire life in the mountains, I questioned whether it was the right thing to do. However, I couldn't refuse the request to commemorate the hundredth year of Keun Sunim's birth by sharing the stories in this book of our meditation and practice alongside the faithful followers at Seongnamsa.

Looking back, not only did Keun Sunim teach the path to truth, he also shared his wisdom on how we should live our lives. I think of all of this as karmic connections, and I shall be grateful if even just one person may be able to live a life of eternal truth through his teachings in this book.

I would like to extend my warmest gratitude to Gimm-Young Publishers and everyone else who has been so generous with their encouragement and support, as well as to Professor Eunsu Cho for her translation and revival of the interest in this humble story.

When I was just a young schoolgirl searching for his guidance, Keun Sunim said to me: "Look at the white snow in the pitch-black night."

I shall end the preface pondering this question.

—Respectfully written by Bulpil
Seongnamsa Meditation Hall
At the end of the summer retreat, Buddhist era 2556 (CE 2012)

Chapter 1

Karmic Connection

Where Will We Meet Again, and as What?

Mukgokri, My Hometown

The village of Mukgokri in Danseongmyeon, Sancheonggun, where I was born, is surrounded by Eomhyesan, a hallowed peak of Jirisan (Jiri Mountain) that stretches from the north to the east, and cradled by the Gyeongho River, which flows west to south into the Nam River in Jinju. A large forest with chestnut, oak, pine, bamboo, and willow trees on the banks of the Gyeongho River encircles the village like a folding screen, and on warm summer nights the villagers would often gather on the white sands of the riverbank to have wrestling matches.

Two mountain peaks overlook our village. One is Munpil Peak, to the east, while the other is known by the locals as Turtle Hilltop, because of a large boulder shaped like a turtle that lies on top, its head casting over to the south like a guardian protecting the village.

The deep blue river that flows swiftly by our village was nicknamed "Queen's Place." The story is that a scholar and his wife built a mud hut on the riverbank a long time ago and gave birth to a baby girl who grew up to become a queen. Beyond the river is Antae Peak, which is named after a prince whose umbilical cord is said to have been buried there. Next to it is the small Pipa Island, so named after a scholar who, after severing ties with the rest of the world, spent his remaining years there playing the pipa (an instrument resembling a lute).

I had a wonderfully innocent childhood growing up in the village that my ancestors had lived in for generations, listening to the stories of Queen's Place, Antae Peak, Pipa Island, and many others. In the spring my friends and I would play in the hills behind the village and pick azalea flowers. In the summer we splashed and swam in the clear waters of the brook that flowed from the mountains. After dinner we would join the grownups by the riverbank, where we lit mosquito coils and enjoyed the cool evening breeze, watching shooting stars fly across the night sky as we marveled at the mysteries of the heavens. Autumn meant going into the forest to hunt for the round chestnuts that lay scattered one by one, more fun than any game in the world.

Our home was surrounded by a chestnut forest, and near the wide field in front of our house my grandfather grew peach, pear, and persimmon trees, the fruits of which we would pick and eat depending on the season.

My grandfather built a two-story wooden house in the chestnut forest by the river where he lived with my grandmother, while my mother and I lived in a house on the large tract of land next to their home. They were both beautiful *hanok*[1] buildings, grand enough to be mistaken for temples if seen from a distance.

My grandfather taught my father the *Thousand-Character Classic* and *Xiaoxue* (The Elementary Learning).[2] I, too, studied the *Thousand-Character Classic* under my grandfather before I entered elementary school. Grandfather's large villa-style house was filled to the brim with books, and the countless varieties of medicinal herbs that he kept on the second floor where he stayed made the place resemble an oriental medicine shop. I can still remember clearly how he would prepare medicine for me by referring to the *Dongeuibogam* (Principles and Practice of Eastern Medicine).

In the warm months when the trees were at their fullest, nightingales would come and flit from this tree to that, singing their beautiful songs, while cuckoos kept the beat with their cries. During cold winter nights, my grandmother would read me old stories by the light of a kerosene lamp as I fell asleep, warm and cozy under a thick blanket. Growing up the way I had, it might have been perfectly natural that I never felt the absence of my father. After all, he had entered the monastery while my mother was still pregnant with me, so I grew up without ever knowing my father's face.

When I was six years old,[3] I was at my grandparents' house playing with my cousins when my aunt came over and gave us each half a sweet persimmon. She had cut the persimmons in half because there were so many of us, but I cried for the whole day afterward. The ridiculous reason for my tantrum was that I wasn't the kind of person who should ever have to eat half a piece of fruit. No end to my tears in sight, my aunt offered me an entire basket of persimmons, but my hurt feelings remained, so I just kept crying and crying. It must have been because I was always treated like a princess by my grandparents growing up.

I think I was quite tomboyish in my childhood. Hanging around my boy cousins, I would see them lifting weights and pick one up myself, not wanting to be outdone. Everyone in my family is quite tall except for me; the weights I'd lifted while I was still growing must have been what kept me short. Even my father, Keun Sunim[4] must have felt I was smaller than the rest of the family because one day he told me, "Short people are that way because they were arrogant in their past lives!"

Here's another memory. One day during the year I was to start elementary school, I tagged along with my youngest aunt who was going out to pick mugwort with her friends. I wasn't very good at harvesting greens, so my basket at the end of the day was almost empty. Returning home, just as we arrived at the front gate, I asked my aunt if I could hold her basket for a while. No sooner had she handed it to me than I ran inside with it, boasting to my grandmother, "Look, Grandma! I dug all these up by myself!" She of course praised what a wonderful job I did, and my aunt never let me come along with her again.

Since I was very young, adults always called me the child with moon-shaped eyes. A face-reading fortune teller once came to our house and, looking at my face, said, "This child's destiny lies outside of the secular world."

In 1944, during the Japanese colonial era (1910–1945) and as the Second World War was raging on, I enrolled at Danseong Elementary School. On my first day I took an entrance exam in front of a teacher, where I was given a physical examination and then told to write my new Japanese name in Chinese characters. During the colonial period, Korean people were forced to change their names to Japanese ones, and though all I had to do to pass was to write my name, I failed the test that day. The official reason was that my body was too frail. In reality, though, it was because my grandfather had refused to yield to pressure and did not change our names. In the end, one of my uncles had to invite the teachers to our home and entertain them with food and drink for me to be accepted into the school.

Korea gained independence on August 15, 1945. The bells of freedom rang loudly in every corner of the country, and in school we sang songs of independence and learned our own language and writing.

If it wasn't for my older sister's sudden death, my happy and innocent childhood might have gone on a little longer. She left this world when I was nine years old, so I don't know how she ever felt about our father's absence or about his entering the monastery.

My sister took after my grandfather's good looks, so her forehead was straight, her nose was sharp and delicate, and her eyes were large and beautiful. She was tall and slender so everybody praised her as a beauty, and she had a wonderful personality as well. Needless to say, she was loved by everyone, especially by our grandparents. The adults brought her along wherever they went, and I watched from a distance as she was showered with love by those around her.

I was more outgoing and tomboyish than my sister. Every time I came home with the ribbon on my dress undone after playing with the boys, my composed and ladylike sister would be my protector, tying it back in place without a word. I was the type to stubbornly push ahead if I didn't agree with something, while my sister was meek and dutiful and would always follow what the adults said.

When my kind and gentle sister was in sixth grade, she read Gyeong-heo Sunim's "Song of Seon Meditation"[5] and wrote a letter to our father, Keun Sunim, at the monastery of Daeseungsa[6] where he was staying, announcing that she wanted to follow in his footsteps as a nun. Although I don't know what was truly in my sister's heart about Buddhism and the monastery, or about our father, I do remember watching her sew a pair of pants which she said she would wear at the temple.

Keun Sunim had severed all ties with his family after he entered the monastery. Perhaps this was why my sister's letter to him was instead delivered to Elder Cheongha Sunim, who wrote a reply saying, "In order to become a great monastic, you must first graduate from school." Receiving this response, she gave up her mission to enter the temple to focus on her studies, eventually going on to pass the entrance exam for Jinju Middle School. The standards for this school were high, and my brilliant sister was the first person from Mukgokri to be accepted there.

My sister was fourteen, and it was Chuseok (Korean Thanksgiving Day, usually late September to early October). After the traditional memorial ceremony, she got all dressed up in pretty clothes and went out with her friends, but when she came home she told us she wasn't feeling well and lay down on the spot. She looked at the palm of her hand and then turned to our mother.

"Mom, you believe in me, right? Don't believe in me."

And three days later, like something in a dream, my sister passed over to the other world. When she died like that, leaving behind her middle school uniform, brand new and beautifully tailored, never once having tried it on—my grandparents' grief and my mother's agony were beyond words. Not a single mouth had words to speak, and our house was plunged into a despondent silence.

A week after she passed, my sister appeared in my mother's dreams, saying she wanted to try on her uniform, so we burned her uniform where she was buried and performed the forty-nine-day funeral ritual for her at Tongdosa.

My father had become a monk by then and was practicing at a small hermitage called Baengnyeonam in the mountains near Tongdosa. Perhaps this was why my grandmother chose this temple to hold the forty-nine-day funeral rite. My father would have known that my sister had passed away. However, he has always been steadfastly silent on family matters or events in his past, so there is no way of knowing how he felt about the death of his fourteen-year-old eldest daughter, who had also wanted to enter the monastery.

The evening of the forty-ninth day, my sister appeared in my aunt's dream and told her, "I'm going to the heavens now. I wouldn't have died if you had made me a nun." She disappeared into a forest lit with a brilliant light, as if on fire, my aunt told us.

My grandfather said the name Seoksun would bring great riches, so our family had called my sister Seoksun at home, rather than her real name of Dogyeong. I was given the name Sugyeong, meaning "live a long life and achieve renown." I feel my sister chose to leave us as early as she did to change her body and be reborn as a monk as quickly as possible, rather than stay in this material world to live in riches. My sister was cremated because she was too young for a grave plot. She became a handful of ash and was buried by a large tree in the mountain behind our home.

"My sister has returned to a handful of dirt. Where did she come from and where could she have gone? What is death, that I can long to see but never see again, and call out to but receive no response? Just what is this existence called 'human'?"

The question "Where do people come from, and where do they go?" that would run through my mind from time to time since I was six or seven years old began to increasingly consume my thoughts after my sister died. The empty space that the sister I had loved so dearly left behind made me realize the futility of life at an early age.

There has been an empty corner in my heart ever since my sister's death. Many years later, during a visit to his dwelling at Cheonjegul, Keun Sunim studied me as I sat in silence before asking, "What are you thinking about?" I was again pondering the question I had been asking myself since I was a child: "Where do people come from, and where do they go?" Keun Sunim suggested I read Lee Eun-Sang's "Impermanence,"[7] a plaintive expression of sorrow after the death of the author's younger brother. I have read it many times since, and I'll quote a few lines here.

> Anitya [Impermanence]! Why, heaven and earth are imperma-
>   nent. Just what is impermanence?
> A songbird greets us in the morning, but before we know it
>   the sun is casting steep shadows over the garden. Is this
>   impermanence?

You see fragrant flowers blooming on a peach tree, but before
you know it you hear the rustling of autumn leaves scattered
about the tree. Is this impermanence?

Last night, without looking, I grabbed one of the books I was in the
middle of reading; it turned out to be Master Songun's[8] book of poetry!
Letting it fall open where it would, I read one verse.

Look at all those graves in that mountain—
In the city, people are born, and die again.
Without learning the secrets of immortality, how sad it is to become
a handful of dust resting underneath the pines.

Lee Eun-Sang wrote these words after his own younger brother
passed away. I remember that their powerful expression of his feelings
toward life and death helped to comfort my own.

After my sister died, all the attention from my family naturally
shifted to me. Whenever my grandparents had guests, they would point
to me and say that I was too precious to even look at. Living at the center
of everyone's world, I was stubbornly convinced I was always the most
important person in the room. Whenever I visited someone else's house
I would act like I owned the place, and it was only when I was older that
I realized how embarrassing this behavior was.

Figure 1.1. Where do we come from, and where do we go? At Haeinsa. Photo
by Kim Minsook.

Meeting Seongcheol Sunim, My Father, for the First Time

It was January of the year I turned thirteen. I was in the sixth grade when I first met my father, Keun Sunim, a figure who until that day had existed only in my imagination. By this time, I had moved from my hometown to the capital, Seoul, and was busy studying for the middle school entrance exam.

My uncle persuaded my grandfather to let me study far away in Seoul, using the old saying "When people are born, you send them to Seoul, and when horses are born, you send them to Jeju Island." But behind all this was my family's grief from my sister's death, especially that of my mother's. My grandfather sent me away out of his love for his daughter-in-law, whose heart must have been torn apart at the mere sight of the white shirts and red neckties worn by girls at Jinju Middle School. Grandfather told my mother and I, "You're not meant to be in Jinju," and he sent us off to Seoul. This was when I was entering fifth grade, while my youngest uncle was a university student in Seoul.

Up until this point, my life had consisted of taking a small wooden ferryboat between the school and my house deep in the forest, so my first train ride to the huge city of Seoul was astonishment itself. Hyehwa Elementary, a fairly renowned school in Seoul, was incomparably more challenging than the school back in my hometown village.

I was busy trying to catch up at my new school but my mind was relieved. Despite the love my grandparents had always showered on me, I was preoccupied with anxieties about the identity of my father, the monk. I didn't show it, but on the inside I think that fact weighed heavily on me.

"Why don't I have a father?" The first time I noticed the absence of my father and asked that question was probably when I started elementary school. Nobody ever told me that my father had left home and become a monk, yet as time passed I naturally understood what had happened. The first image I had of Keun Sunim, the man whom I'd never had the chance to call "father," was that of a beggar.

"What kind of person turns his back on the world and abandons his family to go live deep inside a mountain?" I wonder if little resentments and hateful thoughts toward him began to gradually accumulate by thinking like this. But on the other hand, there was probably also a feeling of longing for the father I had never seen. So when I moved to

Seoul, where nobody knew my father was a monk, my mind finally felt at ease, as if I had let go of a huge burden.

While I was thus busy with my life in Seoul, a nun named Myoeom Sunim came to visit me.

"Keun Sunim is in Busan. Let's go pay him a visit."

Myoeom Sunim was the daughter of my father's close Dharma friend, Cheongdam Sunim. She had gone to her father to avoid being pressed into sexual slavery by the Japanese. While there, she heard a sermon by Seongcheol Sunim and was amazed by the depth of his teaching. After extracting a promise from him that she would leave home if he taught her everything he knew, she shaved her head and became a nun. When we met, she had been a nun for five years; she was five years older than me, and the same age as my dead sister Dogyeong.

My youngest uncle told me, "I'll get permission from your teacher for you to take a few days off school, so let's go." Though I was bewildered by these totally unexpected events, I set out with my uncle, half curious about what my father looked like and half hating him for abandoning his family. I also wondered, "Why am I going to see this person when I hate him so much? Is this what family means?"

Myoeom Sunim suggested that we stop by Daegaksa in Seoul to pay a visit to Vinaya Master[9] Jaun Sunim, a close friend and peer in practice of Keun Sunim. I hated my monastic father, so I didn't much like Myoeom Sunim either, who also wore monastic robes. I therefore chose to go to Daegaksa not with her, but with my uncle, in a separate car.

Apparently, the next day as we sat across from each other on the train to Busan, I asked her this question: "Sunim, do you know how this train is moving?"

It seems I thought monks and nuns living in the mountains didn't know anything about the world. Although I have no memory of this incident, she must have been unable to forget that arrogant little girl, and she regaled me with this story when we met again after I had become a nun.

"You must've thought I was some nun who didn't know anything at all, huh? After that question, you even finished by explaining to me that trains run on steam!"

I must have seemed so childish to Myoeom Sunim, who had been studying under so many great masters.

The sun was almost setting by the time we arrived at the entrance of the temple. After hiking some distance up a mountain ridge beside the ocean, we came face to face with a craggy-faced, scary-looking monk.

This was not the image of my father that I had pictured in my mind. I later found out that he was in fact Hyanggok Sunim, a Dharma friend of my father's, who had been part of the three-year intensive retreat at Bongamsa[10] with him. Anticipating the coming Korean War, Keun Sunim had come down to Busan to join Hyanggok Sunim there.

Hyanggok Sunim told us this after greeting us: "Practitioner Cheol said, 'Some crazy people are coming today,' and disappeared somewhere. Wait a second while I go hunt him down."

Apparently Keun Sunim had already heard about our coming and went off somewhere to avoid us. A short while later, a monk with an

Figure 1.2. With Keun Sunim (*center front, author on the right*) in front of Jang-gyeonggak at Baengnyeonam in Haeinsa. On the left is my teacher, Inhong Sunim, and in the back is Myoeom Sunim. Author provided.

intense stare, dressed in tattered rags, appeared with Hyanggok Sunim. The moment I wondered to myself, "Is that him?" he shouted in a loud voice: "Get out! Go!"

As soon as I heard those words, I gripped my uncle's hand hard and turned away without a moment's hesitation.

"Let's go, Uncle!"

My father, whom I was meeting for the first time in my life, had shouted at me to go away and disappeared inside the moment he saw me. With an angry scowl on my face, I started badgering my uncle to take me home. As I did, Hyanggok Sunim squeezed my hand and led me inside the temple. He assuaged my hurt and disappointment, joking in a kindly voice, "You can be my daughter!" and bringing me all sorts of tasty snacks and treats. I was quickly consoled, and in my innocence, I soon forgot all about the incident with my father.

After evening prayers, Hyanggok Sunim came back and asked me a question: "So, what do you wanna be when you grow up?"

"I want to be an inventor."

When I was little, the person I respected most was the American inventor Thomas Edison. After reading a biography of Edison, who discovered electricity after countless failures and made a great impact on mankind, I thought I should become someone like him when I grew up.

"Oh yeah? Well, what kind of things do you wanna invent?"

"I want to be an inventor that researches people," I replied. "I want to study the question, 'Where do people come from, and where do they go?'"

I think that answer came out of me without my realizing it because those questions were always on my mind since my sister died. He must have found my answer quite funny, and he laughed aloud.

"You're gonna be greater than even Practitioner Cheol!"

It was obvious that the other monks practicing in the Dharma Hall were trying to listen in, wondering just what this little kid was saying. Myoeom Sunim and my uncle began laughing too.

But Keun Sunim, who yelled at me to go away, never did show his face that day. Even after such harsh treatment, I guess I still hadn't abandoned the hope that maybe he would come out to see me again.

Hyanggok Sunim gave me one thousand won as an allowance, and I used the money to buy a pencil case, which I kept for a long time and used all through middle school. My uncle had a long talk with my father that day, who told him, "The world is going to change." I think he had a sense of the coming Korean War, which would begin in the next few months.

My uncle was a man of good stature, and deep thinking too. Wondering, *Just what is he doing in the mountains instead of coming back home like he said he would?* he had set out with some exasperation to find his older brother. But once they met and talked, my uncle started to wonder if perhaps he, too, should become a monk. Considering that my uncle had set out on this mission to destroy his brother's delusions, Keun Sunim must have been a very persuasive man indeed.

My uncle, who acted as my guardian in my father's absence, always called me "pumpkin" when we were out and about. When I would ask, "What's a pumpkin?" he would tease me by saying, "Pumpkins are ugly little things!" But my uncle loved me as if I was his own daughter, and I depended on him as I would my father. In elementary school, I once went on a field trip to the Agricultural College of Seoul National University in Suwon, some thirty-two kilometers away, and had forgotten to take my lunch with me. My uncle was the kind of person who hurried all the way there just to bring me my lunch box.

I spent the night at Myogwaneumsa. The next morning, when I looked out from the temple grounds, I saw the horizon stretching out endlessly. As I faced the blue ocean for the first time in my life, I made a resolution.

"I will throw away my yearning for my father."

He'd shouted at me to leave—his daughter who had grown up without even knowing his face—the first moment he met me. The scales had fallen from my eyes and not a trace of affection or illusion remained. The longing I felt for my father, the hatred and resentment, and everything that had happened at the temple—I released them all into the sea before I returned to Seoul.

Now that I look back, I think it was truly for the best. If my father had been kind to me then, I would not have been able to release my attachment to him, but because he was cruel instead, I was able to bury everything in the sea and turn my back on it. I don't second-guess my decisions; once I make up my mind, I never look back. When he shouted at me to get out, my fantasies and yearnings for a father, my relationship to him as flesh and blood, all of these attachments were put to rest in one moment. After all, who in this world has not been my father, has not been my mother?[11]

Feeling the Transience of Life in the Experience of War

Sunday, June 25, 1950. The year after I went to meet Keun Sunim, Seoul was suddenly engulfed in a state of unrest. Trucks filled with soldiers raced through the streets from Hyehwa Rotary to Miari Hill. Everyone was in a clamor, saying that war had broken out.

By evening the sounds of cannons and gunfire were creeping closer. My mother and I trembled in fear as we stayed up all night in the basement under a blanket, listening closely to the news trickling from the radio.

"Our forces are advancing into Pyongyang [North Korea]," said President Rhee Syngman in a quivering voice. But when we stepped outside in the morning, we saw corpses scattered here and there in the streets while North Korean soldiers, led by units of tanks, marched past the Hyehwa traffic circle. Crowds gathered by the roadside to welcome the North Korean army. Overnight, the Republic of Korea [South Korea] had become the Democratic People's Republic of Korea [North Korea].

A few days later, People's courts were held at Seonggyungwan University and the palace of Changgyeonggung. Taking advantage of mob mentality, these kangaroo trials were over in just one hour. Spectators, knowing nothing of the accused or their supposed crimes, cheered and applauded when they heard that "such and such person is an undesirable element because of these crimes." One by one, those accused were then tied to pine trees and shot to death right in front of the crowd. Even as people were murdered right before them, killed in the blink of an eye, the spectating crowd cheered and clapped. I fell into deep shock as I watched these brutal scenes, where neither conscience nor compassion could be found.

Some days later, the People's courts were held again at the old palace. Countless people continued to die. It was lawless chaos; nobody could be sure of tomorrow. The fields behind Seoul National University Hospital were littered with the corpses of our soldiers.

At school, instead of studying, we sang songs about General Kim Il-Sung [the founder and first leader of North Korea]. Young middle school students were forcibly drafted into the militia; they were so short that their guns dragged behind them on the ground as they walked.

Seoul was consumed by fear, and my mother and I felt unable to stay in the city any longer, so later that month we joined a mass of people fleeing the war. The distance from Seoul to Jinju, the nearest city to my hometown village, was just over 480 kilometers south. A rumor spread that some refugees who had fled before us, unaware that the Han River Bridge had been blown up, drove their cars straight off the bridge and into the river to their deaths.[12] A group of three hundred, we crossed the river by boat and set out to the south on the shelterless path of refugees. Occasionally North Korean soldiers would come marching along the right side of the road, while we kept to the left.

Whenever we heard the sounds of an airplane, soldiers and refugees alike would crouch in the soybean fields or woods by the side of the road and hide. There were people who died by bombs that hit as they crossed a bridge. There were college students who were shot to death on the spot by North Korean soldiers because they said something that angered them.

We slept in abandoned houses and on riverbanks. We begged for food. In the face of a destiny that flickered like a candle in the wind, all we could do was continue walking toward our unknown destination.

Sometimes we would accidentally stumble onto an encampment of North Korean soldiers. When they would shoot us a look and demand, "Who are you?" we would all throw our hands up in surrender and pass them by. Because none of us knew what might happen in the next moment, every day when I awoke from sleep I would pray to myself, "Please let us be safe today as well . . ."

After ten days or so, some of our group had parted ways, heading for different destinations. Many others had died. After marching southeast through Yeoju City and the mountain pass, we finally arrived in what looked to be Sangju, near the Nakdong River. When we took a wrong turn in the mountains, we stumbled onto a battlefield where North and South Korean soldiers had been locked in brutal combat with the Nakdong River between them. The countless bodies could not be told apart as they lay in masses on the ground.

It was about one month since we left Seoul in late July when we arrived at a bridge across the Nakdong River near Daegu. We were at the historical battlefield where military historians would later call the "Battle of Dabudong" took place. The shores of the river were filled with throngs of people like us, a sea of refugees who had gathered from all across the country.

An American reconnaissance plane circled low overhead to protect the refugees. The North Korean army's greatest fear was the airplanes that dropped bombs from the sky. Our group crossed the river to the south on rafts. There were many South Korean soldiers who, even as they prepared to fight, were still kind toward us refugees. In their presence, even my innocent mind was put somewhat at ease.

Even though we were on a battlefield, a general gave me a ride in his jeep because I was young, while my mother followed behind in a military truck. Once we got to Daegu, a military policeman announced that we were refugees from Seoul and assigned us lodgings.

After sleeping by riverbanks listening to the sounds of the water, gazing at the stars on a mountain or field with the sky as my blanket, sleeping in a roofed shelter actually felt stuffy and cramped. Hearing that the members of our group from Seoul all wanted to head for their own hometowns, my mother and I decided to go back to ours in Jinju. The next day, we went to see a relative, a congressman, who was able to put us on a train to Masan. When we arrived at my mother's family home in Masan, her relatives were only then starting to evacuate due to the war; but my mother and I, exhausted from our long journey, stayed there for the next three months. Finally, around Chuseok [Korean Harvest Festival, usually late September to early October], when the North Korean troops began to retreat, we began our walk to Jinju. The road to my hometown was long and arduous. Only the cities of Busan, Masan, and Daegu remained part of South Korea; the rest of the country was the domain of North Korea.

The four months of fighting that had raged were long and intense. When we reached Jindong Hill there were piles of dead bodies stacked one on top of another, and my heart was saddened beyond words at the thought that they were the corpses of our brothers.

We arrived in Jinju to find the city burned to ashes. When we asked an acquaintance about any word from our hometown village, we were told that my grandfather had passed away. Stunned by this unexpected news, my mother nevertheless suppressed her rising grief and dressed me in a white mourning gown. As she dressed me, I couldn't stop crying at the thought that I would never see my grandfather again. Bursting out all at once were the tears of the pent-up sorrow and pain of experiencing the horrors of war at such a young age.

And so, with a mournful heart we walked on to our village. But to our great surprise, we were greeted by my grandfather, alive and unharmed! The moment they saw me, my grandparents wrapped me in their arms and rejoiced. I am told that they had wept at even the sound of a bird singing, as if it were a message that their little Sugyeong had died. The members of our family, who had thought each other dead on the refugee trail or on the battlefield, were awash in a sea of tears at the relief of our reunion.

Our household had been under surveillance by North Korean soldiers as possible reactionaries, but when they descended on our home and told my grandfather they were going to take our cow, he had apparently bellowed at them, "You damn people! Did you eat all your cows up North and come down South to eat all the cows here too?" The North Koreans aimed their guns at him, but my grandfather did not lose his nerve and stared them down. A relative standing nearby quickly carried my grandfather away on his back and they escaped. Just then, the sound of gunfire rang out somewhere, and so the rumor had spread in the village that my grandfather had been killed.

Innocent and ordinary lives were lost in those days. Without even a moment to reflect on the preciousness of life, we lived in fear, not knowing how we made it through each day. Even though I was only fourteen, I think this bitter experience of the fragility and transience of life in war became an undercurrent for my meditation on life and death, both before and after becoming a nun.

Chapter 2

Entering the Monastery

Eternal Happiness and Temporary Happiness

"What Is Eternal Happiness?"

Once Seoul was recaptured by the South my mother and I returned to continue with my schooling. But when the UN and South Korean armies began their retreat from the Chinese border of North Korea on January 4, 1951, my grandfather urged us to hurry back south to Jinju. He gave a strict command that I was never again to be sent to Seoul, even if it meant that I wouldn't be able to study.

After packing away our life in Seoul, I returned to Jinju and graduated from Jinju Middle School. In the spring of 1953, when I was seventeen years old, I enrolled at the Jinju School of Education, a school with a deep tradition where the brightest talents in Western part of South Gyeongsang Province gathered.

One day while I was attending the School of Education, I came home to find a small but solidly built monk waiting for me. Greeting this perfect stranger, he gave me this message: "Keun Sunim says you should come visit. Come to Cheonjegul (Cheonje Hermitage) and see him during your school break." That stranger was Beopjeon Sunim (1925–2014), who would later become the spiritual master of Haeinsa and patriarch of the Jogye Order. He was practicing at Cheonjegul as Keun Sunim's attendant at the time and had come on Keun Sunim's missive: "Go pay a visit to that child."

This was when I was living in downtown Jinju with my aunt. I remember that she wasn't at home that day and, not knowing how to prepare food myself, I couldn't offer Beopjeon Sunim a proper meal. After he left, I thought, "I guess my father isn't completely indifferent to me," but my feelings of discontent toward him remained.

Once summer break started, my grandmother suggested that we go visit Seongcheol Sunim up at Cheonjegul in Anjeongsa. She seemed worried when I responded with silence. Since my meeting with him in the sixth grade I had erased the notion of "father" from my heart and I didn't have much desire to go see him.

At the time, I was actually going to church with my best friend. Though it had started as a form of defiance against my father, from a deep place within my heart, a curiosity had risen about religious people. "What kind of things does a monk do, and what kind of person is a priest?" Perhaps I had wanted to learn what monks were all about through another spiritual person, like a pastor.

When I told my grandmother that I was going to church, she readily allowed it, saying, "Jesus and Buddha were both wise sages." Still, it must have been uncomfortable for her to let her granddaughter go to church when her son had already gone off to become a Buddhist monk. I suppose she was worried about what might happen if I kept at it and told my father about my going to church. Despite Keun Sunim's careless treatment of her, she would visit him occasionally to bring him clothes and food.

I eventually feigned defeat to my grandmother's repeated pleas one day, and we set off to Anjeongsa together. This time, my youngest aunt, four years older than me, accompanied us.

As a matter of fact, I had actually tried to go visit my father once before without anyone knowing. The year before my father sent Beopjeon Sunim for me, I had gone to visit my mother's family in Masan with my friend during summer break. I heard that my father was staying at a monastery in Masan too, and I wrestled with myself for a while trying to decide whether to go see him while I was there. Eventually I thought, "Why on earth am I trying to seek out someone who treated me so coldly?" and I took the train straight back to Jinju. My friend held my hand tightly on the train ride back. She had understood everything, though I hadn't said a word. I may have sworn that I had forgotten my father, but there was no way I could cut away all attachments to flesh and blood at such a young age. I've been holding this story inside my heart, not sharing it with a soul, for decades. Only now am I finally telling it.

When the Korean War broke out, Keun Sunim left Myogwaneumsa, going south to Goseong and staying briefly there with Cheongdam Sunim at Munsuam, before moving to Anjeongsa in Tongyeong during a lull in the war. Anjeongsa is on the southernmost tip of the Korean Peninsula, nestled in Byeokbangsan overlooking the blue sea. A monastery with a storied history, it was founded in the seventh century by Wonhyo, one of the greatest monks of Korea.[1] Keun Sunim built a small thatched-roof house in a cave above the monastery and named it Cheonjegul, where he lived with Beopjeon Sunim as his attendant. The name Cheonje means "a being unable to become a Buddha," or "a being without Buddha-nature." It reflects the philosophy that, in order to set out on the Path, one must take the mindset of such a humble being who has no chance of becoming a Buddha.

We followed my grandmother as she set off on the trail to the monastery, balancing a large basket of food and fruits on her head to bring to Keun Sunim. Watching my grandmother climb over the steep mountain ridges while carrying this heavy load, I thought, "Are mothers the kind of people who can't help but sacrifice themselves like this?"

Just before the sun began to set we took a wrong turn somewhere and got lost. Eventually, unable to continue in the dark, we found a place to sleep at the foothill of some nameless ridge. When we opened our eyes in the morning, we turned out to be right next to the hermitage.

Meeting my father in the early morning outside of his hut, he was still as unfriendly as ever. As soon as Grandmother set down all the food and fruits that she had carried, he commanded me and my aunt, "Go back and share this with the poor people down the mountain." This was before anyone had even said hello.

I gritted my teeth at his indifference to my grandmother's devotion, her sleeping a night in the dark mountains carrying that heavy load, and not even inviting us inside. Still, we had no choice. My aunt and I went all the way back down the mountain with the bundle full of food and gave it all away to total strangers before returning to the hermitage. I'm sure my feelings of discomfort and anger were obvious on my face.

"You should say hello to Sunim."

At the urging of my grandmother, I bowed my head a little and said hello. Standing in the front yard of his hut, the first words that came from his mouth were this: "Well, aren't you a little brat!"

Instantly, I thought, "You got that right!" Without the chance to voice my dissatisfaction, he continued straight to the point once we were seated across from each other.

"So, what do you live for?"

With my grandmother's whispers of my churchgoing habits lingering in his ear, he must have been wondering just what this child was thinking.

"I live for happiness," I replied, under his intense stare, thunderous and full of steel.

"Oh yeah? Well, in happiness, there's an eternal happiness and a temporary happiness. So, which kind of happiness are you trying to live for?"

Until then, I knew that I wanted to live happily, but I'd never thought there were two paths to happiness. My thought was that a happy life is one where you had everything you wanted in this world.

"What is eternal happiness and what is temporary happiness?" I asked.

Keun Sunim's voice suddenly became quiet, a change from the loud one he had used until now.

"Happiness is within your character, not in material things. Even if you're wealthy, you'll be unhappy if you're lacking in character and even if you're poor, you'll be happy if you have a brilliant nature. We are all absolute beings with infinite ability, so the Buddha teaches that you should cultivate this character to its true and complete perfection. Someone who's enlightened like the Buddha is a being of great freedom who enjoys eternal happiness. But if you spend your days chasing after the five desires of this world, then that's just temporary happiness."

The five desires that humans seek out are the desire to eat, the desire to sleep, sexual desires, the desire for wealth, and the desire for fame and power. In Buddhism, these are called the five desires and pleasures. Generally, we say people are happy when they fulfill these desires, but Keun Sunim was saying that this is a temporary happiness, which can only be enjoyed for a brief moment, not an eternal one.

When he told me the distinction between an eternal and temporary happiness, I had already decided which of these paths my life would take. The moment I heard his words, I resolved to myself that, unless I was an idiot, I'd live for eternal, not temporary, happiness. Despite my dislike of monks, my inner heart had been touched by a karmic connection to this Buddha-nature. I organized my thoughts and brought forth another question: "How do I study to become enlightened like the Buddha did?"

"You can become enlightened by meditating on a *hwadu*."[2]

I can say with certainty that I lived many previous lives as a practitioner in Keun Sunim's congregation. The first thing I felt when I started life at a monastery was, "Oh! So I was a meditating monastic in the past!" How else would words like *hwadu* or meditation sound familiar, as if I had known them all along, even though I was hearing them for the first time in my life? Hearing just that one phrase—"the pursuit of eternal happiness"—I felt the pent-up feelings of hatred toward my father melt away like snow in the spring sunlight, and committed my life to understanding it.

Keun Sunim then gave me the *hwadu* called "Three Pounds of Flax."

"A long time ago in China, there was a great master named Dongshan. Once, when a monk asked him, 'What is the Buddha?' the master replied, 'Three pounds of flax.'"

My grandmother, my aunt, and I listened quietly to Keun Sunim's words.

"Why did he say three pounds of flax? From now on, think about that every day, whether you're awake or asleep. Buddhism is about cultivating your mind. You meditate upon *hwadu* in order to do this cultivation. If you keep asking the question, 'Why did he say three pounds of flax?' you'll be able to see the original nature of the mind. No matter what you're doing, whether you're eating, studying, or going for a walk, always be suspicious, questioning. Why did he reply with 'three pounds of flax' when asked 'What is Buddha?' Why?"

After he talked about *hwadu* like this, he asked me a few more questions.

"Look at the white snow in the pitch-black night. What does this mean?"

"As two people were walking down a road, the one in front said he heard sounds of sword-fighting. The one behind gave the one in front a towel. Why did he give him a towel?"

He asked me ten such questions that day; the last one was Master Nanquan's famous story, "Nanquan Kills the Cat."[3]

"Monks in the congregation of Namjeon [Ch. Nanquan] Sunim had split into eastern and western camps, fighting about whether a cat had Buddha-nature. Nanquan grabbed the cat, held it up, and said, 'You monks! If any of you can say anything, I'll spare the cat. If not, I'm going to kill it.' When none of the monks could say anything in reply, Nanquan Sunim grabbed his sword and ruthlessly chopped off the cat's head. When Nanquan's pupil Zhaozhou returned that evening, Nanquan told him what happened that day. Zhaozhou, without any reply, took off his shoes, placed them on his head, and walked out. Upon seeing this, Nanquan slapped his knee and said, 'If only Zhaozhou were there, the cat would've lived!' So, what would've you done?"

He had told me a fairly high-level Seon dialogue,[4] and I replied with my own answer.

After he heard my answer, he said, "You're better than a monk who's been carrying his traveling sack for ten years!" and smiled broadly for the first time.

"Is this kind of questioning and answering what practice is?" I asked.

"No. Practice is awakening your mind through *hwadu* meditation."

How quickly and deeply those words buried themselves inside me! "Practicing is awakening your mind." I wanted nothing else but to devote myself to this study. It was probably fated by my past life. The instant I heard those words I said to myself, "This is the path I should take!"

Ever since I was little, I had always ignored the demands others made of me, but whenever I made a decision myself I went for it without hesitation.

"I'd like to just practice meditation and not go to school."

I was on summer break, three semesters shy of graduating from the School of Education. Keun Sunim told me to finish school first.

"If you can't finish even the smallest of tasks, you can't succeed in the big things."

My youngest aunt, sitting next to me, was apparently moved by Keun Sunim and proclaimed on the spot: "Sunim, I'd like to become a nun too."

"No, your body's too weak," he replied, shaking his head.

At these words, my aunt gave up her desire to enter into the monastic life and went back home. Later when I became a nun, she confided in me her dissatisfaction: "I guess even enlightened masters discriminate, huh? Letting his own daughter become a nun but telling me not to . . ."

My youngest aunt was tall and good-natured, but a little frail. Four years my senior, she never really received much attention from her family

Figure 2.1. With Keun Sunim (*rear, with the author front right*) at Baengnyeonam in my youth. Keun Sunim taught me that "the only life for a practitioner is a life of study." On the left is Hyeonggak Sunim, with whom he spent his first season at Cheongnyangsa. Author provided.

because of me, her niece. Ever since she was young, my aunt always had to make sacrifices for my sake. Perhaps for me that was an upside of having an absent father, but I can imagine just how upsetting that would have been for her at a young age. Now, my aunt has left home to become a wife, not a nun. She and her husband, who worked at the Ministry of Construction, later helped me a great deal when I was building Geoboesa at Keun Sunim's birthplace. If my aunt had also decided to become a nun that day, my grandfather probably would have collapsed and become bedridden with pent-up rage.

From that day on when I met my father for the second time, the name Seongcheol meant to me not "my father" but instead a true teacher, who set me on the path to becoming an eternal being of great freedom.

Later, Keun Sunim used this conversation about "eternal happiness," which had decided the course of my life, and presented it to a community of monks at the famous Haeinsa Hundred-Day Dharma sermon.[5] Just over thirty at the time, I sat among the crowd and listened to the talk.

> If you look at the reality we live in, everything is relative and finite—we see contradiction upon contradiction, a world of conflict. Even if we find temporary happiness in this world of conflict, the happiness soon ends. It is human instinct to think about how we can live in this moment right now in comfort, even if we were to die an hour later. But, as long as we're alive, it is impossible to be completely satisfied with this temporary happiness. You might say that this is why people search for eternal happiness. Since we can't attain eternal happiness in this relative and finite world, we conceive of an absolute and infinite world and strive to enter that world to become eternally happy. This is the foundation of religion.
>
> . . .
>
> Buddhism tries to find this absolute and infinite world—one that transcends the relative and finite world—within our own minds. The position of Buddhism is that we are already equipped with the absolute and infinite world inside our minds, rather than outside it or beyond this reality. Therefore, the fundamental prerequisite of anyone who wants to believe in Buddhism is to believe that one does indeed possess that absolute and infinite world, that one's mind is that of the Buddha. Before you develop the eternal life and infinite ability that resides within your mind,

it is impossible to know the path ahead in detail—you must trust and follow the words of the Buddha and the Seon patriarchs.

From beginning to end, the purpose of Buddhism is centered on the human being, to perfect the human being. Buddhism teaches that the human being is an absolute being. It is only because we are absolute beings with infinite ability that the Buddha teaches us that we should cultivate our characters to their true and complete perfection.

My second meeting with Keun Sunim was in the summer of 1954, when he was forty-three and I was eighteen. It was the greatest and most unforgettable connection of my life. If he had just treated me coldly like our first meeting and didn't tell me about "eternal happiness," could I have walked the path of becoming a nun? How can I explain that karmic connection in words?

Perhaps if you hold the premise that the being called "me" is a living thing that has been reborn through thousands and tens of thousands of years, this might be easier to understand.

Before Leaving Home

I'm quite straightforward; as soon as I hear one word, I have a tendency to jump straight into action without bothering to hear the rest. I was like that when I was little, and I'm still like that now.

"Why did he say three pounds of flax? Why?"

Since my meeting with Keun Sunim, I had no doubt that this question was the key to obtaining "eternal happiness." I spent every moment of my days and nights lost in this question, even at school. In music class, I sat at the very back and worked on my *hwadu*. During physical education, I would sit underneath a tree deep in my *hwadu*, my friends bumping me on the shoulder as they passed, asking, "What are you thinking about so hard?" The deeper I delved into my *hwadu*, the more I had the thought that my school studies were unnecessary.

The first one in my family to detect the change within me was my grandmother. Not only was she naturally sharp-minded, she went to the monastery every retreat season for *hwadu* practice since Keun Sunim became a monk, so she understood the practice of meditation and recognized the meaning of the changes she saw in me. On top of that, she was there when I received my *hwadu* from Keun Sunim and had always regarded my habit of constantly being lost in my thoughts as a special quality, even before we visited Keun Sunim.

Ever since my sister died, I always felt alone even when I was with my family. I became even lonelier and more withdrawn after I went to see Keun Sunim, and I wonder if my grandmother had a premonition of my departure from secular life.

Even my grandfather had noticed the changes in my behavior and made plans to pay a visit to the hermitage.

"There's no way he's going to come down here, so I'd better go up there myself."

Using me as an excuse, my grandfather finally set out to see his son who had been gone almost twenty years—after he had said he would come back in ten. After entering the monastic life at Haeinsa in 1936, Keun Sunim had never again set foot in his home village. My grandfather too was such a stubborn man that he hadn't gone to visit his son until now.

My grandmother later told me, "Your grandfather went up there to settle a score—what kind of person had his son become that he would drag his one and only granddaughter off too?" My grandfather had so much bottled up in his heart that the moment he saw his son for the first time in twenty years he screamed, "Sakyamuni [the Buddha] is my mortal enemy!" He was a Confucian scholar who had lost his eldest son to Buddhism, a religion he looked down on, and had been ostracized by his Confucian colleagues because his son had become a monk.[6] One can only imagine the resentment he had accumulated over the years.

But even my grandfather ended up being awed by Keun Sunim's imposing strength of character. My grandmother told me that he didn't say much when he returned, other than marveling, "He really was like a sage!"

It seems as though my grandfather's icy resentment toward Keun Sunim too thawed like spring snow after their short meeting. As my grandfather prepared to leave after seeing his son for the first time in twenty years, Keun Sunim comforted him by saying, "You must stay healthy and live a long, long time."

When my grandfather came home, he rounded up the servants of the house and went down to the river flowing beside the village. With a scythe, he personally cut down the fishing nets he had installed in the river. They were the nets he had cast when Keun Sunim left home to become a monk, proclaiming, "Since Sakyamuni thinks that it's wrong to kill, I'm going to kill to take revenge on that Sakyamuni, who took away my son."

Once I began my graduating year at the School of Education, my thoughts about becoming a nun became much clearer. I became an intern elementary school teacher and taught first-grade children in my first semester. But now, the *hwadu* that came to me so easily when I sat in class began flitting out of my grasp when faced with the pressure of having to teach.

The conflicting feeling that something wasn't right remained throughout my second semester when I was sent to teach at Danseong Elementary School, the school I attended for four years as a child. Although the setting was as beautiful as ever, the only thought in my mind was that I should study my *hwadu*. I made up my mind to quit my teaching internship and focus only on my *hwadu* at a monastery. I sent a letter to Okja, a friend of mine who was attending the Busan School of Education: "I could concentrate on my *hwadu* when I was listening to lectures, but I just can't get into my *hwadu* now that I'm trying to teach. What could be more important than the *hwadu*? I can't shake the feeling that I'm just wasting my time. I'm thinking about going to Wolmyeongam Hermitage to practice. You should come too."

Okja had also felt the emptiness of life after experiencing the death of her younger brother when she first met Seongcheol Keun Sunim with her mother. From him she learned about the path of becoming an eternal being of great freedom—a path of life and not death—and she too was trying to find that path. She was also an intern teacher like me, but she dropped everything and came running as soon as she received my letter.

In fact, Wolmyeongam would be the first time Okja and I met face to face. The only thing we had in common was the resolve we gained after meeting Keun Sunim to practice and become an eternal being of great freedom. We lived far apart, but we knew of each other through Keun Sunim. Even though we had never met, we already thought of each other as Dharma friends, which was why I felt comfortable sending her such a letter and why I believe she agreed to come right away.

Okja and I began our meditation practice at Wolmyeongam, close to Jinju and my hometown. My grandmother often went there for meditation retreats and in fact was practicing there at the time. As for me, it was like a trial run before I set out to be a nun in earnest, but there was no way this rehearsal could proceed as planned without the permission of my family.

When I, an intern teacher who was supposed to be with my students, went and secluded myself in a monastery, a huge commotion naturally broke out, not just at the school but also at home. My uncle came looking for me after receiving word from the school that I had disappeared. "Come on, Sugyeong. Let's go back. Shouldn't you at least finish your studies?"

My uncle gently tried to convince me to stay in school. I was torn between the need to practice my *hwadu* and my family's pleas for me to return home. I could not have felt lonelier as I sat beside a small pond in the pitch-black night, pondering this and that. I was anxious and did not know where to rest my mind.

"Where is my place in this great wide universe?"

Sitting there, deeply absorbed in thought, Keun Sunim appeared clearly in front of me and stared at me with his deep, wide eyes. As I met his gaze, my resolve to focus solely on practicing my *hwadu* once again gained strength. I was confident that my place could not be anywhere but here.

The next day, my uncle went back home alone, while I stayed at the monastery to practice over the winter retreat. Afterward I returned to school and told my worried teacher, "I learned a lot." He gave me a dumbfounded look in return.

When Okja and I said goodbye to each other at the end of our retreat, we promised to leave our homes and go to Keun Sunim one month after we graduated. Although I was burning to leave home and go practice the moment I finished school, I was worried that this might prove to be too great a shock for my family.

The spring I turned twenty, one month after I graduated from school, I was offered a job as a full-time teacher. Though my family told me to accept, my heart was already someplace else.

My mother and the rest of my family noticed the signs that I wanted to go back to the monastery to become a nun and tried hard to keep me from doing so. They said, "Shouldn't you at least graduate from university if you want to become a great nun? If you decide to leave after you finish university, we won't stop you." But there was no chance such words could sway my mind when I had already chosen the path of eternal happiness over temporary happiness.

The evening before I left, I made a suggestion to my uncle, who was pressuring me harder than anyone to accept the teaching position. I couldn't bring myself to simply ignore the request of the man who had taken care of me and loved me in place of my absent father.

"If you listen to my wish, I won't leave home."

"Really? Okay."

Uncle summoned a family meeting. My grandparents; my mother, who had lost her husband to the Buddha and lived only for her one surviving daughter; my uncle, who had played the role of my father in matters large and small; and my aunt all gathered around to listen to me.

"I don't know whether I'm going to die today or tomorrow. If anyone can die in my place, I won't go to the monastery."

After a moment of stunned silence, my grandfather's lament finally pierced the air.

"Our family is ruined!"

Tears rolled down the face of my grandfather, a man who had never bowed down to anyone in his life. The reason why Keun Sunim was called the "Tiger of Gayasan" was because he had inherited this strong spirit from his father. My grandfather was principled and unyielding—he did not bat an eye when North Korean soldiers pointed their guns at him during the Korean War, and I had even failed the elementary school entrance examination during the Japanese colonial era because he refused to change my name to a Japanese one. I could not express how sorry I was to drive such a man to tears.

"Grandpa, don't worry. The Buddha attained enlightenment in six years, but I'll practice extra hard and come back after attaining it in just three."

It was a time when I was consumed only with the thought that I needed to understand my *hwadu*, to become an eternal being of great freedom, and that I didn't want to be the kind of idiot who merely chased after the five desires and pleasures. I truly thought I would return in three years, and I was confident that I could. I did not think about the possibility of leaving home forever.

Grandfather was probably reminded of Keun Sunim, who had left home to become a monk twenty years ago. He had also said he would be back in ten years when he left. Grandfather likely thought to himself that the apple wouldn't fall far from the tree and didn't expect to see my return. I only hope that the reunion with his son, who had already become quite a sage since he entered the monastery, helped to cushion the blow of my leaving home.

The morning after the family meeting, I said my final goodbyes to my grandfather. He told me, "When you go to the monastery, don't eat any mushrooms other than pine mushrooms, okay? There are many poisonous mushrooms in the mountains." After I left, he must have missed his granddaughter and wondered how she was doing; so much so that he asked my grandmother, "Do you think I could go up to where Sugyeong is with some marinated crab to eat while I stay for a few days?" Since he knew he would only be fed mountain vegetables at the monastery, he must have wanted to bring a side dish that he liked while he stayed by my side for a few days. Once I left my ancestral home, I did not return for another forty years, and my grandfather passed away only three years after I left. The day I left home was the last time I saw him.

Since I left, my heart has always been grateful for my grandfather, who believed in his granddaughter and sent her off with his blessing. Grandfather was an broad-minded and deep-thinking philosopher who, heedless to the restrictions of flesh and blood, generously cared for his entire community.

My grandfather's name was Lee Sangeon, his courtesy name, Samun, and his pen name, Yuleun. He was born on November 1, 1881, when the fortunes of the Joseon dynasty were rapidly crumbling, in the house where I was also born. The house had been passed down through the generations by our forebears, and he lived there his entire life. He took as his wife my grandmother Gang Sangbong and had four sons and three daughters between them. Keun Sunim was his eldest son.

Fiercely proud and direct, Grandfather never bowed down to anyone in his life. He made an even more impressive figure than my father, and when he hit the road with a cane and straw hat, he was the very image of cool. Whenever he attended the local Confucian gathering, they say his very presence would light up the room. My father's towering figure and well-defined features were no doubt inherited from my grandfather.

Grandfather could be scary, but he often showed a considerate side. Around the grounds of our house was a grove of chestnut trees. When the neighborhood kids snuck up the trees to pick chestnuts, he kept an eye on them without saying a word, waiting until they safely came down from the trees to sternly scold them. He was worried that the kids would fall out of the trees if he yelled at them while they were still up there.

He was careful and thoroughly attentive to detail. He planted a goji berry tree by our well, which he would drink from first thing in the morning before giving some to us. When a goji berry tree's roots run deep into the earth and surround a well, beneficial substances leach into the water, and he knew that drinking this water early in the morning would help us live longer.

In the sandy soil around our house was a field of white bellflowers over ten years old.[7] Grandfather had cultivated this field for a long time, saying that eating six-year-old ginseng was good for your health. But when Grandfather passed away, the field stopped flowering even in the springtime and eventually died out. There is an old folk saying that honeybees and ginseng plants are mystical creatures that recognize their owners.

He was so tough and steadfast that during the Japanese colonial period, when officials went around town confiscating items such as brass silverware for the World War II effort, he wouldn't let them touch even a single spoon from our house. With him blocking the door like a mountain, the officials were cowed by his intimidating presence and couldn't do a thing.

How, then, could a stubborn Confucian scholar such as my grandfather have accepted his eldest son becoming a Buddhist monk? Our hometown also happened to be an area with an especially strong conservative Confucian tradition descended from a famous Confucian scholar, Nammyeong Jo Sik (1501–1572). Back then, the Joseon dynasty policies and traditions that revered Confucianism and persecuted Buddhism meant that monks and nuns were regarded poorly. Naturally, the fact that Keun Sunim became a monk became such a huge scandal that it flipped our family and the entire village upside down.

It was this stubborn and prideful Grandfather, so overcome by his feelings of anger, bitterness, and frustration, who cast a net across the Gyeongho River and had spicy fish stew made every evening from its catch. And it was Grandmother who would put the leftover fish in a pail and set them free in the river come nightfall. Her heart must have felt like it was being torn to pieces, trying to live with my grandfather's uncompromising attitude while concealing a pain much greater than his.

My Grandmother's Sacred Maternal Love

My grandmother lost one of her eyes because my father became a monk, though I was too young at the time to remember. My grandfather became so enraged at how my grandmother kept preparing clothes and food to take to Keun Sunim one day that he hurled a burning brazier at her, exclaiming, "Don't go looking for him!" One of the flying embers struck my grandmother's left eye, blinding it permanently.

My grandfather celebrated his sixtieth birthday[8] five years after my father entered the monastery. Family and neighbors gathered for the boisterous festivities, which lasted the whole day. As the sun set, the family had gathered to take a commemorative photograph, when tears suddenly began to fall from my usually proud and imposing grandfather's eyes. Though no words were spoken, everyone knew what those tears meant. The banquet soon turned into a sea of weeping, and eventually the only ones who posed for the picture were my grandfather and grandmother. Looking at that photograph many years later, I felt a poignant sadness as I looked into my grandmother's eyes.

Even with just one eye, my grandmother never hesitated to make the long journey to her son, if just to tend to him for a brief moment. It was because of her that I realized why mothers are compared to the bodhisattva Guanyin, who is the embodiment of compassion.

My grandmother, who gave birth to her first child at the tender age of eighteen, was born the only child of a family of scholars from Hachon, a village that neighbors Mukgokri. She learned Chinese, etiquette, calligraphy, and other subjects with her uncles in their home, which was also the village school. Naturally intelligent, once she learned something she wouldn't forget it. She was highly praised for her exceptional teaching ability and was in charge of writing the letters that were given as wedding gifts whenever there was a marriage in her village.

I have been told that when my grandmother arrived in Mukgokri on the day of her wedding, she descended from her palanquin and pledged that she would give birth to a great man. Ever responsible and meticulous, once pregnant she refused to eat cucumbers or radishes that were bent or disfigured, nor any bumpy or ugly fruits, and always avoided the corners when sitting on a bench or in a room. For ten months, she didn't even step foot outside the front gate in order to avoid seeing or hearing any evil influence, and she prayed day and night with all of her devotion to every god and ancestor to send her the most exceptional son in the world.

My grandmother's devotion to her children that began in this way remained tranquil and unchanged until her final days. She raised seven children, including Keun Sunim, yet she never once raised her voice to teach them, nor used harsh language to scold them. She always spoke to them in such a manner that they would learn and come to understand

Figure 2.2. My grandfather's sixtieth birthday, for which his eldest son was absent. In the end, only my grandparents posed to take a photograph. Author provided.

things for themselves. Ever since they were young children, she always held a firm belief in their character. Thinking back today, I think she must have been a naturally gifted teacher.

My grandmother read to me a great deal when I was young. I remember her patiently telling me stories of the famous characters Kim Chunchu and Kim Yushin from the book *Memorabilia of the Three Kingdoms* (Kr. *Samguk Yusa*).[9] Perhaps these books that she read in her own youth gave her the hope that she too would raise children of great character someday.

My grandmother probably played an important role in Keun Sunim's early love of books. It's widely known that once he got a hold of a book he wouldn't put it down. Having learned how to read by the age of three, he studied the *Thousand-Character Classic*, *The Elementary Learning* (Ch. *Xiaoxue*), and *The Great Learning* (Ch. *Daxue*)[10] under my grandfather, who was himself a learned man. Keun Sunim was exceptionally intelligent and even won first place in a writing contest at the age of five, evidence enough for many to regard him as a child prodigy. It seems my grandmother's extreme prenatal efforts in raising an exceptional son showed their effectiveness quite early.

Once, when Keun Sunim was in elementary school, he bought the four great classical novels of China, including *Journey to the West* (Kr. *Seoyugi*) and *Romance of the Three Kingdoms* (Kr. *Samgukji Yeonui*). Picking a sunny spot on the slope of a mountain on his way home, he buried his nose in them, so engrossed that he didn't even notice the sun go down. Keun Sunim learned everything through his own rigorous study: he once said, "The only time I learned from another person was in the village school and my six years of elementary school. I learned everything else by teaching myself."

The year Keun Sunim turned nine years old, his teacher at the village school closed his book and exclaimed that there was nothing more he could teach him because of his genius. However, according to my grandmother, although my father was highly intelligent, he was a sickly child. She made a great deal of herbal medicines for him and frequently took him to a monastery in the foothills of Jirisan for a change of air to improve his health as a child.

I think Keun Sunim was around twenty years old when he first came across Buddhism. Although he was extremely well read, he had only studied the classical Chinese literature of Confucianism and Daoism, and western philosophy books; he had never even touched a book on Buddhism.

Reading every great book from the East to the West, he had still been unable to find the fundamental answers to life and had no sense of direction. That was until a sunim gave him a copy of the *Zhengdaoge* (*Song of Enlightenment*), a classic work of Chan literature composed by Yongjia Xuanjue, a Chinese Chan monk of the seventh century. When he read it, he felt a deep shock and marveled, "Ah, so there are teachings like this!" Keun Sunim described his feelings in that moment: "It was like I saw a bright light in the darkness, like seeing the sun rise in the dead of night." Yongjia Xuanjue's *Song of Enlightenment* contains descriptions of his state of mind when he attained enlightenment overnight after listening to the important points of Seon from the sixth patriarch Huineng (638–713).

When I was about to enter the monastery, Keun Sunim lectured us on the book that had moved him so deeply. Lifting up a six-ringed staff high in the air, he gave us a convincing impression of Yongjia [Kr. Yeongga] Xuanjue, and told us, "You two are the future Yeongga Sunim!"[11]

They say that Keun Sunim wondered from a young age whether a person could live eternally without dying. His voracious reading habits, as well as the phrase "From Eternity to Eternity," which he wrote in the notes he kept in his twenties, must have arisen from his search for the path of life without death.

After entering the monastery, the book that played a crucial role for Keun Sunim as he contemplated the problem of eternity was Han Yongun Sunim's *Lectures on the* Tale of the Vegetable Roots (Kr. *Chaegeundam gangui*).[12] Of all its passages, one in particular drove itself into his mind.

> I have a book
> That is not made of paper and ink.
> Though there's not a single word inside,
> It always shines with a great radiance.

In this way, the road he traveled in search of the scripture at the center of his mind led him to Daewonsa and all the way to becoming a monk. According to traditional customs, he married early and had his eldest daughter Dogyeong in his early twenties, but his yearning to seek the truth only grew deeper. At Daewonsa he took on the "*Mu*" (Ch. *Wu*; "no" or "not") *hwadu*[13] for himself, based on Dahui Zonggao's[14] *Letters* (Ch. *Shuzhuang*) and a magazine called *Bulgyo* (Kr. *Buddhism*) that was popular among intellectuals at the time. It is said that in just forty-two days he was able to attain the state of "continuous awareness whether moving or still" (Kr. *dongjeong ilyeo*) where one can maintain the *hwadu* throughout the day without interruption, even through talking and thinking.

One can only guess how intensely Keun Sunim must have practiced meditation at the time in order to attain the state of *dongjeong ilyeo* in a mere forty-two days. It's a near-impossible task if one does not lay down his life to practice with all his might. Though he was still a layperson, after that sort of dedicated intensive practice, returning home to secular life must have been unthinkable.

At first, they say Keun Sunim thought only of practicing meditation and had no intent to become a monk. As he practiced at Daewonsa, however, word spread that "this layperson is practicing splendidly" and compelled the master sunims of Haeinsa, including Kim Beomnin[15] and Choe Beomsul,[16] to personally visit him and invite him to Haeinsa.

Dongsan Sunim,[17] a great Seon master of the time, was then staying at Baengnyeonam at Haeinsa. Dongsan Sunim recognized that Keun Sunim was a vessel of great potential upon first glance, and he told him, "You must enter the monastery to meditate well." Keun Sunim believed that the pursuit of achieving enlightenment came before the formalities of religion and still had no intent of becoming a monastic, but his heart at last began to stir after hearing Dongsan Sunim's teachings. "The path is here. No one will reveal its key. Not until you open the door yourself and enter. But there is no door on that path. And finally there is no path either."

Then one day, Dongsan Sunim left a piece of paper next to Keun Sunim, on which he had written the Dharma name "Seongcheol." That led Keun Sunim to go see Dongsan Sunim, and after speaking with him, finally decided to leave home and become a monk. This was March of 1936.

When Keun Sunim discarded his secular name, Lee Yeongju, to be reborn as a Buddhist monk named Seongcheol, the atmosphere at our Mukgokri family home turned into that of a funeral. My grandfather was unable to keep his frustration and embitterment contained, which my grandmother suffered in turn with the loss of her eye. And one can only guess the betrayal my mother must have felt toward her husband, who had left her pregnant with their second child without a second thought.

But I never once heard my grandmother grieve or complain about Keun Sunim leaving home. She was so tender and kind to us, her grand-children, and the sight of her reciting a Buddhist prayer or reading a book under a kerosene lamp in the winter always brought me warmth and comfort. Watching as she fastidiously prepared food to bring to her son, I felt a dignity bordering on holiness.

I remember my grandmother teaching me in great detail the dif-ferent forms of greetings and letter writing after reading a letter I had written when I was in elementary school. Having moved away to Seoul in the fourth grade, I would come back to my Mukgokri home during every holiday and stay with my grandmother in her room. I was closer to her than I was to my own mother. When I would joke, "It would have been nice if we looked like Grandpa, but we're ugly because we look like Grandma!" she would laugh and reply, "Exactly! But in my eyes you are still the most beautiful children in the world." My heart stings and bleeds like a wound when I think of my grandmother, who lost her son to the monastery and bore with her body the brunt of my grandfather's rage.

My grandmother was an intelligent woman who was well educated about the world, and when her son left for the monastery, she began practicing Seon meditation, to such devotion that she would go into meditation retreat every season. After immersing herself in meditation at a monastery for several months out of the year, a mysterious fragrance would emanate from her body when she returned. It seems as if my father Keun Sunim took after my grandfather in his striking figure and after my grandmother in his clever mind.

My grandmother would prepare clothing and medicine according to the changes in the season to bring to her often-sickly son where he was studying. But Keun Sunim never once showed his face. Left with no choice, she would leave what she brought on top of a rock in front of the monastery and come home empty-handed. After a long while, she would go back to the monastery, and if she saw nothing on the rock, she would return home with relief, thinking that her son had taken what she had brought. But she told me how much her heart would ache if she saw what she had carried strewn messily over the ground, until the world seemed so dark that she couldn't tell the earth from the sky.

Once when she went to Wonhyoam at Beomeosa, where Keun Sunim had been staying, she received word that he had left for the Geumdang meditation hall at Donghwasa, then traveled through Eunhyesa and Unbuam to Geumgangsan. Keun Sunim practiced at the monastery of Mahayeon in Geumgangsan (Kŭmgangsan; Mount Kumgang) in 1940, so it must have been around four years after he left home.[18]

My poor grandmother faced every trouble imaginable as she made the unfamiliar and arduous 400-kilometer journey all the way to Geumgang-san Mahayeon, but when she finally arrived, Keun Sunim's coldness was unbelievable, bellowing at her, "Why did you come from so far away?" My grandmother said, "No, I didn't come to see you! Everyone always talks about how beautiful Geumgangsan is so I came to see for myself!" Even Keun Sunim couldn't say anything to that.

What more could he have said in that situation? This was during the hard times of the Japanese colonial era, when transportation was nothing like what it is today. Who could have known what the mother, who had traveled such a colossal distance, and her son truly felt when they faced each other in that breathless moment?

In the end, a monastic assembly with the entire meditation hall in attendance was held because of my grandmother. The assembly gave Keun Sunim a strict order to either show his mother, who had traveled a long way, around Geumgangsan, or to leave the monastery. The will of the assembly, which even the Buddha must obey, had fallen upon Keun Sunim. In a monastic community, the word of the assembly is a Dharma law and rule of monastery life that must be followed by everyone, no matter who they may be.

The next day Keun Sunim prepared lunch boxes and accompanied my grandmother to the mountain. He held her hand as they crossed streams and carried her on his back when they came across steep inclines. When they came across a nice flat boulder they would sit and rest together, as they explored all the beautiful sights of the mountain: waterfalls, hermitages, monasteries, peaks, and valleys.

"My son carried me on his back or held me up by my hand or arm to guide me through dangerous spots. I don't know if the week I spent with him was a dream or real life. There's no happiness like that. I was so glad I wondered if I was really in paradise."

A few years ago I had the opportunity to accompany Gosan Sunim, who was the administrative head of the Jogye Order at the time, and visit the famous Geumgangsan, which I had before only seen in paintings and photographs. As we entered Geumgangsan, I was greatly moved and thought, "Ah, so this is the place where Jaun Sunim, my father Keun Sunim, and other masters came to meditate long, long ago."

Thinking of my grandmother, who made that long journey that was difficult even with a car, I felt a thousand emotions all at once. In those days one had to prepare many things to set out on the road, and my heart ached as I thought of the single-minded devotion that gave her the strength to bear that burden and come here all the way from the foot of far-off Jirisan.

My grandmother, who had turned to Buddhism, received the Bodhisattva precepts from Jaun Sunim at Haeinsa. The Buddhist name she received then was Choyeonhwa.[19] From then on, my grandmother lived a devout and upright life as a Buddhist in the secular world. She observed the precepts, became a vegetarian, and during the winter and summer retreats she would practice diligently at Wolmyeongam, Jeongchwiam, and other hermitages in Jinju.

One evening while she was practicing at Jeongchwiam, she and a few sunims were on their way back to the hermitage after walking meditation when they saw two large, glowing lights through the bamboo forest—what looked like the eyes of a tiger. The laywomen accompanying them, too afraid to even look, held their breath and crept along nervously, but my grandmother, with her nerves of steel, put their minds at ease by telling them that the tiger was there to lead the sunims home, and to continue practicing diligently, since there was nothing to fear.

Twenty years after Keun Sunim became a monk, and the year after I had left home, my grandmother passed away at her Mukgokri home surrounded by her family and Elder Seongwon Sunim from Gugiram. Not long before she passed, I heard that Seongwon Sunim asked if she still had *hwadu*, to which she responded, "My *hwadu* is clear." Seongwon Sunim later told me that my grandmother announced, "I am going tomorrow, so please shave my head before I die," and that "In my next life I will leave home and become Bulpil's disciple."

> A lasting connection of a thousand, ten-thousand lifetimes,
> In the eternal seasons that flow without end,
> Become reborn again.
> You have made a firm resolution
> To be a disciple of the Buddha and escape the cycle of life
>   and death
> And become an eternal being of great freedom.
> With endless devotion and practice until the end,
> You have freed yourself from the entanglements of an empty world,
> Resolving to attain Buddhahood.
> The proud mother of the great Seongcheol Sunim,
> Who leaves behind unshakeable faith and an admirable legacy.
> My grandmother; no, mother of Seongcheol Sunim, bodhisattva
>   Choyeonhwa!
> I thank you, grandmother.[20]

As I write this book, here is a letter from my heart I have addressed to my grandmother.

My Mother's Dreams, Buried in Her Heart

The person who was most shocked by my decision to enter the monastery was my mother. My mother, who was left trapped in a house full of in-laws and no one she could be open with about her husband's departure, had no choice but to swallow her sorrow and frustration alone. My mother, Lee Deokmyeong, had a smooth round face and was a stylish dresser, whose clothes and appearance were always neat and fashionable.

When she first arrived in her marriage home, she cut such a slender figure that the village people nicknamed her "Miss Lark." She came from a wealthy household and she brought a handsome dowry that included several cows and a servant.

When she was young, my mother was clever enough to fluently recite the Chinese poetry that she had overheard at her grandmother's side. Once she learned hangul, she would often regale her friends with stories from the novels she read. At the age of sixteen she was married to my thirteen-year-old father and gave birth to her first daughter, Dogyeong, when she was twenty-three; and to me at the age of twenty-eight.

On their wedding day, according to tradition, my father sang a song in front of family and friends.

Oh, bright and shining moon, where Li Taibo[21] would play,
A laurel tree grows on that moon so far away.
Chop it down with a silver axe and prune it with a gold one.
Build a little cottage and bring both your parents,
And live happily ever after, happily ever after.

Some of the village elders who heard his song declared, "He isn't one for this world," and their intuition proved correct, when my father left my mother to enter the monastery before she had reached the age of thirty. And not ten years later, when her eldest daughter left my mother to go on to the next world, she buried her within her own heart.

Much later, after Keun Sunim had passed away, a reading list that he had compiled when he was twenty-one years old was discovered. The list includes more than seventy books on philosophy that span all eras and places, including *On Happiness, Critique of Pure Reason, Philosophy of World History, Zhuangzi, Xiaoxue (The Elementary Learning), Daxue (The Great Learning), Heine's Poetry, Das Kapital, On Materialism*, the Old and New Testaments, and many others. Though his body lived in the mundane world, it would have been difficult for my ordinary mother to understand that his mind, reading all of these books, lived in the eternal realm; their married life would have been far from peaceful.

In her revenge against her husband, who had left home with only a flippant promise to come back in ten years, she had vowed, "I'll raise this daughter properly and turn her into a great woman, and present her to him proudly!" But even that daughter would cruelly trample her dream and leave the secular world.

My mother always dressed me in the finest silk clothes and would wash all my clothes and even my underwear for me until the very day I left. Even when I was studying at the Jinju School of Education, she would worry about my tutor being a man and followed me around to my lessons to try to protect me. The betrayal she must have felt when I left her side, her daughter whom she had cherished so dearly but who had never once opened her heart to her, might have in some ways been greater than the pain she felt at her husband's abandonment. Maybe a woman's heart is more tender as a mother than as a wife.

She implored me many times when she realized that my heart was at the monastery: "I won't stop you from leaving, as long as you graduate from university first."

Perhaps she had harbored some hope that I would change my mind as I continued my studies. On the other hand, my grandmother, who herself had practiced meditation deeply, was well aware of how special it was to enter the monastery. Perhaps my grandmother was cheering me on my path to the monastery through her silence on the matter.

When my grandmother was getting ready to go to Geumgangsan to look for Keun Sunim, my mother handed her a letter and asked her to deliver it to him. There is no way for me to know what was written in it, but I wonder if it wasn't full of her sorrow and resentment. But my grandmother, who knew her eldest son's attitude, in the end returned home without having been able to deliver her daughter-in-law's letter. My youngest aunt told me exactly what my grandmother said to her: "I was coming back with the letter still with me, undelivered. As I got close to home, I just felt so sorry I started weeping, and my feet could hardly bear to keep walking."

When I decided not to go to university, my mother's worry was written plainly on her face every day, as if she were thinking, *Just what will that girl say today?* When I eventually left home, against her request to graduate from university first, she was plunged into a deeper loneliness and sorrow that she was unable to swallow. After receiving guidance from Seongwon Sunim at Wolmyeongam in Jinju, she went searching for Keun Sunim at the hermitage of Seongjeonam in the monastery of Pagyesa. She wanted to settle the score with him.

At the time, Keun Sunim was practicing in the hermitage surrounded by a barbed-wire fence and prohibited anyone from entering without his express permission. But she couldn't just back down at the gate after coming all that way. At the time there were three postulants attending to Keun Sunim at his hermitage. One of them, Cheonje Sunim, told me the following.

"I thought I heard something and so I went outside to find a strange young woman asking to see Sunim. I told her that Keun Sunim was not seeing anyone and that she should return home, but she just kept repeating that she has to see him. Around sunset, she disappeared without a trace. I of course assumed she'd left and went about preparing the evening meal. Later, Keun Sunim came into the attendants' room; just as he was about to say something, we heard a crashing of the door being smashed open and, lo and behold, the woman from earlier that day burst in."

Keun Sunim immediately roared at the attendants.

"Get rid of her! What are you doing? Get her out now!"

My mother just glared at Keun Sunim in silence while the attendants, completely bewildered, began pulling at her arms to throw her out. My mother shouted a single phrase.

"Sunim! I came to say something to you!"

The attendants, confused by this bullheaded woman who had hidden all day to appear without warning and by Keun Sunim's inexplicable rage, dragged my mother out of the hermitage all the way back to the main monastery. Only then, as if she had given up, did she let out a deep sigh.

"Sir postulants, I won't try to go up there again. Let me go and you can return home."

This is what Cheonje Sunim told me had happened that night.

"We returned to the hermitage and informed Keun Sunim that we chased her all the way down the hill. He didn't say a word in reply, so we thought the woman was just some random devotee."

It was not until several years later that Cheonje Sunim learned that the woman was in fact my mother. When news of my grandfather's death reached the hermitage where Keun Sunim was at, he sent Cheonje Sunim to make a condolence call to our house.

"We paid our respects at the house of mourning and were getting up to leave when we saw the eldest daughter-in-law. She was wearing mourning clothes, but her face looked so familiar. I thought about this for some time when it suddenly hit me: She was that woman we forcibly kicked out that night some years ago. I was so ashamed and sorry, I could have crawled into the first hole I saw."

The reason she'd gone to see him, knowing for sure she would be turned away, was to finally have her say: "If you like the path so much, you can go alone; why do you have to take my only daughter too? If you just give her back I'll raise her to become an exceptional person!" In the end, however, she was dragged out before she could say a single word. How must she have felt returning home with those empty footsteps?

I was always deliberately cold toward my mother, even when I was young. I felt burdened by how much she obsessed over me, and the more she tried to hang on, the more I tried to get away. Even when I returned home from school to Mukgokri during the holidays, I would stay in my grandmother's room and barely spend any time with my mother. My grandmother passed away the year after I entered the monastery, and my grandfather a few years after that. My mother's loneliness and sadness must have only grown as the years passed.

When I left home, the only person who thought I would actually return was my aunt. She tried to comfort my heartbroken mother, saying, "Don't worry. She's so stubborn that she'll never be able to handle the life of a monk."

My mother had believed my promise that I would achieve enlightenment and come back home in three years. When I had still not returned after ten long years, she came to Seongnamsa to look for me.

My practice had been building a fire in me, and though I hadn't seen her in a decade, I treated my mother colder than ever. Forget a simple "How have you been?"; I didn't even show her a warm glance. I believed that I would be leading my parents into hell if they were to remain attached to me, just as Keun Sunim had told me, and so I treated my mother like I would any other passerby.

"The secular world is the path of Samsara,[22] leaving home is the path of Nirvana; you must firmly sever your ties with the secular world for the sake of liberation." I practiced with these words of Keun Sunim's etched deep in my bones. If my mother had come to visit me right at this moment, I probably would have done the same thing. You cannot reach Nirvana and gain eternal freedom without first tearing free of these connections.

My mother muttered, "You're worse than a viper!" and with that she finally turned her steps back home. But it seems my mother could not avoid her karmic link to Buddhism and later came back to Seongnamsa, where after listening to my teacher Inhong Sunim, she too decided to enter the monastery.

My sister, who died at an early age but dreamed of becoming a Buddhist nun. My grandmother, who never lost her *hwadu* her whole life and shaved her head before she passed on. The last words of my grandfather, the obstinate Confucian scholar, who said on his deathbed, "You bastard Sakyamuni! I'm going to Seongcheol Sunim!" And in her fifties, my mother, who abandoned the secular world and entered the monastery. Would anyone disagree that perhaps everyone in my family was a sunim in their previous lives?

Chapter 3

Handwritten Sermon Notes

You Are Inherently Buddha, Yet You Don't Know It

A Practitioner Must First Know Poverty

"Let's meet at Busan Station one month after graduation."

Okja and I had parted ways back at Wolmyeongam with that promise. Finally, when the agreed day came, we boarded the Busan train heading for Daegu. We were on our way to see Keun Sunim.

Okja's mother, who was a deeply faithful believer, was very supportive of her daughter's decision to study at the monastery and even came to the train station to see us off. "Practice well," she encouraged us, and she would often come to visit us after we left and bring us things that we might need.

I asked Okja on the train, "What did you tell your father when you left home?"

"I told him I'd be studying at a temple for the med school exam."

Her father believed her immediately and even bought a lantern and packed it in her bag, saying she would need it in the dark mountains. Okja had wanted to study more and become a doctor or even a poet, but she said she was curious about what Keun Sunim meant when he said, "Going down a single path will lead to something wonderful." Once she realized that she could find true happiness by figuring out her *hwadu*, she left home without a moment of hesitation. Fired up with determination, Okja said to me, "Didn't Keun Sunim tell us that if we let go of our *hwadu*, we might as well be dead? I think living as a corpse is living a life that's *minus*. And we can't be living minus lives."

Keun Sunim had since left Cheonjegul for the hermitage of Seongjeo-nam at Pagyesa, in North Gyeongsang Province and had been practicing intensely there for ten years in total solitude: during that time, he never stepped outside the temple gates, not even once. This "Confinement Practice" is deeply meaningful, not just in Keun Sunim's life story but also in the history of Korean Buddhism. For ten long years, he put up a barbed-wire fence and did not see anyone from the outside world. During that time he not only pored through a vast number of scriptures and the Dharma teachings of past Seon patriarchs, but he researched math, science, and many other disciplines as well. Reading the scriptures and meditating, he was preparing for the future of Korean Buddhism.

Keun Sunim's "Ten-Year Confinement Practice" prepared him for the Dharma talk at Gimyongsa regarded as a lion's roar and his Hundred-Day

Dharma lecture at Haeinsa, but it was also the time he established the innovative Buddhist theories and practical methods that eventually came to be known collectively as "Seongcheol Buddhism." His articulate and comprehensive teachings at Gimyongsa later became famous as the "Undalsan Teachings," while today his hundred-day talks are widely considered to be the crystallization of Buddhism's very essence. While in the outside world the battle between married and celibate monks raged during the height of the Buddhism Purification Movement in the 1950s,[1] these works were the product of Keun Sunim's devoted practice, avoiding the tide of conflict in solitude to bring about the inner purification of Korean Buddhism.

Arriving at Seongjeonam, I offered three prostrations [kneeling bows] to Keun Sunim and told him the news.

"I have left home to study meditation."

"Hurry slowly!"

If there is one thing he and I have in common, it is that we say only what is needed and do away with unnecessary words. Even after I told him I had left home, that was all he had to say to me.

I couldn't understand what his words meant at the time. How impatient my mind must have been, when I felt compelled to find enlightenment in just three years when even the Buddha himself took six? Once I decide to do something, I attack it with tunnel vision. I'm an express train that barrels forward without hesitation. Without that urgent personality, or that burning desire to attain enlightenment in three years, I couldn't have turned my back on the people whom I loved so dearly as easily and immediately as I did.

Keun Sunim knew that urgency in my heart and told me to "hurry slowly." He would have known that we were young, and that we needed time. The path of the Dharma is far from the only one where you need time to accomplish what you want. Countless hours of hard work, dedication, and a high degree of self-control and restraint: is this not the very path of life itself? Faced by that, we were no more than bare-bottomed children, clumsy and reckless, and that was what Keun Sunim excavated in that single phrase.

Keun Sunim did not tell us to become ordained. Instead he said, "Practitioners must first learn poverty and gain humility," and he ordered us to go down to the village and beg for alms.

To us, his words were already law. We immediately went to the village and, entering a random house, asked, "Please give us some food."

The household's young daughter-in-law prepared a whole table spread of delicious food for us, and after eating our fill we returned and reported to Keun Sunim what happened. He tutted and said, "Tsk-tsk, you have a long way to go."

Begging for food from another person must be understood as an exercise in humility. Just as the word *bhiksu* (monk) or *bhiksuni* (nun) means "one who begs," practitioners must live their entire lives without personal possessions, begging for food while devoting themselves to their studies. He wanted us to understand that the foundation of the practitioner is humility and nonpossession, qualities you cannot cultivate yourself without.

Not wanting to waste a single moment, we decided to go to Hongjesa at Taebaeksan where we had heard a number of great sunims were practicing. Beopjeon Sunim, who had attended to Keun Sunim with great devotion at Cheonjegul, offered us the following advice: "At Hongjesa they only eat gruel, so if you go there right away it'll be hard to adapt. I think you should first spend a season at Cheongnyangsa, a branch temple of Haeinsa, before you go over there."

Hearing that, we headed for Cheongnyangsa, at the foot of the mountain of Maehwasan.

Keun Sunim's Textbook for Practitioners

Before Okja and I left for Cheongnyangsa, Keun Sunim handed us a notebook and told us to read it together. It was a book of Dharma notes, written personally by Keun Sunim himself. Written with those new practitioners in mind who had just started on their path, it contained teachings and instructions on the methods of practice in the hopes that they would devote themselves earnestly and resolutely.

Keun Sunim would have thought about how best to instruct the two twenty-year-old beginners who had left their homes to become eternal beings of great freedom, like the Buddha did. Moreover, these young truth-seekers hadn't even been ordained, but were still hoping to finish their studies quickly and return home. He must have faced quite the challenge coming up with a way to teach them the basics of Buddhism and to foster their devotion.

I carried this notebook around, tucked close against my chest, as if it were my own life. I read and reread it until I eventually memorized the whole thing. The teachings in the notebook were pure scripture, like precious, life-giving water.

"Some Words for the Practitioner," "Ten Things Entrusted of Monastics," "The Eight Precepts," and other teachings became my very flesh and blood, and the Dharma notes, which made my faith surge like a great wave, became my textbook, pushing me to never falter on the path of Truth.

To mean that such a teaching could never be given a name, Okja and I wrote, "One Hundred Negations" on the front of the notebook.

When I read the writings in the notebook, I couldn't contain my rising devotion, and I became consumed with the thought of laying down my life in the pursuit of practice. Nothing else mattered to me. Especially when I read about how sunims of the past had studied, my only goal was to hurry up and do as they had done in order to find enlightenment.

"I could be an eternal being of great freedom if I practice like this!"

We were so determined that we made a promise: "We won't go to the hospital even if we get sick. We'll go to the Dharma Hall and do prostrations to the Buddha until we're healed by his life-giving water."

Reading them even now, Keun Sunim's Dharma notes were written in a very modern language that make their meanings remarkably digestible. They were written in the 1950s, when he was in his midforties, and I can't help but marvel at how clear and articulate his ideas are, with not a single unnecessary word or sentence.

The neatly written notebook begins with the following preface:

> The grave of Lord Mengchang,[2] who lived in wealth and
>   luxury,
> Has become farmland in less than a century.
> What, then, is there to mention of accounts more paltry?

This is indeed the case. The mortality of life is an immutable law of the universe. The vastest oceans and tallest mountains will be destroyed in the end, to say nothing of all the organisms, large and small, that inhabit the spaces in between them! Even the greatest hero who enjoys unbelievable wealth and honor will never be able to avoid death, to become nothing more than specks of dust. If so, can we call wealth and honor, no matter how great, anything but an empty dream? There is a song with lyrics that conveys this very message. "There are graves large and small one league south of Luoyang Castle; how many belong to virtuous heroes and how many belong to women of great beauty?"

Oh, fleeting life, transient life, like a dewdrop on a blade of grass!

Although a flower that dies in the winter will bloom again in the spring, humans, once dead, are gone forever. A thousand years will not bring a person back from death. It is truly an eternal tragedy that the universe is merely the tomb of life.

After the ancient hero Emperor Qin unified heaven and earth, he built a grand palace and did everything he could think of to wash away his sorrows; but nevertheless, he too became nothing more than a handful of dust. This struggle is but the meaningless song and dance of a prisoner on his way to the gallows.

Does that mean life ends in eternal tragedy? Is there a tiny sliver of hope? Read on, carefully.

Keun Sunim continues his teachings, giving many examples of how people may live forever.

When the Buddha found enlightenment, he shouted, "How strange and bizarre it is. All sentient beings have an immortal and indestructible Buddha-nature! But people wander about aimlessly and suffer endlessly. How sad and regrettable it is."

These words were the first time it was proclaimed that we humans, living a life of delusion, have an eternal and indestructible life-form within us. Now that all living creatures, submerged in darkness, have gained a path to eternal salvation, how can we repay this debt? Let us celebrate him, and pay our respects for all eons to come.

Even this eternally luminous life-form, before it finds enlightenment and radiates its light, is hidden in perpetual darkness in all directions. Thus, because the happenings of a previous life are forgotten once the body changes, one does not know that true life continues and does not end.

Attaining enlightenment is like a blind man attaining sight. Darkness becomes a thing of the past and the brightness is ever present, even if the body changes tens of thousands of times. Before opening their eyes, a person thinks that the death of their body as it changes is permanent. Upon opening their eyes, they see they are always luminous; changing the bodies that we inhabit is no different from changing the clothes that we wear.

Before opening their eyes, people are pulled around helplessly by their karma, experiencing only suffering without the slightest freedom. Opening their eyes, however, they enjoy eternal happiness through great freedom and great wisdom.

Let us look at this in our actual lives. Regardless of how intelligent or wise an unenlightened person is, their minds are as dark as night while they sleep: they know as much as a dead person. On the other hand, because an enlightened person is always radiant, darkness never descends upon them no matter how deep their sleep.

This is the absolute radiance that transcends Light and Darkness, that is to say, it is the very nature of the Buddha himself.

One only needs to sleep in order to test whether enlightenment has truly been attained. One may very well know all of the Buddha's teachings and feel like they've attained the most enlightened of enlightenments. But if darkness falls upon you while sleeping, this is not true enlightenment. This is why the great masters of the past were the most cautious about this subject.

When realized, the sheer unimaginable power of the ever-present and indestructible Buddha-nature is so great that it is not just secular scholars who are unable to describe it. According to the Buddha, "The Buddha-nature I speak of will be known in its entirety once it is attained. Even if all the Buddhas of the world simultaneously came forth to explain this nature, in ten million years they would have only been able to scratch just the very tip of the surface. That is how extraordinary and mysterious it is. While the empty space in the universe's ten directions may be vast, such vastness pales in comparison with the Buddha-nature. If Buddha-nature were an ocean, the universe would be a tiny bubble of foam in its center. Although the void has endured for billions of years, it is "but a blink of an eye" compared to the life of Buddha-nature. This is how all the Buddhas in the world would describe it.

How could you then describe the happiness it brings us to pursue such a divine principle?

The old masters set themselves on fire just to hear one word of this teaching; but offering this body in flames a million times would still not be enough to repay even one millionth of this lesson. The only way to repay the Buddha and the old masters is to practice diligently and attain enlightenment. So practice hard and with all your strength!

The following are Keun Sunim's teachings on the act of practicing Seon meditation.

The Buddha said to Ananda, "Even if you spend an infinite amount of time memorizing all of my deep and mystical teachings, it still wouldn't be better than spending one day of practice to illuminate your mind."

He also said, "I have walked the Path of Enlightenment together with Ananda from distant, previous lives. Ananda has always loved letters, and it was his focus on reading over all else that prevented him from attaining Buddhahood all this time. Unlike him, I was able to reach nirvana because I only focused on practice."

Laozi also said, "One who seeks knowledge learns something every day, while one who seeks the Way forgets something every day. Less and less remains until there is nothing to lose. This is where one gains true freedom."

An ascetic once said a long time ago, "The heart is clean and as bright as a polished mirror by nature. But specks of delusions build up one by one until they extinguish that brightness, leaving the heart to experience the suffering of death and rebirth in darkness. The original brightness will escape the darkness and emerge once more when all the dusts of delusions are cleared away, leading to the path of great freedom. Focusing on academic learning only serves to dirty the mirror further, and deepens the suffering of birth and death. The dust can only be brushed off through meditation, and continuing down this path will lead to the transcendence of birth and death."

He also said this: "There is a limit to wisdom that is gained through reading. Things outside the boundaries of what was learned continue to exist in darkness. But when enlightenment is reached through practice, the wisdom gained is boundless. The light of that wisdom shines as bright as the sun, while learned wisdom is but the glow of a firefly."

The sixth patriarch of Chan Buddhism (Huineng, 638–713) was a firewood seller and did not know how to read a single word. Because he gained enlightenment, however, his teachings are no different than those of the Buddha himself, and men of even the highest learning would never be able to understand their profound truths.

When Master Tiantai (Zhiyi, 538–597) attained profound enlightenment, his teacher, Master Nanyue, praised him, "Even someone who has memorized the entire Tripitaka[3] cannot hold a candle to your endless teachings."

He has indeed become known as a great master of the ages.

Master Yi was a student of Master Gaofeng (1238–1295). He entered the monastery and was studying the *Heart Sutra*, but after three days he was not able to memorize even a single character. The teacher greatly lamented this, but somebody told him, "This person must have meditated in his previous life." So Master Yi was told to practice Zen meditation where, sure enough, he greatly excelled. He eventually attained great enlightenment and went on to spread the Dharma far and wide. He passed away at the age of ninety-nine and was cremated, but there was not a single wisp of smoke. Instead, countless crystal relics[4] spilled forth and surprised the people even more.

The Buddha said, "Offering food, clothes, and valuables of silver and gold to all the Buddhas of the world and holding Dharma services for the next million years may bring great merits. However, those merits will only be a millionth, even a billionth, of the merit of helping a suffering sentient being for a short moment."

How wise he was. For a disciple of the Buddha, making offerings in front of the Buddha while flaunting his steadfast intentions in personal affairs is an unforgivable heresy. Where will one find the Buddha's vast and boundless mercy if one abandons the offerings of the Buddha Dharma to help others? One can only sigh in despair.

But even such a significant Dharma is a billion times less meaningful than the act of practicing and meditating to feed one's own Buddha-nature with *hwadu*. Facing one who embodies the Dharma of self-cultivation, a thousand Buddhas would be rendered speechless and retreat to a distant corner of the land.

Master Yongming[5] said, "I recommend practice to everyone around the world. Even if the listener does not believe, the seeds of nirvana have already been sown. And even if nirvana is not reached, practice in itself will bestow a fortune far greater than what the human or heavenly worlds have to offer."

These words are not mine, but those of all Buddhas and patriarchs.

Although there are many more such stories that helped me in my practice, I'll omit them in the interest of space and instead copy down the Eight Precepts, the principles that a practitioner must adhere to, that were handwritten at the end of the notebook. They contain to the letter the message that Seongcheol Keun Sunim wanted to impart to us.

The Eight Precepts of Practice, from Sacrifice to Asceticism

The Eight Precepts of Practice

After wandering around for eons, suffering the continuous cycles of birth and death, I have received that rarest of rare gifts—a human body—and I have encountered the teachings of the Buddha. If I do not redeem myself in this life, who knows how long I will have to wait for my next opportunity? With the same indomitable will and resolve of a lone warrior facing ten thousand enemies, I would sooner die than back down from my goal.

1. Sacrifice

Without discarding the insignificant to take on the great, it is impossible to achieve great things. Temporary and trivial wealth and material things must be abandoned completely for the sake of eternal freedom. One must sacrifice one's family, wealth, power, and everything else that are but false illusions, turning away from them completely to focus solely on practice.

2. Severance from secular life

It is conventional wisdom among all Buddhas that the cycle of birth and death is rooted in desire. Without severing all ties to physical desire, enlightenment will never be attained. First, it depletes the body. Second, it destroys the mind. Third, the constant enslavement by one's passions results in endless suffering and torment. Fourth, one becomes be preoccupied with reproducing and rearing. Fifth, desire will succeed death with life, thereby pulling one into the endless cycle of birth, death, and rebirth. Thus it is a fundamental obstacle of practice, and it must be severed completely.

3. Solitude

Empathy is the enemy of practice. Although to be considerate and helpful may seem like virtues, this is the starting point of the cycle of birth and death. One must therefore avoid the bad karma brought about by good intentions and journey in solitude toward the freedom of eternity. The Great Path cannot be achieved without becoming a truly solitary person, a great failure in life from a conventional perspective. This is why a clear line must be drawn to isolate oneself from the ordinary people. The second you breach this line and begin to compromise with civilians, you must understand that you are killing yourself by wasting that time frivolously.

4. Contempt

Receiving the hospitality of others will be your ruin; the eternal path to life is lost to those sold to such things. True life comes only when contempt and scorn is heaped upon us. Those who praise and follow me are the hordes of *Mara*, precisely those who will hinder me the most. There is nobody I can be more grateful toward than those who oppose me, flinging rocks and smearing my name. What could be a greater debt, when they remove all things that interfere with my practice, bolster my patience, and help me continually progress in my practice? Even sincerely prostrating myself before them with hands together would not be enough to adequately thank such a person; how could I bear a grudge against them? This is the true way of the practitioner.

5. Humility

Only when I realize I am worthless do I reach maturity. Age means nothing; I may be eighty years old and still be immature if I am conceited. It is truly difficult to understand those who run around boasting about how great they are, as if they know anything. When I serve everyone as if they were the Buddha and realize that I know nothing, that I am a nobody, is when I take a great stride toward enlightenment. Just as the lowest places on the earth naturally become home to the greatest oceans, the vastness of the Unchanging Path can only be contained by such a land. The admiration and offerings of others must be dodged like a bullet and avoided like a venomous snake. And no matter what question someone may ask, we must answer it with "I know nothing."

6. Commitment

One body cannot walk two paths. Eternal freedom lies in awakening to your *hwadu* and beholding the Buddha-nature within oneself. All other paths lead to death. Talking about food for hundreds of years will never fill your belly; the only way to be full is to actually eat. Thus, in this place of practice even the Eighty Thousand Dharma Treasures (the Buddhist scriptural canon) become only hindrances, to say nothing of other writings. One must only consider the *hwadu*.

7. Endeavor

The degree of every success is directly proportional to the amount of effort put into achieving it. Hoping for maximal results from minimal effort is madness. Eternal freedom cannot be attained through mere ordinary effort. The old masters took vows of silence and did away with sleep, practicing ceaselessly and without rest. It was only through such exhaustive efforts that they were able to attain enlightenment.

8. Asceticism

All failure and corruption stem from laziness. Furthermore, lay believers' donations are like a deadly poison that kills monks. The strict ancient rule of skipping a day of food for skipping a day of work comes from this idea. Thus the Buddha pronounces that to violate this rule is to become part of the enemy nation, serving only to deepen your personal hell, to speak nothing of progress toward enlightenment. We must sweat to survive. It is impossible to achieve Buddha-nature with the rotten attitude of doing what I want while eating your food. This is why the Buddha's True Dharma was transmitted to Maha Kasyapa, the most austere and ascetic of his disciples. One must endure and overcome all suffering for the sake of the great eternal freedom.

Chapter 4

Life as a Postulant

The Bushy-Haired Postulants' First Charge toward Enlightenment

There Is No Tomorrow

I still remember my first determination to achieve enlightenment during my time at Cheongnyangsa[1] as if it were yesterday. They don't say that the first aspiration is the site of enlightenment for nothing. If you keep pushing ahead in the spirit of that first resolve, there isn't anybody who can't become enlightened.

In those days I was strict with myself in a way that almost defies belief. I drew a border as strict as the demilitarized zone [which separates North and South Korea] between myself and other people, and reminding myself constantly that "there is no tomorrow," I practiced barely laying down once for one hundred days. Keun Sunim's notebook was my teacher and the manual for my practice. I strove to follow the teachings within it to the letter.

It was right after the war and the Buddhism Purification Movement,[2] and Cheongnyangsa was old and not much to look at. It has changed a lot since then, but at the time there was only a modest Buddha Hall to the west, a small meditation hall that doubled as the sleeping quarters in the center, a grain mill to the east, and not much besides.

The nuns assembled in the meditation hall were the sunims Jan-gil, Myochan, Hyeongak, Hyeonmuk, Hyegeun, Jisu, Wonmyeong, and Byeokhae, as well as postulant Doeui, and finally Okja and myself, the short-haired postulants (Kr. *haengja*, novice practitioners) who hadn't yet shaved our heads.

When the meditation hall goes into a retreat, individual duties and responsibilities are assigned to each of the nuns. Jangil Sunim, who was both the abbess (*juji*) and head of the meditation hall (*ipseung*), assigned tasks to each of us so the assembly would be self-sufficient. The roles of all the nuns during this retreat were as follows.

The head nun dictated the rules and discipline of the assembly and guided our practice, while the executor and overseer operated daily chanting and ceremonial rites in the Buddha Hall.

The abbess was the representative for the administrative and financial matters of the monastery, while the kitchen head oversaw food offerings for the Buddha as well as the communal meals for the assembly.

One nun prepared side dishes and soups, while another two nuns managed the monastery and kitchen inventory. One nun was responsible for making tea, while yet another attended to the visitors who came to the monastery.

I was made the *maho*, in charge of making the starch paste that the nuns used to iron their robes, something I had never done before. On my first attempt, I just dumped all of the flour I was given into a big tub of water and ended up with something that was neither paste nor porridge, which raised hell with the sunims. Doing something for the first time, I should have asked a more experienced nun to help me, but I didn't and made a mess of the whole thing. These kinds of things happened to me quite often. Perhaps it was because I had grown up with the habit of doing whatever I wanted without asking anybody for permission. In the end, I spent my first retreat with no assigned duties.

My first experience of practice as a postulant, a novice practitioner, officially began. After the nuns were assigned their duties the retreat began in earnest. Although none of us explicitly took a vow of silence, amid our intense practice silence descended upon us naturally. Reading and rereading Keun Sunim's notebook, and with our fervent devotion stretching up to the very corners of the sky, Okja and I made a promise together.

"Let's study without sleep again."

At age twenty during my time at Cheongnyangsa, I had summarized the teachings of the notebook in my head like this: "There is no success without effort. The more I can overcome this physical body, the more I will succeed. I must persevere through all hardships and suffering solely for the sake of the great eternal freedom. A life-or-death effort is needed to practice, and if I am negligent or lazy I will never be able to achieve great enlightenment no matter how long I practice. Do not sleep for more than four hours. Live like a mute and don't chatter idly."

The lives of past masters, who had practiced with bone-wrenching effort, were etched into my mind and became my models. Whenever I felt sleepy I would lie down by the heads of the other nuns, and when I'd open my eyes again, scarcely thirty minutes would have passed. Okja and I never had to wake each other up either. When one of us was getting up, the other would already be out the door. At night we would walk in the front yard of the Dharma Hall; if our legs began to tire or hurt, we would lean on one of the monastery pillars and rest for a moment.

In the middle of the night the cries of wild animals in the mountains were so loud that at first I'd often run away into the Dharma Hall, my face white with fear. Okja wasn't afraid, but I was easily scared. On the other hand, though, I was naturally sleepless and could always wake at any time I wanted to, without the help of a clock.

One day I asked myself how I could continue to practice in the mountains if I was so afraid of the animals, and so in the deep of night I climbed up to the place where I had heard their howls. There was nothing there. I realized I had been afraid of nothing at all, and after that I didn't get scared anymore.

In truth, there is nothing for us to be afraid of. We only feel that way because of our own karma. We are blocked by fear, which in turn prevents us from being free. Only when we realize inherently that not a single thing in this world has true substance can we become free.

Keun Sunim said the following: "Unhappiness and anxiety do not exist inherently. They exist only in our minds."

Sleep would try to take me after practicing hard all day. When Okja and I grew tired, we would pick up our meditation cushions that we used to sit and perform prostrations on and go for a leisurely walk around Cheongnyangsan Mountain. We didn't follow the practice schedule that the others kept, and the mountain itself was our meditation hall.

If we became tired while doing our walking meditation, we would take turns leaning against a pine tree and resting our eyes. After ten minutes we would use a wooden cane to tap the napping one awake. We used this method in order to remain in silence and not speak. I felt like a new person with just ten minutes of rest, no matter how tired I was. If you've never experienced it, you can't know that feeling of reinvigoration.

Keun Sunim said, "You can fool the whole world, but you can't fool yourself. You know the level of your own practice best." The most important thing is one's own determination and resolve. How could I sleep, not knowing if death might take me today or tomorrow? There is a world of difference between living in a monastery just because you like the atmosphere there and doing so with attaining freedom from life and death as your goal. If you find yourself indifferent to this choice, you've forgotten the very reason why you became a sunim in the first place.

I would be very hungry by the time I returned from walking and practicing in the mountains. If a basket of steamed barley caught my eye, I'd run over and shamelessly start scooping it into a lettuce wrap and gobbling it up. The monastery was going through hard times back then, so you don't know how grateful we were even for some coarse barley.

Fortunately, I think that ever since I was a child, sleeping and eating had never been that important to me. I woke up whenever I wanted and couldn't lie still for very long. I was perfectly happy eating my rice with only kimchi as the side dish. Even if there were a mountain of delicacies on the table, I'd always reach for the kimchi first. I ate kimchi and rice with such gusto that anyone who saw me eat would say, "I want some too!" Even now, I love some refreshing *dongchimi*, white radish kimchi, and just that is enough to make me happy.

There is an episode from those days that I still remember clearly. Along the path where we would take a stroll, there was a field of cilantro that was left to overgrow in order to harvest its seeds. In my postulancy I couldn't stand cilantro and so I chopped it all down, thinking only about how disgusting it smelled. In moments like those, Okja and I knew what the other was thinking just by sharing a glance. As if we planned the whole thing, the two of us began hacking away at the cilantro plants and even tossed the knife that reeked of cilantro into a ditch afterward.

When the abbess later discovered what we had done, we received a severe scolding.

"We needed to collect the seeds so we can sow them in the spring, and you're telling me you just cut the whole thing down?"

We just did it because we didn't like the smell; we still didn't have the age or the maturity to think about the consequences. Today, I actually like cilantro. Though the smell would make me retch when I was a postulant, once I tried it a few times I eventually fell in love with its unique fragrance and flavor.

One day, we went out with the sunims to weed the red chili pepper field. But when Okja and I looked back down the rows at our handiwork, we discovered that all the chili plants in our wake were broken. Neither of us had weeded in the field before, so we had unknowingly been crushing the peppers with our behinds. Again, we got a talking-to by the abbess, but perhaps she knew it was our first time, because we didn't get into too much trouble.

Although I was clumsy when it came to doing chores, I didn't spend all my time being scolded by the elder nuns. When she saw me pacing in the front yard of the monastery at night in order to fight my sleepiness, Jangil Sunim, the abbess, would tell me I was doing a good job and feed me a piece of candy. Candy was a rare treat back then, so in her actions I felt a great mercy.

I also once avoided some trouble thanks to something my grandfather had told me when I left home. Toward the end of the retreat, one of the nuns returned from the mountains with some freshly picked mushrooms that were prepared for our evening meal. Remembering my grandfather telling me, "Don't eat any mushrooms other than pine mushrooms," Okja and I didn't eat any, but it wasn't until the other nuns and the village workers who ate them with gusto all began keeling over that we realized the mushrooms were poisonous. Okja and I had to nurse the nuns for a full seven days, and we were only able to leave Cheongnyangsa once they had all recovered.

I practiced so diligently during that retreat that Hyeonmuk Sunim, now the rector at the Seongnamsa Seon meditation hall, said to me as she reminisced on those days:

"Seeing how diligently two girls who hadn't even entered the monastery were practicing, us ordained nuns felt embarrassed for ourselves. So as soon as the retreat ended, Hyeongak Sunim and I immediately went to Jeju Island [a large island to the south, isolated from mainland Korea by a fair distance]. We wanted to go somewhere totally remote without any people and just meditate in solitude."

Afflicted by the Malady of Meditation

During those days at Cheongnyangsa, I slept for an average of only thirty minutes a day and gave everything I had to not let go of my *hwadu*. Practicing like this for one hundred days, all my delusions fell away. Although in the beginning, useless thoughts about nothing in particular floated through my head like clouds in the summer sky, after some time my *hwadu* became all that I ever thought about in my everyday life, and I wouldn't have been able to let it go even if I'd tried. What I realized then was that when you do the things you want to do, there is no such thing as fatigue or suffering.

Practicing like this, as the retreat drew to a close my gums started to become swollen and painful. I had gotten so used to living without talking that even when I noticed it, it didn't occur to me to tell anyone. So I just continued to practice, undeterred.

It was very hot that summer and there was a great deal of rain, especially around the time the retreat ended, but when it rained I refused to take shelter under the eaves of the monastery roof. The sheltered porches under the roof serve as a quiet resting place for sunims, but I was so driven by the urgency to finish my practice quickly that I didn't think about the necessity of rest.

In his notebook of teachings, Keun Sunim wrote down twelve ascetic practices (The Twelve Austerities) that represent the fundamental attitude of a practitioner toward food, clothing, and shelter:[3]

> I do not accept anything new or whole even if it's given to me.
>
> I do not hoard extra clothes.
>
> I do not ask for anything, and only eat food that is offered to me.
>
> I accept food from both the rich and the poor without discrimination.
>
> I eat in one sitting and do not eat twice.
>
> Even if I only receive a little, I am satisfied with it and do not beg for more.
>
> I do not drink juice or honey water in the afternoon.
>
> I live in remote and distant places, like mountains or fields, and do not mix with other people.
>
> I remind myself what impermanence is by looking at the bones in the graveyard when I practice to further my devotion.
>
> I do not live inside a house and always practice under a tree.
>
> A spot under a tree can almost feel like being inside and therefore lead to attachment, so I live in a place that isn't covered by anything.
>
> Because failure comes from laziness, I always sit, not lie down, in my dedication to my practice.

Why was the Buddha's True Dharma passed on to Maha Kasyapa, the most austere and ascetic of his disciples? It is because only the one who puts in the most effort will be able to receive the deepest of the deepest of the Buddha's truths. That is why the True Dharma can be found in ascetic practice, and one must strive to overcome any and all hardships with a firm resolve.

Even if you're unable to follow all twelve ascetic practices, you must never forget the fundamental spirit behind them. If one forgets this, that person is not a practitioner but, as the Buddha said, a great enemy of the Dharma. Clothes should be just enough to only cover one's body; if one wishes to eat and dress well like the rest of the world, what use is there for one to enter the monastery? One should eat just enough food to not suffer from malnutrition, and one's dwelling should be just enough to keep out the winds and rain so as not to fall ill. Not the slightest hint of indulgence can be permitted.

Believe deeply in the laws of karma. You must think of donations and offerings as poison. The three meals we eat each day were given to us as alms, but ultimately they are the blood and sweat of those who offered them to us. And so it follows that we eat and drink three bowls of their blood each day to survive. What a fearsome thought it is that if we fail to attain enlightenment during this lifetime, we must pay all of these offerings back, down to the very last drop of water.

You must resolve to live as much as you can by your own work and effort, for a life spent relying on others without thought is another form of hell. One must fear donations and offerings as if they were poison and to dodge them as if they were arrows, all for the sake of striving and striving for the great eternal freedom.

To us, this notebook was our master, and so we tried our best to live our lives according precisely to its teachings. One day, a storm was passing by, and though the wind and rain raged around us so fiercely that it broke the branches and shook unripe fruits off the large persimmon tree in the yard, we paid it no mind and continued our walking meditation in the pouring rain. Although this wasn't the type of intensive practice where practitioners never lie down, we pushed ourselves even beyond that point. These were our lives at Cheongnyangsa, never looking back and only looking forward.

These days, when I'm in the meditation hall (the Simgeomdang at Seongnamsa)[4] during the end of a retreat season, young disciples will often come to ask me, "How should I be practicing?" Each time I hear this question I remember my first determination to practice at Cheong-nyangsa and tell them this: "Everybody needs to experience practicing with all of their strength. If you want to find your own practice, you must work intensely, so that even the sound of the bamboo clapper that signals the end of the session means nothing to you. You must know your own practice before you can call yourself a practitioner."

To a practitioner, *hwadu* is life. With your mind unaffected by any circumstance, if you practice with the great belief that you are a Buddha,

Figure 4.1. In the meditation hall at Simgeomdang where I spend my retreats each year. "The person who spends their whole life sitting on a meditation cushion and dies there to attain enlightenment is the happiest person in the world." Seong-cheol Keun Sunim would say this often while he was still living. I wish to live in the Simgeomdang until the end, and then leave quietly. Photo by Kim Minsook.

harbor the great resentment of living as an ordinary person even though you are a Buddha, and possess the great suspicion toward your *hwadu*, you will become one with your *hwadu*. Great belief, great resentment, and great suspicion; if even one of these is lacking, you can't call yourself a practitioner. The will to practice rigorously with these three states of mind is true determination.

Nothing is accomplished easily. That goes without saying for the path to enlightenment. I gave every ounce of my life to work as hard as I could during that first season, and I have no regrets. I believe it's why I am the person I am today.

I finally fell ill right before the end of the retreat. I had what was known as meditation fever. There are two illnesses that are most feared by practitioners: "upper-energy" fever, where the body's energy flow, or qi, rises up to the head and causes migraines, and the other is "cold sickness." In the summertime, practicing while sitting on a boulder can sometimes give you cold sickness. The boulder's surface might be warm, but if you sit for too long, its cold energy permeates your body, and it's quite difficult to reverse. But compared to upper-energy fever, this "cold sickness" is nothing.

To me, meditation fever is the most agonizing illness in the world. The whole body feels like it's burning up, but it's totally different from a regular fever; the tightness of your chest, and the pain that makes your head feel like it might explode can't be described in words. The agony of being unable to let go of *hwadu* even in the midst of that boiling heat, is something you can't understand if you haven't experienced it yourself.

When you practice for a hundred days straight with no sleep, meditation fever is practically inevitable. Even so, Keun Sunim's advice to "hurry slowly" didn't occur to me. I only thought, why would he tell us, who practiced like there was no tomorrow, to take things slowly?

After the winter retreat at Cheongnyangsa, I went to Seongjeonam where Keun Sunim was staying and complained about my illness.

"My head hurts so much I am unable to practice."

"Isn't that why I told you to hurry slowly?"

Keun Sunim told me how to bring down the fever.

"Send qi downward to the abdomen, legs, and the arches of the feet."

As he wrote this for me in Chinese characters, he gave me this advice: "Sit on the meditation cushion and focus on lowering your qi downward to the bottom of your feet like water crashing down from a tall waterfall, and your fever will go down."

I focused as he said as hard as I could, and soon enough the ardent questioning, *Why?* loosened its grip on me and my fever began to come down. Keun Sunim's advice continued to be a great help to my practice over the years.

As this story has spread, several monks who were afflicted with meditation fever have come to visit me to ask about the details. Even today, there must be many people still suffering from it. I have told my own disciples who come down with meditation fever about Keun Sunim's method so they could overcome it, but I still keep for myself today the words that he wrote for me.

When I had recovered from my fever, Keun Sunim chose my next place of practice, telling me, "Go to Inhong Sunim at Hongjesa in Taebaeksan." On the way there, I stopped by Gimyongsa in Undal Mountain. It was because I wanted to meet Elder Wolhye Sunim, who was renowned for her rigorous and razor-sharp style of practice. Myoyeong Sunim, who was Inhong Sunim's senior disciple, guided us on our visit.

When we arrived, Elder Wolhye Sunim was with her own senior disciple Myojeon Sunim and some other nuns. When I greeted her, she welcomed me warmly, asking if I was "that student from Jinju." It seemed rumors had spread about the girl who went to the monastery to practice with her hair still on her head.

Elder Wolhye Sunim was extremely thin and frail, but she exuded grace and dignity. At the age of forty-two she had heard Cheongdam Sunim give a Dharma talk at a Buddhist center in Andong, and just three days later decided to enter the monastery. Though her son, a successful judge, tried desperately to dissuade through the night, she broke free from his clinging hands and took off for Yunpilam where she shaved her head. A happy life and harmonious family that wanted for nothing: she cut herself off from it all in a single stroke, so you can imagine how fearsome her practice was. When her son got married, he wrote her a letter saying he wanted to visit her at Yunpilam, but such was her dedication to severing her connections with the secular world to focus solely on practice that she flatly refused to see him. Before long she had become a role model for monks and nuns across the country.

Elder Wolhye Sunim came to know the eminent masters of the time, including Gobong Sunim, Hyobong Sunim, Seongcheol Sunim, and Jaun Sunim, and frequently sought their advice in her studies. This is how she first met Seongcheol Sunim and came to respect him after hearing his Dharma. Although Elder Wolhye Sunim entered the monastery at an older age than usual, she took Seongcheol Sunim's teachings to heart and adhered as strictly to them as my teacher Inhong Sunim, his own disciple. She kept her vigilance over her disciples' practice as sharp as a razor's edge, while always showing indescribable generosity and compassion to others.

Elder Wolhye Sunim was skinny as a skewer due to her bad lungs, and she passed away just one week after our visit, in the fall of 1956. She was sixty-two. In accordance with her will, she was cremated on a pyre the day after she passed, with no coffin or mourning guests, under the watchful eyes of the nuns of the mountain assembly. They say her dying request was, "Don't even buy a casket: just roll me up in a floor mat and cremate my body as it is."

Her material body burned up like a lotus flower within the roaring flames. Red sparks soared up into the sky and Elder Sunim's Dharma-body departed, leaving behind a silent teaching about the forms of life and death.

Life and death are like the waves of the ocean. Just as the waves of the sea rise and fall back down without end, we repeat the cycle of birth and death over and over again. But the ocean itself never grows nor shrinks. Our lives and deaths are the same. Freedom from life and death is understanding that life and death are one. Once the cycle of birth and death has been escaped, transcended, there are no more obstacles, and without obstacles great freedom can be achieved. We call those who have achieved this Dharma masters and sages. Because they have transcended the cycle of birth and death, the sage lives in eternity, eternally. They are forever a being of great freedom.

The image of Elder Wolhye Sunim, who saw even death as a form of nonpossession, as she departed from this world became a great lesson for me. Watching her final moments, free of all hindrances and obstacles, I wondered if this was the way all practitioners should end their time on the earth. I have witnessed the cremations of many sunims since I entered the monastery, but I have still never seen one as simple and humble as hers.

"Just like Elder Wolhye Sunim, I'll dedicate myself to my practice, living a pure and simple life as a nameless sage, and return to the long silence when the time comes."

Witnessing the cremation of Elder Sunim, who had lived her life as a true practitioner, so unexpectedly and at such a young age, became an opportunity for me to really think about how a practitioner should live, and how they should depart.

Who is the one who is left behind, and who is the one who leaves? When your body becomes just a thing in the fire becoming nothing but a fistful of ash, what use is fame, fortune, and the pursuit of the five desires? I was young when Elder Wolhye Sunim passed, at an age when you think of death as some far-off and remote thing. But my memory of her funeral lives on in me as a powerful inspiration.

Being seventy-six now, I can't avoid thinking about how I should be leaving this world myself. I hope to die in such a way that shows exactly how I had lived, just as Elder Wolhye Sunim's death showed how she lived hers. If I am fortunate, my departure will be simple like hers; if I surrender myself to this world's causes and conditions, I'll end up leaving with a big fuss like the others.

You Self-Absorbed Cook!

Hongjesa is buried very deep in Taebaeksan. As we followed Myoyeong Sunim on foot to the monastery, we could see fields plowed by slash-and-burn farmers here and there. Although the stinging hot sunlight of early autumn still lingered, deep in the mountains the thick forests shaded us from the heat, and we took our time on the path, resting and starting up again. We arrived at Hongjesa just as the evening light began to fall behind the mountains to the west.

Inhong Sunim greeted us warmly. She was already by this time a prominent nun whose leadership and dedication to practice were well recognized by all the preeminent sunims in Korea. With her tiger-like appearance and dignified bearing, I could feel that she was a great sunim just by looking at her.

Seeing our threadbare clothes and worn-out shoes, before anything else she gave us a change of clothes and prepared bathwater for us. Not only did we have no interest in anything other than contemplating *hwadu*, but we had vowed to live by the twelve ascetic practices, so we must have truly looked like beggars among beggars. Our hair was cut short then: we must have been the first to popularize the "short-cut" that most postulants have today. At the time we had made an ironclad vow to shave our heads only after we had attained enlightenment.

Coming out into the courtyard after bathing, we saw a few sunims in the distance returning to the monastery carrying knapsacks full of mountain greens. They looked relaxed and at peace, and my heart felt drawn to them.

Inhong Sunim, the head of Hongjesa, had resolved to solve the problem of birth and death before she turned fifty, and as the winter retreat began, all the sunims of the assembly likewise approached their practice with incredible ferocity. Practicing at the retreat that winter were Inhong Sunim and her companion practitioners Seongu Sunim and Hyechun Sunim; her disciples Cheolma Sunim and Beophui Sunim; grand-disciple Hyeongak Sunim; and Okja and I. Inhong Sunim was never careless with a single word or action.

There was no separate Dharma Hall in Hongjesa; there was only the living quarter that doubled as a Dharma Hall. Next to the meditation hall was a small living room and a room for the head nun. Although the circumstances were what they were, I still wanted a space of my own. I had a do-or-die attitude and the confidence that if I practiced for just one week without eating or sleeping, I would be able to attain enlightenment.[5]

One Thing

There is a Thing that has always existed, even before heaven and earth were formed, that will continue to always exist even after they are gone. Heaven and earth can be formed and destroyed a million times, but this Thing will remain constantly, with not even a hair of difference.

It is of unimaginable size, countless times larger than the endless void. If we think of It as an ocean, the boundless space of the ten directions is but a single drop of water in the middle of it.

It illuminates the countless worlds of the ten directions with a light of wisdom that shines trillions of times brighter than the sun. This absolute light, which transcends brightness or darkness, illuminates always all things in the universe.

This is an absolute Thing that transcends all names, forms, and discriminations. Even the label "absolute" cannot be attached to It, but it must be, out of necessity.

Also out of necessity, that which cannot even be labeled as a Thing must be labeled as such. And so that label has become a lie as soon as it was attached to It.

And so, even if all the Buddhas from all ten directions appeared simultaneously and spent eons to try to describe what this Thing is, they would be unable to even come close to succeeding. You can only be enlightened to It; It cannot be described or conveyed by someone else. Those who have become enlightened to what this Thing is are known as Buddhas. They have been forever liberated from the suffering of cyclic existence, and they will remain free until the end of time.

The unenlightened multitude who have not realized this Thing, who remain lost in the wilderness of birth and death and who continue the cycle of transmigration, will continue to suffer for eons to come. But all sentient beings, no matter how insignificant they may seem to be, are in possession of this Thing. From an enlightened Buddha to a tiny insect, we all have It. The only difference is whether enlightenment has been attained.

Even the Buddha and Bodhidharma were unable to see this Thing with their eyes or describe It with their words. Even the Buddha and Bodhidharma will become blind if they try to see this Thing, and they will become unable to speak if they try to describe It. One can only be enlightened to It. This is why the old masters said, "The Tripitaka [Buddhist scriptural canon] is nothing but a piece of paper used to scrape pus off a wound."

But I declare: "Trying to save someone with the Eighty Thousand Tripitaka is akin to saving them with poison." Among the scriptures are those of the Hinayana and the Mahayana schools. According to the Mahayana scriptures, "A person must sooner be fed poison than be instructed with the teachings of the Hinayana scriptures." But why was it not realized that the Mahayana scriptures themselves were also poison? It was known, but it was unavoidable. And so it is here where you must think very clearly and pay attention.

Believing in the One Thing is referred to as proper devotion. Both the Buddha and Bodhidharma are useless. The Eighty Thousand Tripitaka is just nonsense. You must solely focus your practice to be enlightened to this Thing; everything else is non-Buddhism and is simply your own deluded mind.

Other people might live a good life and then, once they die, go to paradise where they will enjoy endless pleasure. You, on the other hand, must never regret practicing in order to find this Thing, even if something might go wrong and you might end up in hell where you will be subjected to eons of endless suffering.

"I will attain enlightenment no matter what happens!"

Attainment is impossible without such a resolve. According to the old masters, "Enlightenment can only be attained by those who could murder another person without blinking an eye."

And I say, "Imagine a young widow who does not even flinch when she sees her only child be struck dead by lightning. You should not even think about trying to practice if one cannot channel that frightening young widow's mind."

Whether you wish to lift one or ten thousand tons, you must have the strength to do so. The one who does not even have the strength to lift ten pounds but tries to lift a thousand tons is simply foolish, if not crazy. If you lack strength, you must develop it as quickly as possible.

To see one's own parents, the people most deserving of the deepest gratitude, and to ignore them even if they keel over on the streets and die from starvation; this was the ferocious determination of the old masters in their approach to practicing.

The unyielding principles and beliefs of the old masters were such that they would sooner die than to leave their practice to teach even the emperor himself.

All the world's wealth and status are but dewdrops on a blade of grass, and even the Emperor, Son of Heaven, is but excrement in a puddle of mud; only the person with such a perspective may transcend dreamlike, earthly glories to set foot on the path of eternal happiness. The difference between practitioners and those who engage in conflict due to competing yet petty interests is like night and day.

You must put in the maximum effort while living the most minimal of lives, wearing nothing but rags and living in a cave deep in the mountains, eating only the potatoes that you plant for yourself. You must practice with every ounce of your energy, whether you are awake or sleeping, solely to attain enlightenment. You will never be able to achieve the great without sacrificing the small.

It is difficult to gain a human body, and it is even more difficult to come across the teachings of the Buddha. It is said that all Buddhas and Bodhisattvas never stop shedding tears as they look upon the unenlightened multitude who continue to commit sins.

This multitude commits sins knowingly and unknowingly. They wander about in Samsara and must endure unspeakable suffering as punishment for the countless sins they commit. Gaining a human body is akin to finding a blade of grass in an arid desert. And even if a body is gained, the difficulty of coming across the Buddha-dharma is of many more magnitudes because of the sheer weight of their karma. Even though many Buddhas have appeared in the past who delivered countless numbers of people from the world of delusion, you can tell how difficult the Buddha-dharma is to come across when you see that there are still those who are unable to escape the suffering of birth and death.

Having gained a human body with such difficulty and then having come across the Buddha-dharma with even more difficulty, you must leave your life behind and practice in order to swiftly realize this One Thing.

A person's life cannot be trusted because it is illusory. Adults die, children die, sick people die, and healthy people also die. Seeing that it is impossible to know when and how a person will die, how can you remain lazy and not practice?

You may die before realizing this Thing, and be reborn as a beast, a bird, or you may descend into hell. You do not know when you will gain another human body or come across the Buddha-dharma again; even if you do, you cannot know if the Buddha-dharma will lead you to this, the highest Path—practicing in order to find this One Thing. It is truly a lamentable state of affairs.

If you don't strive to redeem your body, the body that was so enormously difficult to gain, in this life, who knows when you will get another chance? The most important thing should be effort; the second and third most important should also be effort. Success without effort is impossible. The extent of success is directly proportional to the amount of effort that was put in; this is true of all things. You must put in the effort, and then put in some more.

This was the time that I had first awakened my determination for enlightenment, and my faith was only strengthened as I memorized this writing above, "One Thing" (Kr. *Han Mulgeon*), and everything else Keun Sunim wrote in his Dharma notes. I wouldn't have regretted laying down my life if it meant I could understand this One Thing. I wanted to do all that was humanly possible to achieve this. I was going to succeed, or die trying.

"I will go for just one week without eating or sleeping and try my best."

Inhong Sunim understood my desperate wish. As luck would have it, there was an empty room that had been used as a storage closet, so I cleaned it up and sat down inside. I was going to practice with all my beginner's determination, all my human strength, as if there were no tomorrow. I fully intended to become one with my *hwadu* in this intensive practice and was determined to reach my goal no matter what, but it came to an end after just two days. When I think about it I still feel frustrated, even today. The regret of wondering what might have happened if I could have practiced just that one week without wavering always remains. The reason I stopped after two days was because Cheolma Sunim, who had experience in the kind of intensive practice I was attempting to undertake, persuaded Inhong Sunim to stop me, saying that I would fall so ill I would never be able to practice again.

Taebaeksan got an unusual amount of snow, and there were many days when so much snow would fall that the roads would be closed. On those days Hongjesa would seem to transform into a different place, completely cut off from the rest of the world.

The assembly meditated sitting up, never laying down. Although usual sleeping hours were from eleven at night to three in the morning, we all stayed awake to focus on our practice.

At night we would light candles on the table and use a Dharma staff as an admonition stick. If any of us began to doze off and our posture crumpled, the sunim sitting across from you would hit your shoulder with a big bamboo clapper. The noise would startle you, and every other sunim in the room, back to alertness.

If my sleepiness started to get really unbearable, I would quietly step outside and meditate while walking in the snow. The snow in Taebaeksan would come up to your knees. I'd tell myself that I would go without sleep and just live standing still in the snow. The snow itself had become my meditation cushion. Under the moonlight, the snow shone dazzlingly white, like in a Seon dialogue. It felt like my mind's eye was being opened.

"Look at the white snow in the pitch-black night!"

Is this not looking directly into one's own true nature?

If I got hungry wading through the white snow up to my knees oblivious to the cold, I'd brush off some spinach or potatoes I found buried in the ground and eat them raw. Practicing with all your strength makes you quite hungry.

The valley where our monastery sat was suffused with our ferocious single-minded practice. When the snow fell and the roads got cut off, it became a place so beautiful and majestic it would make you wonder if these weren't the mountains in India, where the Buddha gave Dharma talks to the Vulture Peak Assembly. Even when Ilta Sunim,[6] who was living at Dosolam above Hongjesa, came down to the monastery to give Dharma talks, I would go out instead of listening and meditate while walking in the snow. Nothing else but my *hwadu* entered my mind there.

At the time, life at the monastery was one of bare minimum. Even a sheet of dried seaweed would be cut into little pieces and shared, and a single apple tree in front of the monastery was our only source of fruit. It was unthinkable for one person to eat an entire apple by themselves. Inhong Sunim would travel far away to and meet with laypeople, introducing them to the Dharma and collecting alms of rice for the monastery, hauling it four kilometers back to the monastery on foot for us to eat.

In those days when every nun did their part for the monastery's housekeeping, Okja and I, along with postulant Gyewon who had come from Gangneung, became the monastery cooks for one season. I had never prepared rice before in my entire life and found myself overwhelmed with worries. When I tried to wash the rice, there was too much millet mixed in and it all floated away as I poured off the water. Elder Inseong Sunim, the monastery's chief administrator who managed the kitchen inventory, couldn't bear to see me fumbling around any longer and told me, "You can just light the fire." I figured it was probably for the best.

But I still managed to cause trouble every time I walked into the kitchen. For some reason, I found it easier to concentrate on my *hwadu* while making the fire than when I sat in a room. So one day, completely lost in my *hwadu* as I stoked the fire, I heard someone call out, "Cook!" Tending to the fire, I had completely forgotten that *I* was the cook and didn't respond when Elder Inseong Sunim called out again.

"Hey, you self-absorbed cook!"

At that moment it suddenly occurred to me, *Oh no! This isn't my house!* Thinking about it, I realized that back home, there wasn't anybody who called me away to work, or anyone who put me to work at all, for that matter. After I realized that day that I was no longer living at home, I was quick to respond and started asking people before doing things I didn't know how to do.

In later years when Elder Inseong Sunim came to Seongnamsa and saw how much I'd changed, she laughed and said, "So all that stubbornness has turned into compassion!"

We were supposed to take turns being the cook for a month each, but with one week left on my shift I got sick. Okja got sick just three days in, and even postulant Gyewon, who came to the retreat right after graduating Gangneung Girl's High School and who followed the teachings of the master sunims diligently, fell off eventually. The three of us were supposed to work for the whole season but didn't even make it a month, so you could say that we flunked our cook duties.

I'm still not very good at making rice and preparing food. But back then as well as now, I was at least pretty good at cleaning, and wherever I go I can't stand to see a mess.

As a cook I was an abject failure, but as a postulant, I remember I once gave a Dharma talk in front of the entire assembly. It was Lunar New Year's Day. We took a short break from practicing to eat traditional rice-cake soup, or *ddeokguk*, for breakfast, and afterward all the sunims gathered to play Seongbuldo, or "Buddhahood Game."

The objective of Seongbuldo is to reach the "Buddhahood" square. Players throw dice to go up or down the stages that lead to Buddhahood. With the holiday atmosphere in full swing, we began to play. Right away my casual roll of the dice landed me in the Gyeongjeol Gate, a high level of practice, and I managed to reach Main Buddha [*Jubul*] in just three turns.

Soon a Dharma seat [an elevated seat on which a teacher delivers the Dharma talk] was prepared in the Great Hall, and I, a bushy-haired postulant, climbed onto it. Inhong Sunim, Ilta Sunim, who had come to deliver a Dharma talk, and all the sunims of the assembly, put on their formal robes and *kasas* (Skt. *kāṣāya*), and performed three prostrations facing the Dharma seat. Ilta Sunim formally requested a Dharma teaching from the Buddha. With brazen confidence I thrust the Dharma staff that was placed on the seat high into the air, then sat stoically still for a moment. I then struck the bamboo clapper three times and climbed off the Dharma seat.

This was the portrait of my days as a twenty-one-year-old postulant that remains painted on my heart. People might be ahead or behind in age when they join the monastery, but there is no order or seniority when it comes to achieving your studies. How sooner or later it takes to attain Buddhahood is determined solely by who is willing to practice desperately, putting their life on the line.

If you follow the stream above Hongjesa and climb upward for about an hour, you'll reach Dosolam. It is a hermitage so far away from the outside world that it feels like it could be the place where the old masters Hanshan and Shide lived when they hid deep away from the world.

Ilta Sunim, who practiced with his hair grown out long like Bodhidharma, would occasionally come down to Hongjesa to give us Dharma talks.[7] He had come to Dosolam after resolving to complete a six-year practice pact and practiced intensely without lying down or leaving the monastery, or even eating past noon. At Odaesan he had performed a seven-day, 3,000-prostration prayer, and making the following three vows—to be a good monk, to melt away the karmic residue of the secular world, and to have a mind dedicated to the Dharma—burned the twelve segments of the fingers of his right hand as a ritual promise and come to Taebaeksan.

Ilta Sunim told me many years later that the six years he spent at Taebaeksan was a period of true practice that he wouldn't have traded for his entire life. After that, whenever a lay disciple came to see him to ask him about the path of ordination, Ilta Sunim would send them to me.

The Hermitage Song

I spent a season at Hongjesa, and when the spring sunlight melted the snow and revealed the road, I set out to find a place to spend my summer retreat. The free season between summer and winter is called *sancheol*; the traveling practice done in this time is called *manhaeng*.

In the spirit of Sudhana's search for teachers [in the *Avatamsaka Sutra*], Okja and I left for Yunpilam, a branch temple of the monastery of Daeseungsa in Mungyeong. I wanted to seek out the places my father Seongcheol Sunim had studied and try to practice there myself. He had spent a summer season at Daeseungsa in 1945, ten years after he had left home, and the winter season of that year at Myojeokam, a hermitage in the nearby mountains. He spent this time practicing with Cheongdam Sunim, Jaun Sunim, and others.

Cheongdam Sunim and Seongcheol Sunim were known to have a unique and unparalleled bond, two lifelong companions in practice. In her biography, *Gray Rubber Shoes* (Kr. *Hoesaek Gomusin*), Cheongdam Sunim's daughter, Myoeom Sunim remembers them this way:

> Seongcheol Sunim sat me down in front of him and told me, "Your father and I are so close, you could pour water between us and it wouldn't leak through, so you should put your trust in me." Being asked to trust someone I was meeting for the first time in my life, I couldn't help but laugh a little. So I told him, "I will trust you as life and experience goes on." He asked back: "Really? Why?" When I answered, "How can I trust someone I've never even met, when I can't even trust my father?" everyone laughed. Although Seongcheol Sunim didn't involve himself in Buddhist politics, he showed other monks and nuns through action that his was the way of a true practitioner. Meanwhile, Cheongdam Sunim showed his own dedication through his involvement in the restructuring of the Jogye Order and in Buddhist affairs. The two of them were always of one mind; water truly did not leak through.

Seongcheol Sunim first met Cheongdam Sunim in 1941, at Jeong-hyesa in Deoksungsan. His intention was simply to spend a season there under Mangong Sunim's (1871–1946) guidance; instead he found a lifelong friend. While Seongcheol Sunim was observing a diet of raw foods, Cheongdam Sunim, who was known then as Sunho Sunim, helped him doggedly, drying foraged pine needles, soaking beans, or pounding rice.

That first friendship led to the practitioner's pact at Bongamsa, and together they went on to become cornerstones of the Jogye Order's doctrinal and religious identity. When the two of them were together it was inevitable they would spend the whole day talking, rarely coming outside. Keun Sunim often said this about Cheongdam Sunim: "To be honest, outsiders might know 'Cheongdam' but they don't know 'Sunho.' He worked so hard to build the foundation of today's Jogye Order; he's a Bodhisattva of patience, so he's endured all sorts of praise and criticism fighting for the purification movement, being guided by many elder monks. Without even knowing it he had become the center of the movement. Before he was ever known to the world as Cheongdam, Sunho's will and devotion was truly unparalleled."

I still sometimes recall the sound of Keun Sunim's hearty laughter as he told stories about his old friend.

Yunpilam, a branch temple of Daeseungsa, along with Jijangam in Odaesan and Gyeonseongam at Sudeoksa, is a hermitage famous as a refuge for meditating nuns; the rocky mountains encircle it like a folding screen, so the mind feels peaceful and unburdened there. Many nuns—Elder Wolhye Sunim, and others like Myojeon, Myoeom, and Myohui Sunim—have studied meditation and practiced under the guidance of great masters in this place. Before my winter retreat began, I spent time meditating there with Jeonghwa Sunim and nine others, living among the traces of the nuns who had come before us. Yunpilam was old and cramped but hummed with the energy of devoted practice.

When I focus my efforts on practicing, anywhere that I go becomes a monastery that awakens me. That's why they say there isn't any one monastery you must visit to become enlightened. If I fell asleep while practicing in the common room, I would be woken up with the large admonition staff—in my dreams! It was a time when I would hear the Buddha and Bodhisattvas speaking the Dharma in my sleep, so it must have been their hands wielding the staff. I learned that when I focused my mind on my *hwadu* and practiced with a joyful mind, I would be protected by their grace.

The season I spent at Myojeokam, higher up in the mountains from Yunpilam, was another unforgettable time. Myojeokam is the hermitage where Seon Master Naong (1320–1376) renounced his secular life, and at the top of the mountain sits a boulder where he was said to meditate. Day and night I would sit on that boulder and sing Master Naong's "Hermitage Song" (Kr. *Togulga*) and it filled me with spirit and vigor, like I had become Naong Sunim himself. I remember singing that song in my youth so well I still sing it to myself sometimes. The song always inspired awe and emotion deep in my heart and aroused my devotion whenever I sang it out loudly.

During the summer retreat at Myojeokam, Okja and I prepared the meals and various side dishes for the hermitage. Just like the old Chinese Zen masters Yandou (828–887) and Xuefeng (822–908), who always carried a hoe and strainer, Okja and I became the kitchen help wherever we went. We'd always heard that vegetables should be washed seven times, so by the time we were done all the leaves would be gone and we'd just be left with stems. At least Okja usually had better luck than I did.

One season at Myojeokam, all we had to eat was lettuce and zucchini. Okja and I got so sick of the zucchini we carried a big staff to the garden and pounded all the zucchini flowers to bits so they wouldn't grow anymore. After that, we just had lettuce. It's a fond memory of the mischief we could get up to when we put our impulsive heads together.

As soon as the summer was over we hurried our footsteps to the hermitage of Seongjeonam in Palgongsan, where Keun Sunim was staying. He had put up a barbed-wire fence there and cut off contact with the outside world, so the only time we could see him was the day after our retreat ended.

If Your *Hwadu* Is Clear Even in Your Dreams

"How arrogant! What do you know about how your studies are going when you've never even studied in your life?"

This is what Keun Sunim told me at Seongjeonam after my summer retreat, his piercing eyes fixed on me, when I had asked him why I might be having difficulty with my practice. When I couldn't think of anything to say, he went on: "The thing about Seon meditation is that even if you can hold on to the *hwadu* clearly in your dreams, it's hard to say you're really practicing." These words, which left me unable to even estimate how far I'd progressed in my practice, stunned me into silence. I had been working without sleep or rest to devote all my thought to my *hwadu*, but all I received was a rebuke, without even asking how my practice was going. Not only that, but I was miles away from attaining the level he was talking about; he made it very clear that it was pointless to even think about right now.

"Before you get to the point where you can practice correctly, you shouldn't even be calling it that. You need to be able to uphold the *hwadu* with clarity and ease for twenty hours a day at least to truly say you are practicing. This is called *hwaducheon*. Don't spare yourself; work harder."

After giving me this encouragement, Keun Sunim wrote me these following phrases. He would write them by hand for people close to him or those who would seek him out, to emphasize the difficulty of practice.

Even if your *hwadu* is constant during the busy day,
And bright and perpetual even in dreams,
If suddenly in deep sleep it becomes obscure,
How will you escape the eternal suffering of life and death?

If you are a practitioner and have meditated on a *hwadu*, then you can probably gauge your own progress by these words.

"You might fool everyone else in the world, but you can't fool yourself."

I had experienced *hwadu* in my dreams once, while I was practicing at Cheongnyangsa, so I asked him, "Is this the state of 'continuous awareness while dreaming' [*mongjung ilyeo*]?" He flatly said no.

"For it to be 'continuous awareness while dreaming,' the *hwadu* must be the only vivid thing in your dreams, with nothing else present. When you can uphold the *hwadu* even when completely asleep, with no dreams, that is 'continuous awareness while in deep sleep' [*sungmyeon ilyeo*]."

He was giving me the teaching of the three stages: that *hwadu* must become "continuous awareness whether moving or still," "continuous awareness while dreaming," and "continuous awareness while in deep sleep," in order to become "continuous awareness at all times."

"Continuous awareness whether moving or still" means that no matter what you are doing, whether you're sitting, lying down, talking, not talking, moving, or just being still, your mind is always filled with that lump of doubt called *hwadu*. This level

Figure 4.2. The note that Keun Sunim wrote to emphasize the difficulty of practice. Author provided.

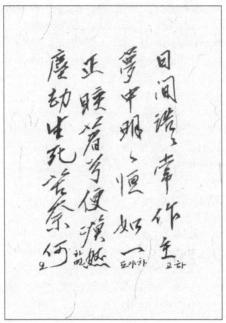

is when you can meditate on the *hwadu* without your mind being distracted or scattered by daily life, and you can hear the *hwadu* constantly and vividly like the bright reflection of the moon in calm water.

Once you attain "continuous awareness whether moving or still" and continue to meditate on the *hwadu*, you will reach a point where you stop dreaming; dreams being the karmic obstacles accumulated over the many eons spent in the secular world. Instead, you will hear *hwadu* just as if you were awake in the daytime. That level is called "continuous awareness while dreaming." If you go one step further from here, you can hear the *hwadu* with clarity even when unconscious in deep sleep; this level is called "continuous awareness while in deep sleep." You must break through these three gateways to understand the *hwadu* and lay down this heaviest burden to become a true practitioner. But Seon practice goes past "continuous awareness at all times"; in order to truly achieve Buddhahood, we must attain "ultimate mysterious enlightenment," or *gugyeong myogak*, clarity and wisdom both inside and outside of the mind. Even once you have achieved "continuous awareness at all times," you might not have reached the ultimate enlightenment, so you must seek out a great teacher who has attained Buddhahood and receive approval.[8]

You must reflect honestly for yourself whether you have attained "continuous awareness at all times" and not deceive yourself for the sake of ego. To get to this point you need to practice without concern for your life. You must work hard and spare no effort.

Once you know this, you know how far you've come in your own practice. I have taken this to be the standard for my own studies.

Keun Sunim had a saying, driven deep into his core like an iron post: "Sacrifice everything for the truth." He understood that if someone wants to follow the truth, they must be willing to give up anything, offer up their whole body, and to hone that willingness like a sharp sword, in order to walk the path of enlightenment. After walking that path my whole life I see that every one of Keun Sunim's sayings became a whip that drove me doggedly forward in my practice.

Jolted awake by Keun Sunim's words, I left Seongjeonam. To visit him from Myojeokam I had to walk down the mountain to Jeomchon, take the bus to Daegu, then walk the rest of the way to Seongjeonam. Walking twenty-eight kilometers a day, of course my legs ached, but more than anything I was hungry. I would eat beans I picked from the fields on the side of the road, or raw eggplants that I begged from the young village women. So when I had to return home along the same path after this rude awakening, it made me unbelievably miserable.

The ten years Keun Sunim spent at Seongjeonam, it was almost guaranteed that every time I came to see him after my winter or summer retreats he would kick me out immediately. This was probably the period in his time as my teacher when he was the most strict. Before I became a nun, whenever we visited, he would bombard us with questions to test the levels of our progress. If Okja or I answered even one question wrong we would both get thrown out. Keun Sunim had a straightforward way of speaking that didn't bother with explanations or pleasantries, so you had to stay alert or a staff would soon be flying at your head. One rainy summer day, Keun Sunim suddenly flew into a rage and began hitting me with his umbrella, covering me in bruises.

"Get out!"

Whenever he said that I would run away as fast as I could, but Okja was slower-moving and didn't always escape the blows. It was alright getting tossed out in the summer at least, but on snowy days in the cold winter we'd really have nowhere to go. One year that I visited him after a winter retreat, he got in a rage about something or another again.

"It's useless leaving these idiots in a temple. Just throw them back to their families!"

He was going to send us back to our families, when we had just arrived after walking all day with no food. Totally at a loss, we fled his room in a panic and slipped out of the temple early next morning during prayers. We were so hungry we snuck into the kitchen and stole a few carrots that were buried in pine needles, washing them with snow and eating them for the strength to escape back home.

The next morning, when Keun Sunim gave the order to "find those girls, and send one to Jinju and the other to Busan," his attendants searched the temple for us but found only some spat-out carrot tops left on a snowy hill nearby. Later, his disciple Cheonje Sunim said to us, "You two postulants stole them? Those precious carrots were meant for Keun Sunim; not even wild pigs would eat them out of respect for him!"

Two summers had passed since I had left home. Once again Keun Sunim shouted, "Get out!" when I couldn't answer his questions. Then he called to his attendants: "Send these girls back to their family homes. If they go back to the temple I'll set it on fire." Then, he told me, "Give me back my sermon notes and go." Keun Sunim's word was law, so I had no choice but to return the handwritten notes I had carried with me like my own life. They went back into Keun Sunim's storage. Years later I implored Cheonje Sunim to let me see them again. He transcribed the contents of the note-book and gave them to me; I never was able to see the original notes again.

When Keun Sunim would chase us out after such a long journey without giving us so much as a spoonful of rice, he was teaching us not to rely on anyone, stoking the fiery indignation in my heart—"Why must I be thrown out?"—that would fuel my studies. He was teaching me to walk alone. It's true. Practice is something that you must do alone, and no one else can do it for you. If there is anything you depend or rely on, it clouds your mind and distracts you from your Path.

When I think about it now, I didn't do anything wrong. Even if I had given a bad response now and then there was no reason to throw me out like that. He was just sending me a subliminal message: that I can't accomplish anything by relying on others. But every time we got chased out all we could do was wonder hopelessly what we had done wrong.

Life is the same way. In the whole world you are the only person who can take care of yourself; when you live with such a desperate mindset, your life truly becomes your own. Something you earned by relying on others cannot be said to be yours; even if it were it will soon disappear. Just like the plum blossoms that survive the harsh winter to spread their fragrance across a hundred kilometers, and the deep-rooted tree that doesn't bend to wind or rain, those who don't rely on others and overcome their own bodily limitations on their own are the ones who succeed. Only as time passed and I learned a little more did I understand that this was why Keun Sunim had treated us so harshly. If he had welcomed us and fed us every time we came to see him, would we have felt so pushed to the brink, have honed the knife's edge of our minds as desperately? It was a truly merciful punishment, borne out of faith in our will to learn.

But this was unknowable to us, two young and clueless postulants, only twenty years old and knowing nothing about practice. All we knew was the fear that, if we were sent back to our family homes, we would never be able to study the Dharma again. In that hopeless, desperate situation, the Buddha was the only one we could turn to.

We had no money to buy even a single candle or stick of incense, so we went alms-begging, *takbal*, in Jeomchon. We had been told that monks and nuns should not carry money, so back then if someone even gave us money for the bus we would surrender it straight away to elder sunims, not leaving a penny in our pockets. *Takbal* was how early monastics fed and clothed themselves; it was one of the twelve austerities (*dhuta*) that all practitioners must observe. *Bal* refers to the bowl or *baru* that holds food, so *takbal* means that your life is dependent on your bowl. Monks and nuns practiced *takbal* in early Buddhism because they were not permitted to engage in commercial business or even any production work for money. Through *takbal*, monastics practiced humility and rooted out arrogance, which was necessary for their practice, and the secular people who donated to them in turn could accumulate merit.

With the money we earned through *takbal*, we bought incense, candles, and rice, and placing them in our sack we walked the twenty kilometers back to Yunpilam. We were planning to do a repentance prayer.

We were so hungry we picked pine needles off the trees on the side of the road and ate the couple of dates rolling around in our pockets to soothe our hunger. We finally arrived at Yunpilam around 11 p.m. For the first time, I began praying instead of meditating.

"I must practice without relying on Keun Sunim, relying only upon the Buddha."

With this ringing desperately in my mind, I did prostrations four thousand times a day for a week. I didn't really know how to pray and wasn't used to bowing at all, let alone four thousand times, so it took me almost twenty hours a day to get through all of them, a time in which others could have done ten thousand. It took a ridiculous amount of time, but as I performed the prostrations without any worldly thoughts to distract me, I realized that humans have unlimited ability. It occurred to me that, if you cultivate this inner power, you can escape from life and death and become an eternally free person. If you don't, you would continue to be trapped in the binding affliction of life and death, resigned to endless suffering.

When you know the truth, it is bright; when you do not, it is dark. When it is dark you are afraid, and when you are afraid you become stuck. So when you become stuck it is because you cannot illuminate the truth. What is this truth? It is knowing that I am an eternal life, a Buddha who possesses infinite ability. So practice is the process of realizing this truth.

One day while I was doing the daily four thousand prostrations, I dreamt I saw my grandfather leaving his house in the dark night forest of Mukgokri. It was the first time I had dreamt of my grandfather since I'd left home, so I wondered if something had happened, but being in my prayers all day I soon forgot all about it. But a few days later, a message arrived from my hometown, bearing the news that my grandfather had passed away.

I was told that he had a nine-day funeral as well as a temporary burial, and the place that he had been buried was where I had seen him in my dream. According to the laywoman who brought me the news, right before he passed away my grandfather called for his son who had left home, roaring, "You bastards! I'm going to Seongcheol Sunim!" as if he had seen the envoy of death right in front of him. After hearing the news of his death, I felt at times grateful to him, at others sorry and remorseful.

After I finished my seven-day repentance prayer, I returned to Keun Sunim at Seongjeonam, but he didn't mention what had happened last time I was there at all. I understood then that while Keun Sunim would never forgive something in the moment, he wouldn't bring it up again either once it had passed.

Since I had received a message about my grandfather's passing, Keun Sunim had to have also known, but he didn't talk about him once. Later I found out that he had sent a disciple to our home to offer condolences.

In all the decades I knew him, Keun Sunim never spoke a word about our family. He had left it all behind when he entered the Sangha [Sk. Saṅgha], so what personal attachments could he have left? When I read his leaving-home poem, which burns with the spirit of a great man who left everything behind to walk the Path of ancient wisdom alone, any question of blame or resentment goes out the window. The thought that he was the father who abandoned me, those matters of our past or future lives; I couldn't hold on to them even if I wanted to.

Reading his leaving-home poem after I too had left home, I couldn't help but marvel in respect at his confidence and boldness in walking his own path. Even now, I find it speaks to me more than his enlightenment poem or deathbed poem.

The Song of Enlightenment

Keun Sunim wouldn't always throw us out when we came to visit. It seemed he wanted to teach us the basics of being a practitioner before we shaved our heads and formally became nuns. When he was in a good mood he would recommend books for us to read or explain things to us. We enjoyed as young postulants the kind of treatment we would never dream of receiving as nuns.

Back then, Keun Sunim told us to memorize books like *Zhengdaoge* (*Song of Enlightenment*), *Xinxinming* (*Correct Inscription of Faithful Mind*), *Togulga* (*The Hermitage Song*), and *Siphyeonsi* (*A Poem of Ten Mysteries*). We were young and our spirits and devotion were sky-high, so whatever Keun Sunim said, we followed.

When Okja and I were postulants, he gave us Yongjia Xuanjue's *Zhengdaoge* and told us, "Memorize this first." When Keun Sunim began searching for the answer to eternal wisdom, devouring books from the East to the West in his effort to solve the problem, this was the book that convinced him wholeheartedly to become a monk, so he must have wanted all the more to pass it down to us.

We had been getting scolded and thrown out daily, but one day he must have been in a good mood, because he said, "You should understand it before you memorize it," and he thoughtfully deciphered each part of the *Zhengdaoge* for us. I still remember the sight of him theatrically hoisting a six-ringed staff into the air as if pretending to be Yongjia Xuanjue himself, saying, "This is what those heroic old monks looked like!"

"You two are the future Yeongga Sunims[9] who'll sing of enlightenment!"

I can't forget the bravery he instilled in me when he said that. I was able to put my life on the line to practice like I did in my youth because I believed his words without a trace of doubt. Because I believed it, I was able to spend every second on working to push myself further.

When you pursue something while thinking positively that you can achieve it, time becomes as precious as gold. The times I spent after becoming a nun were some of the most treasured and precious times of my life. I practiced with the thought that Yeongga Sunim and I were one person, and when I practiced ardently, the *Zhengdaoge* seemed to come even closer to my heart. After that I would walk along the valley at Taebaeksan or up and down Ongnyudong Stream near Seongnamsa, loudly reciting the words of the *Zhengdaoge* and *Siphyeonsi*.

Figure 4.3. Keun Sunim in front of Baengnyeonam at Haeinsa. He was usually known as the fearsome Tiger of Gayasan, but there were times when he would smile like this too. Photo by Kim Minsook.

For people who follow the Dharma, the *Zhengdaoge* is an eternal standard. I heard it again as a Dharma talk given by Keun Sunim at Gimyongsa, ten years after it had first strengthened my devotion as a postulant listening to his interpretation. The lecture united both meditation and scripture and was grounded in the Middle Way; it was like listening to a great roll of thunder. My teacher Inhong Sunim described the moment too: "I felt such joy, such faith. Who could understand that feeling?" She wasn't the only one who felt that way.

The *Xinxinming*, or *Correct Inscription of Faithful Mind*, is a 146-line poem written by the Third Patriarch Sengcan (d. 606) of China. It is often lauded as the finest Dharma writing in history and is an important required reading in Korean Buddhism. Its central concern is the analysis of forty sets of oppositional concepts or dualities, in order to show that the root of our suffering lies in duality and our dichotomous understanding of the world, and that these can be reconciled in the perspectives of the Middle Way.

The *Xinxinming* seems like a straightforward Dharma, but within the simplicity of its writing lies transcendent truth and perfectly embodied meaning.

At his Hundred-Day Dharma talk at Haeinsa, Keun Sunim urged the attending practitioners to learn the *Zhengdaoge* and *Xinxinming*. Of course, in later years I urged my own disciples to learn them too.

Make the Precepts Your Teacher

On the Path to enlightenment, the precepts are your first lifeline. Just like you can't fill a broken bowl with water, if you don't keep the precepts everything else falls apart.

The precepts are a code of morality. So how could they apply only to monastics? The reason the world is in such noisy disorder is because it has deserted this morality. In your personal life too, trying to achieve something when your morality is compromised is like planting brambles and expecting heavenly peaches. I believe morality is the first foundation of a life worthy of a human being.

When Keun Sunim was alive he always emphasized the importance of the precepts, so he wrote some verses on them for Okja and I to read as we resolved to walk the Path of enlightenment. Keun Sunim explained these verses using the story of Maha Kasyapa (Sk. Mahā Kāśyapa) and Myohyeonni (Sk. Bhadra Kapilani).

These verses were exchanged by Maha Kasyapa and Myohyeonni. The two had agreed to marry, but not live together as man and wife.[10] One day, she was taking a nap when Kasyapa saw a viper approaching her and shook her awake with his hand. Myohyeonni said, "Even if I would be bitten by a viper, do not touch my body with your hand. If I were bitten, I would die, nothing more, but if I fell into bodily sin, there would be no end to my suffering."

Hearing this, Kasyapa responded, "Walking into a blazing fire wielding a sword is a simpler task than practicing side by side with a woman. If I can keep this promise and not violate it, it would be the rarest thing in the world."

Keun Sunim finished this story and he said, "If you break the precepts, the Buddha and the patriarchs and all that? It's all useless." He asked us, "So what are you gonna do in a crisis like that?"

Okja answered first.

"I'll take poison and die right on the spot!"

Keun Sunim laughed and asked me. "What about you?"

"That sort of thing won't happen to me."

At that time I hadn't even imagined what a relationship between a man and a woman would be like, and I didn't have the faintest idea why he was even talking about men this and women that.

We left Keun Sunim's room and I asked Okja: "Where are you gonna get the poison?"

There was something Keun Sunim said to me the second time I met him at Cheonjegul, when I was still at the Jinju School of Education. "Men are all crooks. So don't get close to any of them, besides your own parents." I guess I seemed very innocent to him.

After that, I didn't even like my male teachers coming near me. When a boy at school accidentally bumped into me while walking by, I slapped his face before I realized it; I can be a pretty uptight person sometimes. When I was going to school in Jinju and living at my aunt's house, I didn't like how my cousin's friends kept staring at me, so my friend and I left the house and rented a room in town instead. Neither of us knew how to cook, though, so we had to come back the next day.

Keun Sunim wrote, "Make the precepts your teacher," along with these observations in his Dharma notes.

When the Buddha was on his deathbed, he made this final request.

"Even when I am gone, if you take the Vinaya precepts as your master it will be as if I am still alive, so please practice hard with the precepts in mind and do not be sad. If you cannot keep these precepts, then I cannot be of use to you, even if I live ten thousand more years."

He spoke truly. The precepts are like a bowl that holds water. If the bowl is broken, then it cannot hold water, and if the bowl is dirty, then the water will be dirty as well. No matter how clean the water is, if you pour it in a dirt bowl it will become dirt water, and if you pour it in a shit bowl it will become shit water. So if one cannot keep the precepts faithfully, they will fall into Samsara, unable to attain even an ugly and filthy human body.

Knowing this, how can one expect to attain a clean Dharma body after breaking the precepts? This is why it is better to die than to abandon your morality.

Venerable Jajang Sunim was the son of a royal Silla family, and was of such noble stature that the king often sent him emissaries to convince him to leave the Dharma and become a minister. But no matter how much they would plead, he would not go with them. The king was furious: giving his emissary a knife, he ordered him to bring back Jajang Sunim's head. When the emissary arrived and told Jajang Sunim his orders, Jajang Sunim laughed and said, "I would rather die after one day of keeping the precepts, than live a hundred years after breaking them."

When the messenger heard these words, he couldn't bear to fulfill his order. When he returned and told the king the truth, the king's anger calmed and he came to respect Jajang Sunim even more deeply.

There is an ancient saying: "If you commit a crime knowingly, you will fall into hell headfirst."

Practitioners more than anyone must heed these words.

When Keun Sunim was practicing as a young man, he created a set of twelve promises to himself. He called them the "Twelve Self-Promises," and reading them, you can see how strictly he disciplined himself in his youth.

I will not even glance at a woman.

I will not even listen to the meaningless stories of the secular world.

I will not even touch money or riches.

I will not even pick up nice clothes.

I will not even approach the offerings of followers.

I will not even pass my shadow by a nun's monastery.

I will not even chew any meat with my teeth.

I will not even smell the stench of pungent vegetables.

I will not think about the trappings of judgment.

I will not change my mind to follow good or bad opportunities.

I will not discriminate against who I bow to, even facing a little girl.

I will not joke about the shortcomings of others.

Chapter 5

Seongnamsa Monastery

The Tiger of Gajisan Becomes My Vocation Master

Hapil and Bulpil

Keun Sunim told me many times, "Hurry slowly," but I rushed like there was no tomorrow into my practice and eventually came down with meditation fever again. When I tried to send my qi downward to the abdomen, legs, and the arches of the feet as Keun Sunim taught me, my fever began to go down. But the minute I felt better, I'd think about the day I'd wasted and rush back into practice, only to fall ill again. When it got so bad that I couldn't even sit or stand up, I figured I'd had enough and went to see Keun Sunim.

"No matter what I do, my fever will not go away."

Keun Sunim looked at me with pity and told me decisively, "You can't get rid of meditation fever so easily. It can't be helped, you have to take your time and work slowly. Do things in the long-term."

"Long-term." When I heard those words it felt like the sky was falling down on me. When I had left home I'd told everyone I was going to finish my practice in three years, and I'd really believed I could do it, too. But here he was telling me "long-term." In disbelief I asked him again, "Then how should I practice going forward?"

"If you keep walking the same Path you'll eventually find Buddhahood. Take your time."

But that kind of slow-going, resting on the way, "taking my time" was much more difficult for me. It had been over a year since I had left home, but Keun Sunim had never brought up ordination to me; that day, he urged me for the first time.

"If you want to go long-term, you should shave your head. Become a nun."

Having said that, he took out some paper and a brush. Bulpil and Baekjol. These were the Dharma names given to me and Okja.

Okja had always said, "I hope I get a name that will keep me humble," so she was very pleased by the name she received. Baekjol means that one who is incapable of a hundred things can become one who is capable of anything. As Okja delighted in her new name, Keun Sunim wrote her this verse:

Living deep in a high mountain
At sixty years old you become free and unobstructed.
Your name must disappear from the mouths of others,
For today you become Baekjol Sunim.

When I asked Keun Sunim, "Why did you happen to name me Bulpil?" he told me, "If you understand *hapil* [why is it necessary?] you will understand the meaning of *bulpil* [it is not necessary]." Most people interpret my name to mean "unneeded" or "unwanted" and compare it to the name of the Buddha's son, Rahula, which means "obstacle." I figured that might as well be right too, so I never argued with it. However, I think what Keun Sunim meant when he gave me this name was that in order to achieve the Dharma, you must first become a truly unnecessary person to this world. As for the deeper, hidden meaning of the name, I will have to finish my practice to fully understand that.

Keun Sunim always emphasized that one cannot attain eternal freedom without first becoming a useless person, a discarded person, not only to the world but in the Buddha Dharma as well. He taught that practice was the only thing a practitioner's path and life would ever know, and so I have taken the meaning of my name to be "do nothing but practice like a crazy idiot" and lived my life accordingly.

Keun Sunim never comforted me as my father, but he opened my every path to enlightenment. As I grew determined to take the vows and become a nun, he encouraged me to hide away and practice by telling me the stories of Hanshan and Shide. He taught me about the attainments of great masters who had come before me, planting seeds of devotion and courage in my heart. Because I found my way through the channels of my Path by following his guidance to the truth, I have always lived with gratitude to him.

One day, not long after I had shaved my head, Keun Sunim asked me: "Among the Dharma masters, there are crazy masters, hermit masters who live hidden away, and masters who work to rescue the masses from suffering. There are also masters who say, 'Buy my rice cakes.' What kind of master do you want to be?"

"I want to become a master who lives hidden away."

"Hidden masters are always found someday, so they are of middle potential. The master who rescues the masses is one who chases wealth and fame, and the master who says 'Buy my rice cakes' doesn't practice at all and deceives even himself, and is therefore the lowest potential. The master with highest potential is the one who acts like a crazy person."

That day, Keun Sunim told me the story of two such crazy masters, Hanshan and Shide.[1]

"In China's Tang dynasty there was a monk called Hanshan, who was neither monk nor layman and lived deep in a cave near the temple of Guoqingsi on Tiantai Mountain. He would go to the temple with Shide and act like a crazy person, but their behavior reflected the principles of the Buddhist Path. He was also a good poet. One day, the governor of the province recognized he was a great master, and he prostrated himself and offered him clothes and food. Hanshan screamed, "Thief! Thief! Get away from me!" and ran away, never to be seen again. In this world some say that Hanshan is the reincarnation of Manjusri, and Shide is the reincarnation of Samantabhadra [representing wisdom and Buddhist practice, respectively]. After that, Hanshan collected over three hundred poems he had written on the stones and dirt walls around the village as well as some poems of Shide's and made a book out of them, *The Poetry of Hanshan*. You should read it sometime. Those two lived like idiots and were ridiculed in every way, but they were more free and joyous than anyone. Anyone who studies the Dharma should live like them, Hanshan and Shide."

How greatly I was moved when Keun Sunim himself taught me this, before I knew anything of the world, let alone life as a nun. He told the story so vividly and sincerely that just looking at his face I had already made up my mind to live in a mountain cave somewhere, digging up potatoes to eat, just like Hanshan and Shide. I made a promise to Keun Sunim in my mind that I would spend every second practicing, asleep or awake, and that I would never accept official titles or lofty positions, only live my whole life as nothing but a wretched nun. I have held myself to that ironclad pledge ever since I took my vows to become a nun.

When I was younger, reading a book just meant glancing at a few pages in the middle and then closing the cover, but I did always carry one book of ancient poems with me. Of those I most loved to read a poem by Seong Sammun:[2]

When this body dies, what will I be?
I will become the old pine tree at the top of Bongnaesan.
And when the world is covered by white snow I alone will
   be evergreen.

I would gaze upon the solitary pine tree, which stays fresh and green through days of stormy winds and snow, and recite Seong Sammun's poem to myself. Reflecting upon all the aspects of who I am after coming to the monastery, I wonder if these little affectations of mine became what led me down the path to nunhood.

The pine trees that grow in the mountains behind Cheongnyangsa, where I spent my first season after leaving home, are especially green and lush. I would often look at them and remember the ancient poems I recited back home, but once I encountered Hanshan's poems, I put down that ancient book for good. That is how much his poems enchanted me. I like them so much, I carved one of them into the pillar in the Simgeom-dang, where I now live.

> Between the cracks of the boulders is where I live;
> No human walks here, only birds.
> What lies beyond that narrow garden's edge,
> Only the faintest wisps of clouds rolling by.
> How many seasons have I nested here?
> I've seen spring become winter many times over.
> I'll say one thing to you rich folks,
> A false name is nothing but a true illusion.

Figure 5.1. In my youth, when I wanted to become a master who lives hidden away. Author provided.

Even now, when I sit by the window in Simgeomdang and read Hanshan's poems under the clear moonlight, I feel like I've become Hanshan himself. I reflect on myself with Hanshan as my mirror. Within the great natural world I become clouds and become wind. I may leave other books behind when going into retreat, but I always take Hanshan's book of poems. It is my lifelong companion.

It has already been half a century since I received my Dharma name from Keun Sunim. The seasons have seemed to pass in an instant, faster than an arrow that has left the bow. The day I turned seventy, I invited some old friends to have a meal. Afterward, as they were leaving, my old friend Okja, who is now Baekjol Sunim, gave me a letter. Her words took me back to those fifty long years we had spent together since our first meeting as young intern teachers at Wolmyeongam.

Bulpil Sunim,

Your hospitality enjoyed with old friends make this early summer day feel even fresher. The heart doesn't seem to grow old, but seventy is truly here. A half century has passed since we rode the train to Daegu.

Let us always meet in good health.

2006. 5. 5.

Searching for a Place to Practice

After I received my Dharma name, Bulpil, I traveled to Seongnamsa and greeting my future teacher Inhong Sunim, told her "I have received my Dharma name from Keun Sunim and am here to be ordained." Pleased, she said, "I have received two blessings from my dreams." Seongnamsa, in South Gyeongsang Province, is a monastery with a deep history, established by Master Doui in the Silla dynasty, who founded the Gajisan lineage of the Nine Mountain Seon lineage. Inhong Sunim rebuilt the dilapidated monastery and established a teaching community for nuns. Educating the generations of tomorrow, today it is the leading Seon training center for nuns in the Jogye Order, and through its existence you can understand the status Inhong Sunim holds in Korean Buddhist history.

It is standard practice when first arriving at the temple to spend several months, if not years, as a postulant. However, because I had spent over a year in Cheongnyangsa and Hongjesa, Yunpilam, and Myojeokam living as a bushy-haired postulant, I was allowed to shave my head right away. In the fall of 1957, aged twenty-one, with Inhong Sunim as my vocation master and Jaun Sunim as my preceptor, I received sramaneri [Sk. *śrāmaṇerī*, novice nun] ordination in the Buddha Hall of Seongnamsa, formally entering the path of nunhood.

Realizing I had now entered the "long-term" in the search for enlightenment, I felt like I had gotten off the express train and transferred to the scenic route. The fire in my heart to grasp enlightenment in just three years now being somewhat tamed, I began to notice the little things around me more often. I had the freedom to indulge in a wintertime cup of tea with the other nuns in the common hall after lunch. Descending the mountain behind the temple after gathering the stray branches dropped by the wind, I could lean against a rock for a moment and look upon the beautiful landscape in front of me, a sublime blessing enjoyed by those who live in the mountains.

Sometimes I would think about dear friends, with whom I wanted to share the joy of the Sangha [Sk. Saṅgha, community of monks and nuns] and invite to become ordained, and called to them in my mind. Yet I held myself back, realizing they must be living happily as they saw fit.

As spring arrived, all the nuns went out to the field to tend to the potatoes and vegetables and plant seedlings in the rice paddies. For the first time, I worked in the dirt, spreading the manure from the outhouse in the field. The moment I touched the fertilizer, I was struck by the thought that if I had not left home I would never in my life have done things like this. Every day was filled with wonder and gratitude for my ordination.

The rule Inhong Sunim most emphasized to everyone when she opened the Seongnamsa community was, "A day you don't work is a day you don't eat." Baizhang Huaihai, the Tang dynasty master who first established this ancient decree, founded a Chan temple independent of the Vinaya Seminary on Baizhang Mountain and wrote his own book of Chinese Chan precepts, not bound by the orthodox Vinaya literature of Indian Buddhism; these were *The Pure Precepts of Chan Monastery* by Baizhang. Of these, "A day you don't work is a day you don't eat" clearly reflects the ideas of these precepts.

Master Baizhang never rested, every day plowing the fields and chopping wood. He worked tirelessly even into his nineties, and when his disciples expressed concern for him he ignored them, saying, "What virtue do I have that I can rest comfortably and eat?" His disciples felt so sorry for him that they hid all of his tools so he could not work. Instead, he refused to eat, starving the whole day. Thus, the ancient rule "A day you don't work is a day you don't eat" was established and has become the foundation of the practitioner's lifestyle.

Seongnamsa was a rural monastery, buried deep in the countryside, at a time when the national economy was struggling as well, so the task of repairing the slowly crumbling monastery and fixing its leaking roofs fell directly to the Buddhist nuns' community. We would make blocks of mud—cutting hay, adding dirt and water, and kneading the mixture with our bare feet—and haul them onto the roofs. When I climbed the long ladder to the roof holding a brick of mud, my legs started trembling so much that I decided to stay on the ground after that, passing up the roof tiles instead.

Once, the superintendent of South Gyeongsang Province came to the monastery to pay his respects. Seeing Inhong Sunim standing precariously on the high Great Shrine Hall roof, with lines of nuns delivering balls of yellow clay up and down the ladders, he exclaimed, "You are incredible!"

Hearing that, Inhong Sunim answered simply, "A nun must know how to make tiles if she wants to live in a tiled-roof house."

Wherever you go, you become the owner and, in every situation, you are true to yourself: when you do your very best in the place you are in, you live as the protagonist of your own life. At Seongnamsa, Inhong Sunim embodied this principle and taught it to us. I worked and practiced with her until I received my bhiksuni [Sk. bhikṣuṇī, P. Bhikkhuni, Kr. biguni, fully ordained nunhood] ordination later in March of 1961 at the Geumgang ordination platform at Tongdosa.

Usually, after they receive sramaneri ordination at their home temple, nuns go to the doctrinal seminary, which is the educational institution for the novice nuns, and study scripture, preparing for nunhood. However, Inhong Sunim maintained that leaving the temple prevented us from living a monastic lifestyle, and so nuns ordained at Seongnamsa were not sent to the seminary. Instead, she invited lecturers to Seongnamsa to teach us the essential literature for beginners, like the *Admonitions to Beginners* and the *Admonition for Gray-Robed Monks*, and afterward had us study *hwadu*.

Seongnamsa later began sending nuns to the seminary, more than ten years after it was founded, when Myoeom Sunim became a tutor at Unmunsa.

Inhong Sunim said, "I can trust Myoeom Sunim with my students" and began sending the novice nuns to her. Later, Myoeom Sunim renovated Bongnyeongsa in Suwon and established her own seminary there, presiding over it as head instructor. Myoeom Sunim was ordained after receiving a promise from Seongcheol Keun Sunim. In her autobiography *Gray Rubber Shoes*, she says: "Thinking carefully about the things Keun Sunim had taught me over the time I knew him, it seemed to me that he knew more than my teachers at school, and I quite liked the things he said, and how readily they flowed into my ears. So I promised him that I would become a nun if he taught me everything he knew. And Sunim promised me he would do just that. Now that I think back on it, it was a happy time."

In 1945, May 5th in the Lunar Calendar, she received sramaneri ordination from Keun Sunim at Yunpilam and was given the Dharma name Myoeom. For the occasion, Seongcheol Keun Sunim himself painstakingly bound for her an ordination booklet and a copy of the *Eight Grave Precepts for Bhiksunis*; I was so envious of Myoeom Sunim, who treasured these gifts and kept them safe. In order to keep his promise to Myoeom Sunim, Seongcheol Sunim told her, "I am not a person who preaches ordination, but since you are Sunho (Cheongdam) Sunim's daughter, I will make an exception," and he bestowed on her the sramaneri precepts. After that, he never gave sramaneri ordination to anyone again.

The Dharma name Myoeom comes from the first chapter of the *Avatamsaka Sutra*, entitled "Seju Myoeom," and it means "adorn the world mysteriously." Perhaps Seongcheol Keun Sunim foresaw her future as a great teacher of doctrine, providing restful shade for all sentient beings underneath her great branches.

Here is a snippet of conversation between Seongcheol Keun Sunim and Myoeom Sunim from *Gray Rubber Shoes*:

"But Keun Sunim, all the things you taught me when I was younger are already in the scriptures."
"Why, you little—you shouldn't say stuff like that!"

Keun Sunim rapped her on the head and laughed heartily.

Once, Myoeom Sunim visited Seongcheol Keun Sunim at Baengnyeo-nam and, in a playful tone, asked him to make her a Dharma pen name.

"What do you want with a pen name? Well then, you can be Seju, from the chapter 'Seju Myoeom.' It's a great meaning, the character *se* [world] and *ju* [master]."

"Is it okay to use Seju when my Dharma name is Myoeom?"

"Why, it means that you'll become the master of the whole universe and decorate it mysteriously, how great of a meaning is that?"

"Alright, Sunim, I will do as you say."

Like that, both her Dharma name Myoeom and her pen name Seju ended up being given to her by Keun Sunim. My companions, and most of all myself, who wouldn't dare dream of asking Keun Sunim for a pen name, regarded Myoeom Sunim to be surely the luckiest person in the world.

Inhong Sunim's principles being one thing, I was so focused on meditation practice that I had no desire to study at the seminary either. I didn't even learn the *Admonitions to Beginners*, the most basic text for beginning practitioners.

"If I wanted to learn from books, I would have gone to college, not become a nun."

Having told this to Inhong Sunim, I threw myself wholly into meditation study. In those times, Keun Sunim's lecture notes were the sole guide to my practice, and I believed that was enough for me.

When Inhong Sunim first opened the door for practitioners at Seongnamsa to enter the seminary, most of the sramaneris packed their things to go and study there. Meanwhile, I encouraged a younger nun to meditate instead of going to the seminary and suggested she visit Keun Sunim to determine her future path.

She told me that when she asked Keun Sunim at Baengnyeonam what she should do, he responded, "Do you want to learn the *Platform Sutra by the Sixth Patriarch* and study *hwadu*, or do you want to go to the seminary, learn just the *Letters* [by Dahui Zonggao], come back, and then study *hwadu*?"

Keun Sunim also encouraged her to forego the seminary for meditation and to first read the *Platform Sutra* or the *Letters*. During his time at Baengnyeonam, Keun Sunim's standard was to have his postulants learn Japanese on their own, then after their ordination to study the Japanese-language Mahayana and Theravada Buddhist scriptures, the *Shobogenzo* (*Treasury of the True Dharma Eye*) by the Japanese monk Dogen, and various discourses of the Chinese Chan patriarchs for a couple years before going on to the Seon Meditation Hall.

Even after receiving my precepts, my work in the kitchen continued to be a problem. It was not long after my ordination. The nun serving as the kitchen head had immolated her fingers while offering vows to the

Buddha of devotion to her practice. I felt sorry to see her working when her wounds had not yet healed, so I volunteered to become head of the kitchen in her place.

But whenever I washed the pots, all the water would spill out and create a veritable Han River flowing through the kitchen. Back then, instead of concrete, the stove was made of dry yellow clay, and my clothes would get soaked in muddy water; I wouldn't mind if it were just me, but I felt quite embarrassed when it made a mess for all the other nuns in the kitchen as well. I tried to spill less water, but I was more or less unsuccessful. As a result, whenever I stepped into the kitchen, all the other nuns working in the kitchen would shout together, "Sunim, please don't come in! We'll all float away!"

Once, I carried the hot rice water from the rice cauldron, something that would have fit perfectly well in a kettle, into the Great Hall where communal meals were held, in gigantic buckets. Inhong Sunim saw me and said, "You could feed a hundred people!" to the great laughter of everyone in the hall. Thus, my career as kitchen head at Seongnamsa wasn't too successful either.

The Dharma Exchange That Shocked the Monastery

The history of Korean nuns and the history of Korean Buddhism follow a parallel path. When Venerable Ado brought Buddhism to the Silla Kingdom (ca. 374 CE), he stayed at a house owned by Morye; Morye's sister Lady Sa was the first Korean Buddhist nun. You can find a lively bhiksuni presence in the Goryeo period, but entering the Joseon dynasty it stagnates. Bhiksuni practice still managed to maintain a thread of life after that, albeit weak, with support from female patrons of the imperial court; and now in the modern age we are seeing highly accomplished nuns becoming active in the realm of Korean Buddhism.

According to the Vinaya, the codes of conduct for monks and nuns, nuns must keep the "Eight Grave Rules"[3] and receive bhiksuni precepts from preceptors belonging to both the bhiksu and bhiksuni orders, ten each. Vinaya Master Jaun Sunim established the practice of the Dual Ordination Platform for nuns, in which bhiksunis receive precepts from the bhiksunis first, then receive them again from the bhiksus; and this continues today. Along with Jaun Sunim's restoration of the bhiksuni Sangha, Cheongdam,

Hyanggok, and Seongcheol Sunim's recognition and acceptance of bhiksunis as students played a great part in reviving the bhiksuni community and bringing about a new wind of vitality to the tradition. Meanwhile, Inhong Sunim, who presided over the National Bhiksuni Association of Korea, became a great pillar for the bhiksuni community.

When I first made up my mind to live in the temple and study, Keun Sunim instructed me to go to Hongjesa, which was led by Inhong Sunim, and she eventually became my benefactory master when I was ordained. He must have sent me to her because it is rare to find someone of her caliber anywhere else.

Inhong Sunim favored Keun Sunim's form of diligent practice above all and worked hard to embody his ideals in her own life. There was something she always used to say: "One must live by Keun Sunim's Dharma. That is how Korean Buddhism will survive."

And she would sometimes tell her disciples: "When Hanam Keun Sunim was on his deathbed, he thought long and hard about whose kind of Dharma knowledge should be revered and studied, and finally he announced, 'The person I have chosen is Seongcheol Keun Sunim.' So now all you must do is trust in him and study, without turning back."

Inhong Sunim followed Keun Sunim as her spiritual teacher and Dharma master, and she observed his ideals her whole life. The first time they met was in the winter of 1949, at Myogwaneumsa in Busan.

Inhong Sunim, who had been ordained at thirty-four and had been studying under Hanam Sunim in Odaesan, reached a turning point in her practice when she met Keun Sunim. She had come to Busan from Odaesan, which was uneasy with rumors of coming war, and there she had met Keun Sunim, who was practicing there with Hyanggok Sunim. He had been leading the Bongamsa Pact under the flag of the eradication of Japanese Buddhism and living by the Buddha's Dharma, but had traveled to Myogwaneumsa in anticipation of the war. Here and there in Keun Sunim's photo album, the *Poyeongjip* [lit., *Collection of Foam and Shadow*], you can see playful images of Cheongdam, Hyanggok, and Seongcheol Sunim, releasing caged animals on the banks the Han River or climbing the peaks of Samgaksan.

When you read about the Dharma exchanges between Seongcheol Sunim and Hyanggok Sunim during their Bongamsa Pact period, described in Myoeom Sunim's biography *Gray Rubber Shoes*, you can understand how deep their friendship truly ran. I have reproduced the scene from the book here.

On a summer day, while rain poured in buckets from the sky, a bizarre scene was unfolding in the courtyard outside Bongamsa's meditation hall. Barefoot and soaked in rain, Seongcheol Sunim and Hyanggok Sunim were walking back and forth with their arms around each other's shoulders, swaying this way and that.

Hyanggok Sunim slapped Seongcheol Sunim's shoulder and said, "You are Manjusri [Sk. Mañjuśrī]."

This time Seongcheol Sunim slapped Hyanggok Sunim's shoulder and replied, "You are Samantabhadra."

Hyanggok Sunim and Seongcheol Sunim, standing in the rain, went back and forth between each other like this, while all the other monks crowded under the eaves, simply watching the two great sunims eagerly.

Myoeom Sunim too crept unobtrusively into the crowd.

But all of a sudden, Seongcheol Sunim shouted.

"Dig a ditch, let's die in one ditch!"

With that, before anyone knew what was happening, Seongcheol Sunim seized Hyanggok Sunim by the collar and dragged him to the gate. Kicking it wide open with his foot, he began raining punches on Hyanggok Sunim. Hyanggok Sunim, faced with an inescapable threat, fled outside the gate, and bang! Seongcheol Sunim slammed the gate shut and latched the bolt.

It had all happened in an instant; shocked, the monks of Bongamsa could do nothing but watch these two strange monks and their Dharma test in breathless silence.

Finally, Hyanggok Sunim pulled himself up and could be seen through the gaps in the planks, standing up and walking back and forth outside the gate.

He shook the gate with a clattering noise. But with Seong-cheol Sunim bolting it shut, there was no way it would open.

"Open up that gate for him."

Seongcheol Sunim wasn't even talking to anyone in particular, but no one dared to approach the gate. There was no way to tell if another fearsome rage might randomly fly your way. Hyanggok Sunim continued to rattle the gate loudly. That was when Seongcheol Sunim suddenly picked up a large rock, normally used to hold food offerings, and carried it over to the gate. Carefully removing the bolt without making a sound, he stood there quietly, holding the stone in both hands.

Hyanggok Sunim, thinking the gate was still locked, pushed it again with all his strength, and it flew wide open. At that moment Seongcheol Sunim launched that heavy stone at Hyanggok Sunim's stomach, where it bounced off and landed solidly on his foot. It all happened in the blink of an eye.

All the watching monks had to stop themselves from crying out, ack! But truly mysteriously, wouldn't you believe that Hyanggok Sunim simply sauntered back in as if nothing had happened, put his arm back around Seongcheol Sunim, and let out a raucous laugh.

"Ha! Ha! Ha! Ha!"

Seongcheol Sunim and Hyanggok Sunim's resounding laughter rang heartily all throughout Bongamsa.

It seemed like they truly were the reincarnations of Manjusri and Samantabhadra. At some point, as the crowd watched the spectacle of those two strange monks with open mouths, the rain had stopped, and brilliant sunlight was shining down.

At the time, Inhong Sunim found a room in the village by Myogwaneumsa to stay in while she practiced. This was because of the precept that forbids nuns and monks from living together. Inhong Sunim would meditate at Myogwaneumsa at set times and advance her studies while alms-begging; her companions at the time included Jangil Sunim, Seongu Sunim, and Myochan Sunim.

One day, during the winter retreat, Hyanggok Sunim asked Inhong Sunim the level she had reached in her studies. When she replied with her answer, he simply nodded his head. But Seongcheol Sunim, who had been listening to their conversation, grabbed her by the collar and demanded, "Say it again."

Inhong Sunim couldn't say anything. It was as if she was blocked by a great wall and couldn't take a single step forward. That day Inhong Sunim heard the following Dharma lecture from Keun Sunim: "The *hwadu* might stay unbroken no matter how busy you are during the day and remain clear and constant even in your dreams; but if it suddenly becomes opaque while you are deep in sleep, how will you escape the continuous suffering of life and death?"

This was his teaching of the three stages, in which *hwadu* must become "continuous awareness whether moving or still," "continuous awareness while dreaming," "continuous awareness while in deep sleep," and finally become "continuous awareness at all times." It is said that after hearing Keun Sunim speak that day, Inhong Sunim gained determination anew and vowed that she would receive the guidance of this great master and become enlightened no matter what.

After that incident, Inhong Sunim was contemplating *hwadu* while walking around the pond in Myogwaneumsa, when Keun Sunim asked her the level of her studies. When she could not answer, he shoved her straight into the pond. It was a silent rebuke. Without panicking, Inhong Sunim escaped the icy water of the pond, which had slightly frozen over. Inhong Sunim often said this about the experience: "I finally made it out of the pond, but my clothes were already soaked through and ice stuck to my skin. And that coastal wind is so cold. But I couldn't return to my room. I stood right there meditating until my clothes dried. Then my sense returned to me. 'Whatever little I've learned doesn't mean anything. Even that I must throw away.' I have lived my whole life never forgetting the iron determination I felt in my mind and in my heart that day."

After meeting Keun Sunim at Myogwaneumsa and receiving his great admonition, Inhong Sunim went to Seongjusa in Masan and began her own practice community with around forty other nuns. It was an exact remaking of the Bongamsa Pact founded by Seongcheol Sunim and led by Cheongdam Sunim, Jaun Sunim, and others. At Hongjesa, where I first met her, she was still leading the community in the same way she did at Seongjusa.

Inhong Sunim would eventually put the same traditions of Uposatha [Sk. Uposatha, self-examination and public confession] ceremonies, cooperative physical labor, and communal meals from her time at Seongjusa into practice at Seongnamsa, which she led without the slightest deviation from the path of practice. In those days when we struggled to sustain the temple solely on the generosity of devotees, she was a pioneer who saw that the key to creating a community for bhiksunis was in diligent practice, and endlessly pushed her disciples in their studies. Knowing her unwavering dedication, Keun Sunim sent to her women who showed the resolve to follow the same path.

Inhong Sunim put Keun Sunim's ideas directly into practice at Seongnamsa. Often she would say, "Keun Sunim gave appropriate teachings for every situation. No matter how much he tried to keep us away with his barbed-wire fences, his meaning was always clear. I rely solely on his Dharma, and I have led Seongnamsa with my motivation to build a practice community for bhiksunis under his guidance." This is how much Seongnamsa was run in accordance with Keun Sunim's teachings.

At morning service we would recite the *Surangama Sutra* dharani and in the evening perform 108 prostrations. Each month, when the moon had waxed and waned fully, everyone would gather for an Uposatha Ceremony to repent our mistakes. These were the routines done in the large communal practice and retreats that Keun Sunim wished to realize, and which Inhong Sunim put into practice at Seongnamsa. It was something that would have been impossible without her unconditional faith in Keun Sunim.

In the mornings students would recite the *Zhengdaoge* and *Xinxinming*, and when a postulant shaved their head and received their Dharma name and *hwadu*, they were required to stay up and perform three thousand prostrations overnight. No matter what, in order to receive their name and *hwadu*, they would have to meet with Keun Sunim in person. At the beginning of each meditation session, they would read Emperor Shunzhi's leaving-home poem in order to cement their identity as a practitioner and thoroughly learn the *Admonitions to Beginners*, a critical text for beginner nuns and monks.

Finally, they would read Keun Sunim's "Ten Requests for the Monastic." Written in verse, it contains various messages to encourage a practitioner's determined study, from warnings against the swift passing of idle time to admonitions for nonpossession and self-reflection.

Ten Requests for the Monastic

1. Impermanence

The sliver of waning moon lights the winter forest
And white bones litter the ground between the trees.
Where are those delights of the past,
When the suffering of samsara continues to multiply.

2. Poverty

Sitting alone with bushy hair and tattered clothes,
Wealth and fame are mere dreams beyond the clouds.

Though there is no rice in the rice jar,
The ancient light of awakening illuminates the wide universe.

3. Endeavor

Fetching water and chopping wood is the family tradition of
    the ancient monk.
A rice ball after plowing the fields is truly a tiding of being alive.
Finding inspiration in my sleep, I feel nothing but shame.
Having not reached enlightenment, I sigh and soak in tears.

4. Celibacy

In destroying the body and erasing the Dharma, lust is the first.
Tangled and bound by a thousand ropes, fall into burning hell.
Better to approach a viper, so keep it distant,
With one wrong thought comes unending suffering.

5. Honesty

There is no one who sits alone in a darkened room.
The eyes of the gods are like lightning and don't miss a hair.
Even as you serve them carefully with palms pressed together,
They become angered and erase every trace of you.

6. Humility

When the whole world of Buddhism is Vairocana Buddha,
Who could speak words of the wise and the foolish?
If you venerate everyone like the Buddha,
The Vairocana Hall will be adorned by your virtue.

7. Altruism

It is sad, like drifting clouds the foolish sentient beings of
    this world,
Planting thorny brambles and expecting heavenly peaches.

Hurting others to save myself is the path to death,
Hurting myself to save others is the path to life.

8. Self-reflection

When I search for my successes and find nothing,
The whole world will become comfortable.
When I search for my mistakes and always repent,
Even insults become gifts difficult to repay.

9. Salvation

Coveting a grain of rice in a dream,
You lose a golden pavilion with food enough for ten thousand
    lives.
Impermanence is a moment, difficult to even comprehend.
Would you not take back a thought to practice fiercely?

10. Causality

Plant peas and peas grow, shadows follow the shape,
The deeds of past, present, and future are reflected as if in a mirror.
If I look back and diligently reflect,
How can I fault the heavens or other people?
The people who treat me the worst are the true Zen masters.
The gift of pain and affront cannot be repaid even with my life.

What could possibly be added, when he wrote these words while seeing the whole world in a glance? Regardless of whether you are monastic or lay, it is a true Dharma lecture for anyone who disciplines their mind. The days seem like yesterday when I would read this with the other nuns in the Dharma Hall at Seongnamsa, building faith and practicing together.

A Communal Meal for a Hundred People

Inhong Sunim, who during her life used to be called the "Tiger of Gajisan," would often say this: "Take apart the character *seung* (僧), which means sunim. Isn't it the character meaning 'person,' in (人), next to the character for 'early,' jeung (曾)? It means that monastics are people who go before others do, in every aspect. The disciples of the Buddha must become models for the rest of the sentient world. They must embrace a poor but honest life of practice and pray for all sentient beings, endlessly humble and giving."

My vocation master Inhong Sunim was a strict teacher, even when it came to our posture during meals. No matter what, the whole monastery ate the communal meal together in one room, and no exception would be forgiven. There was no salvation for the occasional group of nuns who, busy with work, might eat separately in a back room: "Your character as a monastic must be built by your own hands. Is it proper that ordained disciples of the Buddha eat like laymen?"

She taught us to live as though we were in front of important guests, even alone in a dark room.

The communal meal, baru gongyang, was a crucial custom at Seongnamsa. When Inhong Sunim came to Seongnamsa, she got rid of the traditional wooden bowls and replaced them with steel. In the time after the purification movement, there were no other monasteries having communal meals in formal monastic robes and kasas, and using steel bowls, so some had the not-so-well-meaning perception that we led a strange lifestyle, but Sunim held her ground about the importance of the communal meal. No matter how busy the community might be with monastic work, the sight of the whole monastery a hundred strong gathering in the lecture hall to quietly share a communal meal is one that reveals the dignity of the practitioner, and it remains a Seongnamsa tradition.

Once the morning service is over and the six hundred, if not one thousand daily prostrations are finished, the nuns put on their formal robes and coats, and the morning communal meal begins.

When the bamboo sticks clap once, bow with palms together and recite verses:

A verse for thinking of the Buddha.
The place Buddha was born, the Lumbini Garden outside Kapilavastu.
The place Buddha was enlightened, under a bodhi tree in Bodh Gaya, Magadha.
The place Buddha gave his first sermon, the Deer Park near Varanasi.
The place Buddha passed into Nirvana, under twin sal trees near Kushinagar.

A verse while unfolding the bowls.
This miraculous bowl, which has traveled to me from the Buddha,
I now receive and unfold.
I wish for the sentient beings of the world too,
The three wheels become serene with equality.

A verse for folding the bowls.
At the end of this meal, the body's power is replenished,
In the ten directions and three worlds, radiate the Buddha's
    majestic power.
Transform these merits and do not linger on them,
All sentient beings will achieve enlightenment.

When the bamboo sticks clap three times, bow with palms together and
the morning meal ends.

"Take out your bowls and eat properly, with good posture. With
this good food in front of us after praying in our robes, must we eat like
village people?" At times I miss these little scoldings we heard from Sunim.

Figure 5.2. The sight of the whole monastery a hundred strong, gathering in the
lecture hall in their ceremonial robes and *kasa*s to quietly share a communal
meal, is one of the most important and long-standing traditions of Seongnamsa.
Photo by Kim Minsook.

They didn't stop at eating, though. No one could imitate the harsh punishments she would bring down when a precept was broken. Once, a student who had entered the Sangha at Seongnamsa was visited at the temple by a man she had known in her hometown. Sunim found out and gently admonished her once or twice to make him stop, but she could not put an end to his continuous visits. Sunim told her to take off her *kasa* and, right there, ripped it to pieces in front of her. She didn't stop there. She told her, "You don't deserve to live as a practitioner" and, confiscating her monastic robes, sent her out of the mountain gate.

Though she was the kind of person to look at even the most hopeless of students and say, "To help one sentient being I'd follow them through a hundred thousand lifetimes," she refused to accept even the slightest deviation from the precepts.

In a famous incident, amid the hundreds of nuns she had remembered exactly who hadn't shown up to morning services, went to their room, and dumped a bucket of water on them while they were fast asleep.

And if only that were all. Finding a postulant who had dozed off on her desk, she told her, "People who fall asleep studying are not needed at Seongnamsa" and chased her out of the temple. The postulant, who hadn't even been able to put on her shoes, sat on her knees to receive criticism at the monastic assembly.

There are probably very few monasteries that hold monastic assemblies for as long as Seongnamsa. If a monastic does something wrong, this is the time for every old grievance and overlooked mistake to be exposed and reproached. The assembly is where even an unrefined footstep would be brought up and discussed. It was Inhong Sunim's view that without going through such a severe process a monastic could not become a role model for others. Without such diligence, Seongnamsa would not have earned its place as the exemplary monastery of the bhiksuni Sangha. The word spread that "Seongnamsa is a place of strict rules and hard work, but it's there that you can really learn," and it became a center of practice where many people wished to be ordained.

Rebuilding the monastery out of ruins and transforming it into a place of practice and center of education for the future generations of practitioners, there must have been no shortage of hardships, but my teacher never once showed us these troubles on her face. She was a role model to us, not only as a nun but as a human being.

She was blessed among the blessed. But those blessings didn't come out of nowhere. I believe they came from humility.

One day, a monk with a familiar face came to visit Seongnamsa. He was a woodsman, who had worked odd jobs at the monastery for about a year before becoming ordained at Inhong Sunim's suggestion. After a friendly greeting with palms together, we had all forgotten about him, busy in the course of our individual work, but when Inhong Sunim returned from her outing and heard that he was there, she changed into her formal robes and prostrated herself three times to that young monk, sending him off with great hospitality.

When we asked, "Why did you get all dressed and bow to him when you could have just received his greeting?" she told us, "What are you talking about? That monk was no longer a woodsman, but rather a monastic going the path of a great man."

My vocation master was also not one to worry about matters of "yours" or "mine." Once, I accompanied her to Daewonsa deep in Jirisan while she saw to some matters. Perhaps the abbess there was having difficulty financing the construction of the temple, because the roof of the Main Buddha Hall had yet to be tiled, with only bare wooden rafters. When we returned to Seongnamsa, Inhong Sunim asked the devotees who could afford it to contribute: after that, the roof had new tiles.

She was a person who never lost the resolve to raise the prestige of bhiksunis, even if it meant bowing to a young monk who had been a worker at the monastery, and never strayed one step from the foundational principles of a practitioner.

Seongnamsa's headquarter monastery is Tongdosa, which houses relics from the Buddha's body. Inhong Sunim led Seongnamsa while receiving the teachings of the esteemed monks who resided at Tongdosa. Attending steadfastly to such people as Elder Guha Sunim, from whom it would not be an exaggeration to say all of Tongdosa's modern history originated; Gyeongbong Sunim, Weolha Sunim, who served as the head patriarch of the Jogye Order; Byeogan Sunim, who was the abbot of Tongdosa and former senior council chairman of the Jogye Order; and others, she received their teachings as she guided the new generations of students. I remember the night when Inhong Sunim traveled to Tongdosa to pay respects after having a major surgery. Weolha Keun Sunim himself took care to bring warm water and a lantern to her room, telling her, "Use these, you'll need them at night."

The strict Byeogan Sunim was always the picture of austerity to his students, but whenever we went to Tongdosa to pay respects, he would give us a piece of handwritten calligraphy as a gift. I still have with me a treasured passage of the *Xinxinming* that he wrote for me with his brush. Today, the nuns at Seongnamsa visit Tongdosa to attend the bimonthly Uposatha ceremonies and at the beginning and end of the seasonal retreats to hear the patriarch's lectures.

Inhong Sunim would also invite various esteemed monks to teach her pupils. The students broadened the horizons of their mind, hearing lectures from Cheongdam Sunim on the *Diamond Sutra* and Unheo Sunim on the *Surangama Sutra*, Hyanggok and Jaun Sunim's Dharma talks, Ilta Sunim's talks on the Bodhisattva precepts, and more. These all came from Inhong Sunim's conviction and philosophy of providing a holistic and expansive education. I learned from Inhong Sunim how important the clear vision of a leader is to shaping a monastery into a place of learning and practice.

When I was young I thought all grown-ups were like that. As I have passed sixty and now seventy, I now know that my vocation master had the countenance of a truly outstanding leader, that she was beyond compare. She was a formidable person. Who could hope to match such devotion and inner strength?

The Mortar Monk's Secret to Not Dozing Off

During the time I spent studying as a wandering nun, I journeyed back to Hongjesa in Taebaeksan. Returning to the place where I had once practiced as a bushy-haired postulant, trudging through moonlit fields covered in snow in an effort to stay awake, but now with a shaved head brought back a fresh sense of reminiscence.

Staying at this small temple with the few nuns who practiced there, Baekjol Sunim and I went for a hike and stopped by Sajaam where Beopjeon Sunim was staying, which was at the foot of a peak a little further up from Hongjesa. Beopjeon Sunim, who had been ordained at Anjeongsa Cheonjegul with Keun Sunim as his vocation master under the Dharma name Dorim, had moved here to Taebaeksan to farm and practice.

With logs from the mountain as the walls and plywood sheets for a roof, he had built a small ramshackle shelter and called it Sajaam, or Lion's Hermitage. The name was apt, for it was so remote and deep in the mountains that you might have expected to see lions prowling around. We had been talking about this and that for a little while, when Beopjeon

Sunim handed me a poem and asked me to read it. Sunim, who used to say that if he hadn't become a practitioner he would have been a classical poet, had written dozens of books of poetry during his ten years living in Taebaeksan. I read the poem and told him my honest thoughts.

"Sunim, it's just like reading Hanshan's poems."

Around that time I'd become enraptured by the lives of Hanshan and Shide and went around reciting their poetry. Beopjeon Sunim, having spent no less than ten years in the depths of Taebaeksan, where a great master might have once hidden away, must have been naturally overflowing with poetic spirit when he wrote. Anyone who had studied under Keun Sunim must have dreamed of living like Hanshan as I did, and Beopjeon Sunim seemed to have been no exception.

As we were talking it had somehow become dinnertime. Thinking I would make Sunim a meal, I headed to the kitchen, which was completely empty except for a single pot hanging on the wall.

Picking fresh mountain greens and putting together some side dishes along with a bowl of kimchi, I set the table. No sooner had the three of us sat down and picked up our utensils to eat, when crunch! Beopjeon Sunim cracked his teeth on a rock. Sunim had scooped the rice, and since we were guests he had given us the rice on top while he took the rice from lower down. I must have missed a rock while washing the rice and it had sunk to the bottom of the pot. Sunim had told me, "My teeth are weak so watch out for rocks," but I had given him one on the first spoonful; I felt so embarrassed that we left right after dinner. This was when we were in our midtwenties and Sunim was in his late thirties.

The stories of Beopjeon Sunim's scrupulous devotion to Keun Sunim at Anjeongsa Cheonjegul are still told by many today. He would often brew an Oriental herbal remedy by hand for Keun Sunim, who was quite frail, and so careful was he about the task that he would make sure it was precisely the same concentration and amount every single time. So impeccable was his attention that, since then, when other practitioners would attend to Keun Sunim's medicine, he would ask them to do even a fraction as well as Beopjeon.

"I trusted firmly in my master, and together we spent some important times. Old Master had a quick temper but he never scolded me once."

Only someone who has attended to Keun Sunim knows how alert and conscientious you'd have to be to never hear a scolding from him.

After Beopjeon Sunim's time attending to Keun Sunim at Anjeongsa, he spent time at Dosolam, Baengnyeonam, and elsewhere, practicing and tending farms, then moved to Sudoam in Gimcheon where he lived for fifteen years. There, he restored a ruined temple and established a Seon meditation monastery to educate the next generation, later returning to Keun Sunim's side at Haeinsa. Ten years after Keun Sunim's passing, he rose to become the patriarch of the Jogye Order, so you can tell how greatly he dedicated his life to practice, from beginning to end.

Upon his return to Haeinsa, the monks would watch Beopjeon Sunim sitting in the meditation hall without even the slightest movement and say he was like a hunk of rock sitting there, or that he looked as solid as the horns of an ox. Because they said he looked like a heavy mortar bowl, which doesn't budge once you set it down, he was sometimes called the "mortar monk," so I asked him once: "Sunim, how do you manage to never doze off like that?"

Beopjeon Sunim replied briefly, in his unique pattern of speech: "I don't eat much."

They say that during Haeinsa's traditional intensive Seon practice, where one goes a week without sleep, the only person who didn't fall asleep was Beopjeon Sunim. Among the monastics I practiced with, the rumor was that no one had ever seen Beopjeon Sunim dozing off in the meditation hall in the decades he spent at Haeinsa.

"If you thought you'd die if you lost *hwadu*, could you fall asleep?"

This is what he said to the students who asked him the secret to not dozing off. Beopjeon Sunim was a person who followed Keun Sunim as his teacher and lived his whole life by Keun Sunim's teachings. Compared to Keun Sunim's directness, Beopjeon Sunim was quiet, but when it came to enforcing discipline he was no less ruthless. Seeing a monk using a phone in the temple office at Sudoam, he smashed the phone box, shouting, "What does a monk need with a phone!" and he was said to have told a monk who was practicing in a small hermitage above Sudoam that he should not leave his spot, even if Sudoam caught on fire.

There are probably few people as wordless as Beopjeon Sunim. After I pay respects, he'll ask in one phrase if I'm doing well and then just sit quietly. If I don't start talking first, the only sound would be the wind blowing outside the hall of Toeseoldang. Yet when I presented him with a set of formal robes as a gift for his appointment as the patriarch of Jogye Order, he wore them to the inauguration ceremony, and later that silent monk expressed his thanks to me.

Even today, I'll visit him at Toeseoldang several times a year to see how he's doing. He has always been so careful about his health that though he'll be ninety next year he's still hale and hearty. It seems that Beopjeon Sunim learned his attitude to life exactly from Keun Sunim, who never retreated a step from his principles. Even now he performs 108 prostrations every day, and he observes his meal time and his walking time to the very second.

Ever since Keun Sunim's death, all of my disciples have received their *hwadu* from Beopjeon Sunim. I trust that he will guide them by their side for many years to come.

Saving Our Teacher with a Twenty-One-Day Prayer

Is it not the special privilege of the wandering monastic that they are never tied down and can fly away whenever they feel like leaving? Whenever I felt things weren't helping my studies, I would put on my knapsack and walk out the single-beam gate. I did this sort of wandering practice for about three years after my bhiksuni ordination, traveling here and there, and when I finally returned to Seongnamsa and greeted my teacher Inhong Sunim, she just about fell over sideways. She was very angry with me.

With all the busy work going on at Seongnamsa they needed hands to help, and I had been wandering around who knows where when I could have been practicing right there at the Seongnamsa meditation hall, which must have displeased her quite a bit. But in my young days as a practitioner, I wanted to be free, floating around like the clouds and the wind, and so I had left, pretending not to notice my teacher's feelings. During that time she had been working endlessly to repair the dilapidated temples and open the Seon Hall, as well as practicing. There was so much work that even the nuns who had taken on responsibilities had wanted to run away to somewhere else.

Inhong Sunim pushed the work forward so doggedly that, before she knew it, Seongnamsa had staked its claim as a leading center of practice and enlightenment. Rumors had spread far and wide that monastics could practice very well there.

However, she must have overtaxed her body, and she fell ill. She said her stomach suddenly felt like it was being ripped out, and she wasn't able to eat anything. We took her to hospitals, but neither Korean nor Western medicine could find a definitive source.

I watched over her, reading to her from her bedside and placing warm salt compresses on the painful area. My sister nun Beopui Sunim traveled back and forth endlessly between Seongnamsa and the hospital, and the tears never dried from her eyes. That faithful disciple Beopui Sunim, who had stayed by Inhong Sunim's side and served her since the day she was ordained, was hurt more than anyone by Inhong Sunim's illness. Two months passed without us even learning its name, and there was no change in her condition.

"The life of humans is up to the heavens. I must be receiving the retribution from my family's fishery. It's good that I can settle it like this before I go."

Watching her prepare her heart like this, I decided enough was enough and went to Maryknoll Hospital, which was the most famous hospital in Busan at the time. I met with the foreign Catholic nun who was the director there and, explaining our situation, told her we wanted to get an examination, but the nurse beside her told me that first-time patients could only be admitted after waiting a week. I remembered suddenly that several years ago I had once accompanied Inhong Sunim to this very hospital. They say that when there is a need a solution will arise—the nurse managed to find the records from years ago.

The very next day when I brought Sunim to the hospital, the director informed us, "There is a problem with the pancreas," and she wrote a letter of introduction for us to see the director at Wallace Memorial Baptist Hospital in Yeongdo. The German director there performed his exam and told us that the pancreas was infected and seconds from bursting. Ignorant of all this, I had given her hot salt compresses thinking it would help her, so she had suffered even more because of a foolish nun like me! After booking a date for the surgery, Beopui Sunim and I went straight to see Seongcheol Keun Sunim at Seongjeonam. In our desperation at the thought of losing our vocation master, we couldn't sit still. Keun Sunim happened to be in the middle of walking meditation when we arrived, and we were able to see him right away. Listening to everything that had happened, he fell into thought for a moment, then laid out this plan.

"Your boss can't die yet. You've got to save her. Do this. Go back and do a twenty-one-day prostration prayer and recite the *Surangama Sutra* dharani [Sk. *dhāraṇī*]. For twenty-one days, the sound of *moktak*[4] and chanting can't stop for even a second. Light incense, and have two people do the 108-prostration prayer and two people do the dharani. Don't let any laypeople into the Great Buddha Hall."

After hearing Keun Sunim's words, my footsteps felt lighter on the way back. Returning to Seongnamsa, we passed on Keun Sunim's advice to our eldest sister nun, Myoyeong Sunim. She called a community meeting to plan the teams, and we began praying. The group that would carry out the prayers was made up of sixteen people, subdivided into four squads of four people each: two to do prostrations in a 108-prostration repentance prayer, and two to recite the dharani. The squads rotated every two hours, and the twenty-four-hour twenty-one-day prayer began.

The next day when Beopui Sunim and I went to the hospital, Inhong Sunim had already gone into the operating room. They were going to observe her for a week before the surgery but her condition was so bad that they had rushed her in. Coincidentally it had been at the very same time that the nuns had begun their prayer.

The nuns at Seongnamsa prayed so hard, with every bit of their heart and strength, that Seongu Sunim, who had been overseeing the meditation hall, later said this: "Everyone, even the nuns from the meditation hall, had come out to pray. When they all sat and chanted, the whole monastery ground rang with the sound of *Ji Sim Gwi Myeong Rye* [With devotion and my whole life, I take refuge]."

Inhong Sunim's surgery finally ended after almost eight hours. The director, who had performed the surgery, said, "The fact that she survived when her pancreas had burst from infection is a miracle. This surgery is difficult to do successfully for even one person in a thousand, so I'm planning to report the results in my home country." The singular mind of the monastery that we had to save our teacher had managed to move the heavens.

Saying that her pain would still be severe after the surgery, the director never left Inhong Sunim's side and took meticulous care of her. Pus and blood flowed endlessly out of Sunim's body through a tube placed in her body during the surgery. She had clung to her practice and the temple work until her body was this ruined. She had climbed up roofs to replace their tiles herself, and even returning late at night after walking twelve kilometers and back from Seongnamsa to Eonyang City, she would go straight to the meditation hall and sit.

After three days in a coma, she finally woke up. Sunim looked at us and said this: "Now I'm refreshed. When I was on the operating table, Manjusri and Samantabhadra appeared, as well as Avalokitesvara and Mahasthamaprapta, and all four of them stood around me touching my stomach. I've received the mercy of the Buddhas and Bodhisattvas."

We were told that infections of the pancreas are even more painful than infections in other areas, but after the surgery Inhong Sunim took no painkillers and recovered quickly, getting her stitches removed within a week. Even as her condition improved, the prayer at Seongnamsa continued.

Sunim was discharged on the day that the twenty-one-day prayer was completed, and wearing her formal robe and *kasa* she stood in the middle of Seongnamsa's Great Buddha Hall and did three prostrations. It was in the late fall of 1964. Even now I can't forget how everything came together for that beautiful prayer dedication. The Buddha, who had answered our desperate prayers with mercy; Keun Sunim, who taught us how to pray and told us to save our teacher; Inhong Sunim, who had survived a massive surgery and returned to us alive; the three prostrations I offered in my gratitude to them was a moment I have never forgotten.

Inhong Sunim suffered many more trials with illness after that, and once she turned eighty she had trouble with her legs that made it difficult to walk, but when it was time for the daily service, morning and night she would dress in her formal robes and *kasa* and observe it from her room without fail.

The tradition of a monastic community endures only when an extraordinary teacher and the students who uplift her teachings sincerely become of one mind. After that time it became a tradition every year on the fourth day of the first lunar month for Seongnamsa to hold a weeklong no-sleeping prayer with dharani recitation and repentance prayer, and it has continued from that day fifty years ago to today.

My Mother, Who Became Ilhyu Sunim

"Every mother in the world is an idiot!"

This is how I felt looking at my own mother. My mother, who had believed me when I said I would achieve enlightenment in three years and return home, waited for her daughter for over ten years before going to Seongnamsa herself to find me. Since the day I had left home I hadn't even dreamt of going back, and she must have guessed how I truly felt. My mother may have seemed mild on the outside, but she was a proud woman, and she had a sharp mind.

All that time, with all of her in-laws having passed away, she had been guarding our family home alone, waiting with the sole hope that her daughter might return one day. There never was a more tragic woman. Watching her daughter go off to the temple in her forties, the signs of old age had already begun to rub off on her as she reached her fifties. My mother, who spent so many lonely years, calling out her sorrow like a mourning dove with no one to hear her. Yet when she came looking for me after ten years spent apart, I treated her with more indifference than I would a passing stranger.

"The secular world is the path to a cyclical existence and leaving it is the path to freedom, so for freedom's sake the secular world must be cut off completely."

These words from the precious lecture notes I carried like my very life had become my entire existence, so I had already left all my blood relations in the past. Even before I left home I had watched my mother hang all of her hopes on me and thought, "How much pain she must be in to hold on to me like this." Yet despite all this, I still refused to stay by her side, so imagine my attitude toward her once I had left home. When I met her so coldly, she told me, "You're more poisonous than a viper" and turned her footsteps back home.

It must have been meant to be, then, that my mother came to leave home as well. She came back to Seongnamsa, and after hearing Inhong Sunim's Dharma talk about karmic law and rebirth, she resolved to become a nun. That was also the time when Inhong Sunim's own mother had joined the Sangha as Baekwol Sunim and was staying at Seongnamsa.

In the spring of 1965, her fifty-sixth year, my mother was ordained at Seongnamsa with Jeongja Sunim as her vocation master. Jeongja Sunim had been Inhong Sunim's vocation master and had already passed away; when you receive precepts from a deceased person and have them as your vocation master you become a "memorial tablet disciple." Thus my mother and Inhong Sunim became sister nuns, and to me an aunt nun. She received ordination precepts and the Dharma name Ilhyu from Jaun Sunim, and my mother lived as Ilhyu Sunim until the day of her death.

Jaun Sunim, who gave my mother her precepts, was not only a close companion of Seongcheol Keun Sunim but also my preceptor as well, so I have a deep connection with him. The impacts that Jaun Sunim's grace and kindness have had on the bhiksuni community are too great to enumerate one by one, but his establishment of the dual ordination system is one that is worth paying attention to. At the time, the Buddhism of

Southeast Asia, as well as the Tibetan Buddhism of the Dalai Lama, still had no established rite of ordination for bhiksunis, so the creation of this system to ordain nuns was a pioneering moment in the history of women in Buddhism worldwide. Because of this, even the eldest nuns of the bhiksuni communities now pay respect to Jaun Sunim: "With devotion and my whole life, I take refuge."

The relationship between Jaun Sunim and Seongcheol Sunim shows the highest reaches of the trust that can be built between two friends. In 1980 the Jogye Order was in turmoil after violent action from the military government, but the next year things had settled enough to select the new patriarch. The following are the words of Seongcheol Keun Sunim: "One day they told me Jaun Sunim had called from Seoul. Sunim had never picked up a phone in his life, so wondering what it was all about I picked up the phone and asked, 'Jaun Sunim, what is it?' He said, 'Don't say you won't do it and just listen. There was an election for patriarch and the senior monks have come to an agreement. Just don't say you won't do it,' and without even waiting for an answer he hung up."

When he came to Haeinsa Hongjeam, Jaun Sunim would sometimes stop by Baengnyeonam. Some days he would get up in arms about some problem with Haeinsa's management and unleash a torrent of complaints on Keun Sunim. But their friendship stayed constant, and Keun Sunim entrusted all matters outside of Haeinsa to Jaun Sunim's judgment. I would visit Jaun Sunim when he came by Haeinsa Hongjeam once in a while, and he would always joke, "You don't have to be nice to that guy up there, just be nice to me," and he would receive me warmly.

Even after Ilhyu Sunim was ordained, she couldn't let go of her affection for me and always put me first. All the mothers of the world are like this, so how could Ilhyu Sunim be any different? Of all the people in the world, I thought, the most foolish existence must be that one called mother.

Despite her ordination late in life, I hoped she would practice with sincere resolve, so I tried to watch over her from afar as much as I could. Ilhyu Sunim practiced with determination, as if she didn't want to lose to anybody. She suffered from pains in her knees due to arthritis, but she showed her strength, and with the help of an attendant she worked her way up from one prostration to finally finishing a thousand. Later her pain completely went away and she was able to do walking meditation and advance her practice without disturbance.

Figure 5.3. My mother, Elder Ilhyu Sunim, was ordained late, but she practiced admirably, with true resolve. Author provided.

One time she fell ill and looked like she might pass away. She was sitting leaning on the cushion, but even in her unconscious state she never put down her prayer beads, rolling them in her hand for twenty-four hours. At dawn she opened her eyes and, looking around as if she had awoken from a deep sleep, she said, "You thought I was dead, didn't you?"

It was one rainy day of many during the summer retreat season while I was practicing at the Simgeomdang. Early in the morning Ilhyu Sunim's attendant found me and said that she wanted to see me urgently, and when I went to her she said quietly, "I'm going to go today."

They were the words of an old woman, but it had happened several times now, so Seongta Sunim, Beopui Sunim, Hyunmuk Sunim, Beobyong Sunim, Hyeju Sunim, Baekjol Sunim, and others, all gathered around and talked and laughed with her joyfully for a couple or more hours. That day happened to be the beginning of the midsummer season, when the nuns of Seongnamsa would bathe in the stream of Ongnyudong and eat sticky rice cake soup or potato pancakes to cool off from the heat.

Even while the other nuns went out to Ongnyudong, Baekjol Sunim and I stood watch by Ilhyu Sunim's side.

"I would like to eat some refreshing watermelon."

Just as Ilhyu Sunim expressed her wish for watermelon, a monk came by with a truck laden with mouthwateringly fresh-looking watermelons. When we brought her some after offering them on the Buddha's altar, Ilhyu Sunim readily ate one or two slices.

Baekjol Sunim and I finally went up to Ongnyudong and had dinner with the nuns, and on the way back we had been resting on a boulder for a moment when an attendant ran up. The feeling arose that "she has left," and we hurried back down, only to hear that during the dinner meal she had eaten a spoonful of sticky rice cake soup, and while scooping a second spoonful had breathed her last, sitting right where she was. It was the lunar sixth month and sixth day, sixteen years after she had entered the Sangha.

In her appearance after death, all form had fallen away, and neither her longing nor her attachments nor her waiting were visible any longer. Three days later, flames burned brightly upon the pyre and her material body became a handful of ash. Scattering those ashes in turn to the north, south, east, and west, the life of one human seemed so empty.

"Do not be drawn by glory into a futile world, but enter only into the eternal Nirvana free from life and death," I prayed in my heart. I did not show tears. Life is inherently hollow, so how can one replace freedom from life and death with sadness?

On the day of the forty-nine-day ceremony, the water in the pond outside her residence turned a golden hue. The monks and nuns who had come to attend the ceremony called it an auspicious sign, saying, "It hasn't even rained, but a rainbow is standing on Gajisan." A rainbow had stretched from Gajisan and rooted itself in the pond outside the temple, making the water seem golden. Later, when Ilta Sunim heard this story, he said that it was a sight rarely seen these days. As for myself, I would like to remember Ilhyu Sunim as a practitioner who left home late, but focused diligently on her life in the Sangha and practiced admirably.

Chapter 6

Practice

In Search of the Path to Eternal Freedom

Breaking Ten Years of Silence, the Lion's Roar Sermon

There are probably few sunims who have been as mistreated and pushed away by Seongcheol Keun Sunim as those of us from Seongnamsa. Every year of the ten-year period between 1955 to the mid-1960s when Keun Sunim shut himself away behind a barbed-wire fence at Seongjeonam, the nuns of Seongnamsa would climb the hill of Unmunjae the day before their retreats ended to hear Keun Sunim give a Dharma talk.

There were few means of public transportation at the time, so one expected to walk at least a few hours. You would pack a lunch and some rice cakes in your knapsack to eat on the way and cross the Unmunjae. Taking the bus from there to Daegu, then walking the rest of the way to Seongjeonam, you would arrive at dinnertime. Making a hole in the fence that surrounded the monastery like a steel drum and barely squeezing in, you would sit waiting in the great hall holding your breath, and Keun Sunim would come out and chase you away with his staff.

Running outside to dodge the staff, without a chance to put your shoes back on, everywhere around Seongjeonam would be covered completely in white snow. The attendant monks would put our shoes in a basket and pass them outside to us, but with the sun having set and being unable to make our way back to Seongnamsa, we often climbed precariously down the mountain in the darkness of the night and slept at the main monastery, Pagyesa.

As we returned, we would think, "If I don't practice harder, I'll never be able to see Keun Sunim's true character," and with a new furious spirit we threw ourselves back into practice. Teaching lectures and offering food is Dharma, but receiving scorn and getting thrown out is also Dharma. Practice is the only path to survival because it heightens the pillar of resolve. What earthly grudge could he have had against us to throw us out like that? Only one who has been rebuked and thrown out knows the great strength that can be gained from it.

Forgetting the memories of being kicked out without so much as a drink of water, when our retreats ended we would once more walk four hours and cross the Unmunjae. We repeated this pattern of walking thirty *li* from Daegu to Seongjeonam to get chased out again for ten years, and at some point it had become like a Seongnamsa tradition.

Even with the continuous ejections, my vocation master never stopped going to hear the Dharma talks. She had put her faith in this teacher, and so with single-minded determination she went to him, leading her followers. Thinking about it now, Keun Sunim's staff, as cold as a column of frost, was a lesson of mercy, teaching us that we should offer our lives and our bodies to our Path.

To us, who had faithfully walked barefoot through blizzards without even noticing how cold our feet were, to hear even one word in our desire to practice, the thunderous sermons Keun Sunim delivered were immeasurable teachings that nourished our souls.

Keun Sunim finished his ten-year confinement at the hermitage of Seongjeonam of the monastery of Pagyesa in the mountain of Palgongsan in 1965. That summer, Keun Sunim moved to the monastery of Gimyongsa in the mountain of Undalsan, South Gyeongsang Province, to spend his rainy-season retreat, and the same year during his winter retreat he delivered another great sermon for the monastery audience. That sermon was his *Chojeon Beopnyun*, the Buddha's first sermon.[1]

Except for a few nuns who were tasked with guarding the monastery, Inhong Sunim decreed that the whole monastery should attend the Dharma lecture. We rode the bus all day to the city of Jeomchon, then walked the remaining sixty *li* to Gimyongsa. Splitting our time between Yangjinam and Daeseongam, we stayed for twenty days to hear Keun Sunim's great sermon.

After finishing his Undalsan Dharma lectures, Keun Sunim moved to Haeinsa Baengnyeonam at Jaun Sunim's request and spent the winter retreat there in 1966.

In 1967, as the spiritual master of Haeinsa, Keun Sunim began a Hundred-Day Dharma lecture series for the monks entering the winter retreat at Haeinsa. In daily two-hour sermons, he meticulously explained every aspect of Buddhism; this was the moment that the "One-Hundred-Day Dharma Talk," the catechism of Buddhism containing Keun Sunim's Buddhist philosophy and the complete history of Seon practice, was born.

My vocation master received word that "the master is beginning his Hundred-Day lecture, and only practitioners with at least ten years' experience will be accepted as audience members," and called a community assembly at Seongnamsa to decide who would attend. Around twenty people were selected. Bhiksunis from Seongnamsa, Gimyongsa Daeseongam, and Daeseungsa Yunpilam attended. This was possible because so many of us had already been practicing under the guidance of Seongcheol Keun Sunim's teachings.

In Haeinsa's Great Hall, there was hardly any room to step between all the monks in attendance; meditation monks from the Seon hall, scholar monks studying Buddhist doctrine, and administrative monks who took care of the monastery's livelihood. As the reputation of his Dharma lectures had spread far and wide, monks not only from Haeinsa's various mountain hermitages but from temples across the country had gathered to hear him. Notable monks such as Hyeam Sunim, Beopjeon Sunim, Jiwol Sunim, Dogyeon Sunim, Ilta Sunim, Boseong Sunim, Jigwan Sunim, and Beopjeong Sunim were all in attendance as well. This large-scale Dharma lecture, which over three hundred monks and nuns had gathered to hear, was a rare sight for the time and became a sensation in the Buddhist world.

On top of Keun Sunim's strong Sancheong regional dialect, he spoke very quickly, and the audience complained: "Spiritual Master, your words are too fast. Please speak a little slower."

"I'm talking too fast, huh? I understand. I'll go slower."

But after that, his words started to speed right back up again, and he laughed, as if he couldn't help himself.

"I'm talking fast again, right?"

There was a reason Keun Sunim had become the spiritual master and organized this long hundred-day lecture. He explained that reason thus: "The scripture of Christianity is the Bible, Confucianism has its Classics, Islam has the Koran. The foundational scripture is simple. But since in Buddhism we have the so-called Eighty-Four Thousand Teachings, it's hard to say just what the scripture is. So to begin I've put together at least the things you should know in order of urgency."

These days, as I spend my retreat at Simgeomdang, I listen to Keun Sunim's hundred-day lectures. I listen for one hour a day, but no matter how much I listen it sounds new; and I relive my wonder at how, like a lofty waterfall, he was able to pour forth such endless knowledge for as long as one hundred days.

At that time Jaun Sunim had ordered, "Open the Great Hall at Haeinsa Hongjeam to the nuns from Seongnamsa," so we stayed in Hongjeam, practicing until eleven every night. I wrote down each day's lectures in my notes and gave them to my vocation master. Keun Sunim had said, "If you are a practitioner you must memorize all of the *Zhengdaoge* and the *Xinxinming*," and because of this, every monastic who attended went and memorized the *Zhengdaoge* and *Xinxinming*. Climbing upon the Dharma platform to lecture, come rain or snow, never missing a single day, the sight of Keun Sunim as he strove to instill great spirit into the heart of even one person seemed so merciful to me.

A professional female Go[2] player was staying at Hongjeam at the time, and she said this to me: "Sunims may not be glamorous like actresses, but you're true beauties."

In her eyes, the Seongnamsa nuns who listened fastidiously to the sermons and focused solely on their practice must have looked very beautiful.

With many people living together for a hundred days, there were some unexpected incidents as well. During a short break on the last day of the last month of the lunar year, right before the new year, Keun Sunim overheard Hyechun Sunim singing a song,[3] and she was sent away without being able to hear the lecture to the end. I had been away making a trip to Seongnamsa to prepare for the New Year, and Inhong Sunim was not present at the scene so we avoided a harsh rebuke, but we almost could have all been thrown out without hearing the rest of the lecture.

Following this, the hundred-day lectures were published as a book, to serve as a guide for people who wished to practice, and were even translated into English. I've heard that many monks and nuns used the hundred-day lectures as a textbook for writing their own Dharma talks, and that Wontaek Sunim, the monk who had edited the recordings of the lectures into a book, received many commendations from people saying, "You've published a fine book which is very useful to me." With the hundredth anniversary of Keun Sunim's birth, the book is receiving new attention, so this must be how Keun Sunim's Dharma body still lives on today.

The Gimyongsa Dharma lectures and the hundred-day lectures, which filled my studies with great meaning in my early thirties, are stored deep within my heart, and I trust they will remain a great support to my practice for many lives to come.

The Three-Year *Gyeolsa* at Simgeomdang

One year after I heard the thunderous hundred-day lecture, a three-year *gyeolsa*, or retreat community, began at Seongnamsa. A *gyeolsa*, unlike the reoccurring practice periods of the winter and summer retreats, is when a group of monastics make a pact to perform long, intensive practice in pursuit of a certain goal.

"You should be practicing for yourself, not coming to me for Dharma lectures. Now that Seongnamsa is more or less settled, you should try a three-year intensive retreat."

This is what Keun Sunim told my vocation master when she came to him with all of us in tow to hear his Dharma lectures, ten years after she had restored the Seongnamsa Great Hall, leaky and full of holes, and opened the Seon meditation hall to practice with her assembly. When Seongnamsa's raised pavilion, Chimgyeru, and its meditation hall, Simgeomdang, were built, Keun Sunim named them himself, and wrote this verse of encouragement.

O sword of Chan Master Zhaozhou,
The blade glitters with cold frostlight.
If you ask twice what it means,
Your body will be cut in two.

Returning to Seongnamsa, Inhong Sunim began preparations for a religious pact.

Seongnamsa was not my vocation master's first attempt at a *gyeolsa*. In the summer of 1951, Inhong Sunim and around forty other nuns had reproduced Keun Sunim's methods for his Bongamsa *gyeolsa* at Seongjusa. The 1947 Bongamsa *gyeolsa* hoisted a flag proclaiming, "Let's live by the Buddha's laws": a movement to overcome the crumbling precepts and fading Korean Seon tradition in the wake of the influence of Japanese Buddhism and bring about a revival of Seon Buddhism had begun. After my vocation master met Keun Sunim and was first touched by his influence, she put into practice at Seongjusa the exact pact that he had followed at Bongamsa. Just like the Bongamsa *gyeolsa*, which had started a new practice tradition and became a model for Buddhist reforms, the Seongjusa *gyeolsa* was strict and diligent.

Even in daily life they wore the monastic robes and five-panel *kasa*, and when leaving the monastery they would don straw hats and carry a bamboo staff. Besides their practice, they labored in the fields for at least two hours a day, and every first day of the month and full moon they would recite the *Bodhisattva Precepts*. They always ate gruel in the morning; no food touched their lips in the evening. During the morning and evening ceremonies they recited the *Surangama Sutra* dharani and did prostrations of repentance; they did not change this routine even on days of important religious ceremonies at the monastery. It was the exact method of the Bongamsa *gyeolsa*.

The very fact that Inhong Sunim made such a *gyeolsa* a reality speaks to how much of a pioneer she truly was, at a time [1951] when a religious community of nuns was almost unheard of, not to mention the chaos of the Korean War that still raged around her. The very attempt at creating such a monastic community centered around the upholding of proper practice would have been difficult to realize if not for her steadfast belief that practice alone is the true purpose of the monk and nun.

The Seongnamsa *gyeolsa* took place almost twenty years after the one at Seongjusa, but Inhong Sunim's determination was joined by the powerful energy of the nuns in the monastery who had heard Keun Sunim's Dharma lectures at Gimyongsa and Haeinsa. Our combined spirits could have touched the sky. Keun Sunim told us to perform a 300-prostration repentance prayer and recite the *Surangama Sutra* dharani once a day, and to always practice with a devout mind.

In 1969 on October 15th of the lunar calendar, the three-year *gyeolsa* began in the recently renovated Simgeomdang at Seongnamsa along with the winter retreat. I was thirty-three years old; thirteen years had passed since I had left home. The members of the *gyeolsa* numbered thirteen in total and, with Inhong Sunim, included senior nuns such as Jangil, Seongwoo, Hyegwan, and Hyechun Sunim, as well as young nuns like Beophui, Beobyong, Baekjol, and Hyeju, and myself. The supporting team of nuns chosen to take care of the *gyeolsa* members over the three years were Hyeongak, Yeongwu, Domun, and Doyeon Sunim.

To the assembled nuns beginning the *gyeolsa*, Seongcheol Keun Sunim gave the following lecture: "Practice hard with all your desperation. If you're not strict with yourself now, no matter how hard you work later you won't be able to fulfill your goal. Practice must become one with your daily life, your dreams, and your sleep. There can't be even the smallest break in the *hwadu*."

Keun Sunim then gave us five precepts to follow for the duration of the *gyeolsa*:

I do not sleep for more than four hours a day.
I live as a mute and do not speak needlessly.
I live as an illiterate and do not read anything.
I do not eat excessively or between meals.
I do an appropriate amount of manual labor.

We observed these rules to the letter, performed three hundred prostrations and recited dharani every day, and never left the meditation cushion besides mealtimes. A holy person is someone who has surmounted every suffering and overcome their own material body. Where there is serious practice there is true Dharma, and living through self-restraint and self-denial is the foundation of the practitioner's life.

Hanging in the room where Inhong Sunim, who had now passed sixty years old, resided, were the words "When you are lying down comfortably, think of the sentient beings who suffer the pain of hell." It was a stern lash of the whip aimed at her own practice and a rebuke directing her toward oneness with *hwadu*, which cannot be broken for even a second.

Because Inhong Sunim was also serving as the abbess of the monastery of Seongnamsa while participating in the *gyeolsa*, she would come down from the hermitage when there were matters at the monastery and return later to sit in the meditation hall, no matter how late the hour. During those three years, the only time she left through the gates of Seongnamsa was when Cheongdam Sunim passed into Nirvana. Naturally the rest of the *gyeolsa* assembly never left Seongnamsa once during the three-year *gyeolsa*. I wonder if this three-year *gyeolsa* might not be considered part of a golden age during her tenure at Seongnamsa.

The thirteen of us in the Simgeomdang were not the only ones in *gyeolsa*. Every nun at Seongnamsa, holding to the spirit of *gyeolsa*, were faithful to their tasks. Those engaged in monastic affairs and administrative duties, those working in the kitchens preparing meals with every care, all devoted themselves to their responsibilities fully. The whole monastery was alive with an atmosphere as keen as a knife, and a tension and excitement, as if the negligence of any other would cut your own flesh, surrounded us on all sides.

The monastery, which had already been so quiet that many people wondered, "Are all the nuns at Seongnamsa mute?" became even more silent during the *gyeolsa*. We began the day at three in the morning with three hundred prostrations and a dharani, take a break from meditation and do stretches together at five, and every morning mealtime, rain or snow, we would walk down with kerosene lamps to the Gangseondang, Seongnamsa's Great Hall, and hold the communal meal with the rest of the monastery.

I heard later that when we would finish our meals and begin ascending back to the Simgeomdang, one of the kitchen workers would open the door and bow with palms together toward our departing backs. To those young supporting nuns, Simgeomdang became a place where they were determined to one day practice like that themselves.

Yeongun Sunim, who after her postulancy at Seongnamsa had decided to stay and focus on meditation rather than going to the seminary, had gone to Keun Sunim to receive her *hwadu* and returned with a directive to memorize the *Platform Sutra of the Sixth Patriarch* front to back without stumbling. Lighting the *ondol* fire to heat the floor and boiling pots of gruel, she had memorized the whole thing and returned to Keun Sunim, only to return with an assignment of a million-prostration prayer, so she joined the three-year *gyeolsa* and began her prostrations. She meditated with the assembly in the Seongnamsa meditation hall and performed 1,080 prostrations a day. In the wee hours of the cold winter mornings when we were overcome with sleepiness and hunger, the warm soup of scorched rice boiled for us by the head of the kitchen would warm and thaw our bodies, frozen by the cold drafts.

Yeongun Sunim completed the three-year *gyeolsa* and finished the million-prostration prayer, which wore her robe and *kasa* to pieces. We later worked together when Yeongun Sunim became the catechist while I was the prior at Seongnamsa, and more than thirty years after that she became the abbess of Seongnamsa.

Now, when I sit in the Simgeomdang and listen to the sound of the passing wind, I sometimes remember those times in my youth when I lived within my practice and served my elder nuns. It truly was a *gyeolsa* unmarred by even the tiniest crack or flaw, carried out in accordance with the Dharma. One day, however, close to the end of the *gyeolsa*, there arose a revolt among the young nuns.

Every day at dawn during the morning service we would do a 300-prostration prayer together, but the elder nuns bowed faster than us younger nuns and it was hard to keep up. At dinner time we requested, "Your prostrations are too fast, so we would appreciate it if you went a little slower," but over a week later the pace of the prostrations had not decreased.

Hyeju Sunim, whose spot in the Great Hall was further toward the back, suddenly moved her place over toward Beobyong Sunim, who was performing the service. I recognized it to be a silent demonstration that she could not do prostrations at this speed any longer, and I began to slow the pace of my prostrations as well. At the end of the prayer we found that we had finished exactly five minutes behind the senior nuns, as if we had promised to do it that way.

The expressions of the elder nuns did not look good at all. More than anybody my vocation master seemed very angry. Not only had the fact that her own disciples had led the protest put her in an uncomfortable position in the eyes of the other elder nuns, but in the tense atmosphere of the *gyeolsa* such insubordination could not be tolerated. It looked like there would be trouble, and sure enough the next day she summoned the three of us and asked us to come with her to Ongnyudong.

Holding her bamboo staff and walking ahead of us with large strides, Inhong Sunim looked like she was ready to catch a tiger. A person who had lived her whole life without engaging in idle talk, there was no way she was going to say anything now.

Finally, stopping us in a flat field of grass, she looked at us silently, and the look in her eyes was truly frightening.

"Sit."

In an instant she brought the bamboo staff down across Hyeju Sunim's shoulders and back.

Whap! Whap! Whap!

As the bamboo staff moved onto Beobyong Sunim, the thought occurred to me, "No use in waiting to get hit," so I turned and ran away. I knew better than anyone that when the elders are angry it is only in the moment, and that with a little time their wrath quickly cools. Even during Keun Sunim's rages I would promptly get out of there and hide somewhere I couldn't be seen. My vocation master was no different, so that was the end of the whole affair.

When the revolt that had incited Inhong Sunim's rage was over, a hundred-day intensive practice was waiting for us.

Approaching the last one hundred days of the *gyeolsa*, the whole *gyeolsa* assembly went into an intensive meditation session. Intensive practice, or ferocious effort, refers to meditation practice where one does not sleep or lie down.

"For one hundred days, you must not lie down or lean on anything, and your *hwadu* must not break even for a second. Work hard, then work harder. There is no success without work." Remembering Keun Sunim's words, we in the *gyeolsa* assembly thought only of our *hwadu*. In intensive practice, myself and my *hwadu* must become one, and even the trappings of sight or sound must disappear. This was a time we pushed ourselves to the bloody limit, as if every day would be our last.

Whenever I felt sleep coming over me at night I would go outside and walk the mountain roads endlessly. There were no electric lamps back then so I would fill a glass bottle with oil to make a kerosene lamp, and as I trekked those paths alone, surrounded by complete darkness, there were times I would instinctively feel the presence of some large animal passing right beside me. If my thoughts became fearful, I would say to myself, "I have no mind to hurt you, so why would you have a reason to hurt me? There is nothing to be afraid of" and close my eyes for a moment, and when I'd open my eyes and look to my side, the beast had disappeared and was no longer there.

To say nothing of blankets or pillows, you could fall asleep before you knew it just by leaning your back against something for a moment, so even the chairs were cleared out to the attic. Even the daily three hundred prostrations were expunged, so that besides mealtimes and brushing our teeth all our time went to meditation.

To be silent and cultivate for one hundred days without lying down for even a moment is an impossible thing unless one is truly willing to risk their life. Even now I remember Seongwoo, Jangil, Hyechun, Hyegwan, and all the other young nuns who strived together during that time. Becoming as old as I am now, I understand the fierce desperation of their efforts.

With all of our human strength, we finished the hundred-day intensive practice. When we went to Keun Sunim for a Dharma talk to commemorate the three-year *gyeolsa* completion, all we received was a single cold remark he tossed at us: "What practice could you have possibly done during that time?" "Still," he said, "in the entire Jogye Order, for bhiksus and bhiksunis both, an assembly that has completed a three-year *gyeolsa* all the way to the end is rare."

Knowing Keun Sunim, who by nature used scoldings as his warning stick, I wonder if what little he said was not indeed great encouragement and praise. His gaze, which I have faced over a lifetime, was always razor-sharp and harsh. He didn't need many words. If he had spoken the key point, that was that. It was up to the listener to figure out the rest.

After my vocation master passed, I was organizing her study when I found a handwritten letter from Keun Sunim. We were all seeing it for the first time, and the date was not written, so there was no way to tell the reason it had been sent. I speculate it might have been written around the time of the three-year *gyeolsa*, so I've recorded it here.

This life is for a moment, the future is eternal.
To become ensnared in the empty fantasies of this fleeting world
And lose the eternal happiness of the future,
There is nothing more sorrowful than this.

I will leave the world behind and strive only to practice.
When the *hwadu* is realized, for eons to come
I earn boundless great happiness.
If you cannot awaken and continue to suffer eternally repeating
    life and death,
What use, then, is there to regret?
Do not tend to your body and life, but diligently search for truth.

Intensive Practice, without Even Leaning on a Chair

In 1972, after the three-year *gyeolsa* had ended and four days before that year's winter retreat, I had sat down in a chair and must have dozed off for a moment, for I saw a brilliant light, as if from a great fire, shining in the mountain facing the Simgeomdang. It may have been a dream, but my *hwadu* was so vibrant. My confidence and dedication was strengthened, and a resolve grew inside me to truly apply myself to intensive practice.

More than anything, the fact that my vocation master and Seongu Sunim, who had served as the rector of the meditation hall during the *gyeolsa*, had departed to Chilbulam in Jirisan to further their practice, became my igniting force. Watching Inhong Sunim now in her sixties finish the three-year *gyeolsa* and head right into practice again, I simply couldn't just lie down and fall asleep.

In the Simgeomdang, the young nuns regrouped and began a summer retreat of intensive practice. The practice community included Cheongjo Sunim and six others, and I became the rector of the meditation hall.

The rector, or *ipseung*, is the representative of the meditation hall and thus has the responsibility of leading the assembly in prayer. They are guides not just in meditation practice but in all aspects of life, so when the leader practices diligently they build the strength of the assembly, and when they are neglectful they steal strength away.

For the one hundred days of the winter retreat, we meditated and did not lie down or take off our *kasa*s, except for meals or bathroom breaks. The reason we did this was because we had heard Keun Sunim's Dharma talk about an intensive meditation retreat in Hieizan in Japan, and we wished to strengthen our will even more firmly.

This Dharma talk by Keun Sunim emphasized that the goal of Buddhism is to find release from life and death by attaining eternal freedom, and that there are real-life examples of this happening. He was encouraging us to trust the eternal freedom the Buddha showed us and practice intensively even further.

I resolved to reach my goal once and for all by the end of the season, and after forty-nine days of intensive practice we traveled to Haeinsa Baengnyeonam. Around forty-nine days is when I usually start to lose a little steam, so I wanted to hear Keun Sunim's Dharma talk and renew my strength and courage.

After finishing his talk, Keun Sunim asked, "Do you practice without leaning back even a little?"

"There were times when I was so tired, I leaned back on the chair."

"You must not even touch your back to the chair. To lean back on a chair during intensive practice is the same as lying down."

The assembly that went to Baengnyeonam came back filled with determination, and gathering the chairs that we had rested on once in a while when we really thought we might die of exhaustion, we stowed them all up in the attic. For the remaining fifty days, we practiced without chairs exactly as Keun Sunim had told us.

With the summer retreat comes unwelcome guests called mosquitos. The moment the sun begins to set and it gets a little dark, they come stealthily flying in and hover mercilessly around the assembly. When we did walking meditation we would light mosquito coils outside Simgeom-dang and they would buzz away, at least for a little bit.

Around 10 p.m., the sleepiness would rush in like the tide. When it did, the assembly would rise together, pick up kerosene lamps, and walk from Simgeomdang to the nearby deer farm and back, returning in time for the morning service.

The summer of that year, we did five hours of walking meditation a day, for one hundred days, not missing a single day. In my midthirties, I had the strength to transform any thought I had directly into action, so even through raging storms I pushed forward. I was full of confidence that I could do anything at any time, so during those five hours of walking meditation I never sat down to take a break, even when I wanted sleep more than anything.

It was dark around us when we would set out, so as the rector and the most senior nun in the assembly, I would stand at the front, and when we returned at the break of dawn, the younger nuns would be sent ahead and I would walk at the very back.

"Once you begin to practice, you must see it through."

It was a promise to myself, a promise to Keun Sunim, and a promise to the Buddha, so in the throes of practice, even at the risk of death, I couldn't stop. Thinking about it now, my will to finish what I'd started, through rain or snow or anything else that might have befallen me, seemed to have owed a lot to the strength of my youth.

Since I've passed the age of seventy, I find conflicts arising in me: *It's raining, can't I stay inside today?* That was when I had the acute realization, *Ah, so this is what getting old is.* I could understand what Master Wonhyo meant when he said, "A broken chariot cannot run." Once the desire arises to make your body comfortable, the age when you become a broken chariot has set in, where you cannot dedicate yourself fully to practice anymore.

Those who have experienced it know that age is the biggest enemy to a practitioner. Therefore you have to be able to push forward with any

Figure 6.1. A few years ago, when I was invited to the Blue House. Author provided.

kind of practice while you're young, and cultivate with everything you've got while your confidence is still sky-high. You can't be afraid of anything, and while your spirit is overflowing you must put your life on the line and focus everything on the work you must do. When you forge ahead wholeheartedly and without doubt, the path becomes clear.

After the long hours of walking meditation and morning service, sitting down on the meditation cushions felt as comfortable as lying down. When we would go back out for more walking meditation after the service, Mr. Choi Kiyun, the proprietor of the Seongnamsa Inn, which stands across from the monastery's gate, and his wife would come stand outside and offer us cups of coffee. In those times when coffee was a rarity, they made coffee offerings for one hundred days. Just as in the old saying, "While three sparrows might starve to death during a famine year, the monks and nuns do not go hungry," it seemed as though they were sent to us by Indra for our sleepless nights of practice. On those melancholy days, fighting through the fatigue or the rain, that cup of coffee was true ambrosia.

Living on your feet and performing walking meditation, with no chairs or blankets, not your eyes but your legs are the sleepy ones.

"Holy people are those who have conquered their own bodies!"

Because I had practiced in this way, fighting fatigue and sleep, I could understand these words that Keun Sunim would speak often. If you don't struggle with all your living might, it doesn't matter if a thousand or ten thousand years pass; you won't achieve your practice. The words "There is no success without effort" are an ancient truth.

The spring of 1972, after the three-year *gyeolsa*, we planted two bodhi trees at Simgeomdang. One of them has grown tall and thick with leaves over the last forty years; in the spring the air is full of the smell of its flowers, and in the summer its shade cools the heat. In the fall its fruits grow ripe, and we greet new nuns with rosaries made from their pits.

As I practice in the Simgeomdang every summer and winter retreat, I miss my old companions who once studied with me. Guided by the words of their desperate hearts, *This season is my last, and there is no tomorrow,* they were nuns who practiced bravely with everything they had.

How the years have passed since then. Now that we've all become old nuns, I offer a prayer thinking of those companions who walked with me during youthful times.

I pray thus
To hone meditation with ironclad and proper faith.
And with great wisdom and virtue, and vast bravery,
To redeem all the world's sentient beings, without exception,
And that the sea of Dharma will forever be pure and peaceful.

Living Communally in Harmony

To be happy in this world, you must be grateful for everything that happens to you. As you draw the great picture that is your life, if you lack the tracings of gratitude underneath, you will live unhappily. When turmoil holds your heart, like troubled water, examine the inner flow of your consciousness and you will find someone who lacks a grateful spirit, or has forgotten it entirely.

To be grateful not only for good things, but for that which is difficult or painful, is the mark of a wise person. Within affliction is found enlightenment. People grow and mature in difficult times, so on the contrary you must appreciate what is painful. No matter what anyone says, when you are grateful for it and let it go there is no quarrel left that can stick to you. Aren't all of this world's happenings a result of these quarrels?

In a monastery, too, one cannot live without conflict. But we can further grow from these conflicts, so when we bump up against each other, we speak aloud, "Thank you." You must think gratefully to live a grateful life.

When I first said I would become a nun, Keun Sunim told me, "Always live gratefully among the assembly," and he gave me this writing to help me appreciate all things and govern my heart.

> True nature is free of corruption and is always pure,
> So, precious or crude, old or young,
> Even little children, serve everyone the same as if they were
>   the Buddha.
> Respect to the utmost those who are very bad
> And love and protect the enemies you resent.
> Slander and insults against me are true Dharma teachings,
> Invasions and violations are great Dharma services.

So wordlessly, with a heart that is always glad,
Be grateful for everything.

In our monastery we called this the "Gratefulness Dharani," to mean
that we wanted to always pray for such a grateful heart, and we learned
these thoughts of gratitude for all the happenings at the monastery like
they were the words of the Buddha: "A grateful lifestyle must become
everyday for the practitioner. We must be grateful so that the community
will cooperate and live well together."

Just as Keun Sunim taught, from the largest communities of hundreds
of monastics to the smallest with only a few dozen, a monastery where
many live together cannot progress if they can't cooperate harmoniously.
I imagine families, and even countries are no different.

I still give this writing as a gift to those who are newly ordained
and to laypeople I might encounter. My vocation master took these words
that Keun Sunim had written in his own hand and hung them in the
middle of the Great Hall, where the whole monastery eats and practices
together. She must have wanted to engrave them upon the hearts of the
whole assembly.

I had vowed to never even dream of being an abbess or taking administrative positions, living only as a wretched nun who does nothing but
practice, but around twenty years after I had been ordained I took on the
position of prior of Seongnamsa. In a monastery the prior can also have
the role of acting on behalf of the abbess.

In living a communal life, harmony is a crucial virtue for maintaining
order overall. As a result, taking on these responsibilities is in some ways
unavoidable. Before becoming prior, I had been the catechist, responsible
for the education of the postulants and students at Seongnamsa. As she
assigned me the role of prior, my vocation master said this: "Out of the
whole assembly you have the most fortune. So the one who has much
fortune must help when there is work to do at the monastery."

With the mindset that my practice and my duties were not separate
things, I worked as best I could for a year. It was nothing compared to
what my vocation master had to live with as the abbess, but Seongnamsa
was overflowing with projects at the time and it was very difficult.

While I was prior, Yeongun Sunim was the catechist, and we agreed
that all the money we personally received would be used for good deeds,
and we spent it to help others.

That time was truly a great era of Seongnamsa's history. The Great Buddha Hall, Amita Buddha Hall, and Patriarch Shrine were all completely torn down and rebuilt, while the Jeongsuwon, our meditation hall, the bathing house, and mill were newly constructed. With Inhong Sunim at the fore of the construction, we climbed up to the roof of the Great Hall, lugging tiles and hammering nails. It wouldn't be an exaggeration to say that there wasn't a single place in Seongnamsa that our hands hadn't touched.

There was a mother and father who had come to visit their ordained daughter at Seongnamsa but left, full of sorrow, after seeing her carrying heavy A-frames on her back, never to return again. The tilemakers who worked alongside us marveled at the sight of the young nuns, college graduates who had never even known the smell of dirt, toiling diligently on the rooftops.

Attempting such a huge temple construction while the economy was struggling, we were in short supply of everything. One day, I was walking Tongdosa's Weolha Keun Sunim back to the parking lot after a visit to Seongnamsa. I told him, "Sunim, as we've been working on the temple construction, we've run out of rice." He replied, "Go to Tongdosa and take twenty pallets of rice."

In the midst of this great temple construction, I ended up going to a movie theater of all things for the first time since I had left home. My vocation master had decided on blue tiles for the construction, and she enlisted Mr. Sangmoon Choi, who owns a tile factory in Ulsan, to try to make them. Compared to standard tiles, which don't resist cold well and can freeze and explode, blue tiles are strong against the cold. The sample of blue tiles were perfected after many repeated failures, but the factory was suddenly flooded by orders from all over the country, and they were even exporting to Japan.

When we arrived at the factory office to pick up the tiles, we found that they were not yet ready. Director Choi apologized and said he would bring the tiles over himself, and he escorted us to the movie theater in the meantime. So myself and Yeongun Sunim, who had accompanied me, watched *Papillon* together, in which Papillon is framed for murder and must survive the most extreme conditions as he attempts countless escapes from prison. His resilience was so great that it occurred to me that if he had applied such incredible determination to meditation practice, he would have achieved enlightenment without a doubt.

In my middle school years, I remember once that my whole class of students snuck out during after-school activities to watch the play *Ondal the Fool* at the Jinju Theater and were scolded by the teacher when she found out. It was the first film I had been to since then, and *Papillon* became the first as well as the last movie I watched after being ordained. What business does a bhiksuni have at the movie theater, after all?

Once in a while, Yeongun Sunim and I would also go to the market. Because our community was quite large and the housekeeping for it so substantial, whenever we would go to the market we'd end up with a lot to carry, which the merchants would load into instant noodle boxes for us. But I couldn't bring myself to pick them up.

"Sunim, you should carry one to the bus stop as well."

"I can't carry it!"

Yeongun Sunim asked, "Why, Sunim?"

"They'll mock me if they think a nun is eating ramen!"

Even with Yeongun Sunim staring at me like she couldn't believe her ears, I wouldn't pick up the ramen box.

Even so, I later heard that because I had stocked up on an abundance of treats and had been so generous as the prior, the nuns still had plenty of their favorite noodles to eat several years after I'd left.

While I was prior, there was a time when my vocation master entrusted Seongnamsa to us and left to practice at Doseongam. Yeongun Sunim and I made some of Inhong Sunim's favorite mugwort rice cakes, packed them in a knapsack, and climbed up to Doseongam to see her. My vocation master's smile of pleasure as she looked at the rice cakes, her face shining brightly like a wild rose blooming by the riverside, is a memory I still hold on to.

I also served Inhong Sunim as her attendant. Whenever she went out of the monastery I'd follow her around, running errands and looking after her needs. Hearing about it later, I found out that the newly ordained nuns used to call me Venerable Ananda. Ananda was Buddha's disciple, who attended him his whole life. However the real Ananda for my teacher was Beophui Sunim, my sister nun. Since the moment she was ordained she had been by Inhong Sunim's side, acting as her hands and feet without a moment of rest.

One busy day, in the middle of helping with the construction, Inhong Sunim asked me to take a trip with her to Seoul. I later found out that we were going to the house of Mr. Hurak Lee, who at the time was the chief secretary at the Blue House, the presidential residence. Seongnamsa is in Ulsan, Mr. Lee's family home, and his wife would occasionally visit

Seongnamsa as a devotee. At the time, the construction was being financed by the combined small generosities of the devotees. Going to an individual personally and asking for help was a very rare occurrence, so I imagine Inhong Sunim's footsteps were heavy with reluctance.

Arriving at Mr. Lee's home, we found that his wife, whom we were there to see, was out of the house. Watching Inhong Sunim's quietly seated and waiting form, I could feel the torment that comes with being a leader. When an hour had passed, his wife finally appeared. Inhong Sunim scolded her as she apologized for making us wait: "How can a devotee make a sunim wait like this?"

As she continued to chew her out, for quite a long time no less, she looked just as imposing and dignified as she did when she scolded us, her students in the monastic assembly. After we had finalized the matter we came to discuss, Mr. Lee's wife booked us plane tickets back to Busan

Figure 6.2. Together with my teacher Inhong Sunim in front of Haeinsa's One-Pillar Gate, during my time as her attendant. Author provided.

as an apology. For the sake of her disciple who had never been on a plane before, Inhong Sunim sat on the window side. I went with Inhong Sunim the second time she went to see Mr. Lee as well, and as we were on the way back from the meeting she told me this: "He asked me what we wanted help with, so I asked him to help us with the translation of the whole Buddhist canon into Korean."

I was startled. It was a difficult time at the monastery, with the whole assembly constantly working, and resources were short. It was to the point that the administrative nuns were hiding out from the lay workers because we couldn't afford to pay their wages on time, so I thought surely she would have asked Mr. Lee to help with the construction work.

"At the recent Jogye Order Council meeting, I heard from Unheo Sunim that the sutra translation business is struggling. And isn't Unheo Sunim the one who first established the Tripitaka Translation Institute, in the confidence that the revival of Korean Buddhism depends on the translation of the Chinese canon into Korean? He was saying that there was too much financial strain within the Jogye Order, so there hasn't been as much progress as he'd expected. On the way over here I suddenly remembered what he said. I'd be requesting something anyway so I did it because I thought I should talk about more important things. After all, the Seongnamsa construction is Buddha-work, so won't it somehow find a way to work out?"

At the time, sutra translation was a matter important enough to rank among one of the three highest priorities of the Jogye Order, along with proselytization and training disciples. Faced with a situation where the Buddha's words, engraved in the stone tablets of the Tripitaka canon housed at Haeinsa but obstructed by the language barrier of Chinese characters, were not being read widely, the business of translating them into Korean was more urgent than any other. This was when the Dongguk University Institute for Sutra Translation was founded, to translate and publish the Korean canon in its entirety.

"Mr. Lee said he wanted to help with the Seongnamsa construction, so I told him we, the disciples of the Buddha, would take care of the monastery work and asked him to focus his interest on bigger things."

After that, Mr. Hurak Lee helped to propel the sutra translation project to a federal level. A bill to nationally subsidize sutra translation through the Ministry of Education was passed in Congress, and with the Center for Sutra Translation continuing its work for thirty-four years, in September 2000, all 318 volumes of the hangul [Korean written language]

Buddhist canon were finally completed and published. Hyobong Sunim, the patriarch of the Jogye Order at the time, presented my vocation master with an Award of Commendation and named her "A truly exceptional hero."

The reason she could walk upright and confident even when traveling to ask for financial help must have been because her principle and integrity stood above any ulterior motives or greediness. As I've lived I've worked to learn that principle and integrity for myself, and however little it may be, I believe these teachings have rubbed off on me. Because of this, I think which teacher you meet, what they teach you, and how you put it into practice are all important questions in determining your life.

Once the construction was completed, through the good merit of my vocation master and the cooperation of the nuns in the monastery, Yeongun Sunim and I decided to spend our summer retreat at Jijangam in Odaesan. We were preparing to depart when my vocation master told us to regild the statue of the Buddha, which was being temporarily housed in the raised pavilion while the Great Hall was being rebuilt.

We had neither the money nor the time, but Inhong Sunim's word was law so we had no other choice. Right at that time, Daean Sunim and Daeseong Sunim, who had just graduated from Busan Girl's High and Seonggyungwan University together, were ordained after hearing Keun Sunim's Dharma talk, and their parents, saying that they wanted to at least hear their daughters' voices if they couldn't see them, handed over thirty million won [ca. 30,000 USD] to install a phone line at Seongnamsa. Back in those days when phones were a rarity, you would have needed that kind of money to drag the phone lines from Eonyang all the way to Seongnamsa.

We met their parents and, asking for their understanding, used the money to start the gilding project instead. Then, serendipitously, one month after the gilding was complete, the government came and did the phone line construction for us, and we were able to put in the phones for just one hundred thousand won [ca. 100 USD]. I had the thought, "So this is how Buddha-work is fulfilled."

After all my work was completed, I withdrew from my position and packed my knapsack, ready to embark again on the path of the wandering gray-robed nun, impeded by nothing. What else does a nun need in all the four seasons besides her one bag?

Going from Seongnamsa in the south to Jijangam in Odaesan in the north is naturally a long journey, so when we arrived a day later than expected we found the twenty-four members of the retreat had all gone to forage ragwort up in the northern area above Sangwonsa and weren't at the monastery. We were a day late but it felt like we had gotten there before anyone else. After two days, the nuns returned from deep within Odaesan, each with a bundle of mountain greens on their back. The winter retreat began three days after that.

We woke up at three in the morning and practiced for eleven hours a day until we went to sleep at eleven. During these times we would all stay together, but besides that we were free to practice as we wished.

I decided to do walking meditation after the meditation break at 11 p.m. Past the fir tree forest of Woljeongsa on the path toward Sangwonsa, another young nun and I would go walking without a trace of fear. The dense and thriving forest path through the firs was a beautiful gift in itself, given to us by nature. Maybe it was because I was practicing after the end of my administrative tenure, but my heart couldn't have been more expansive and calm.

Perhaps because Odaesan is a deep mountain range, Jijangam's supplies weren't very plentiful. My vocation master was in fact ordained at Jijangam, but since that was in the mid-1940s their lifestyle must have been even more destitute. Inhong Sunim would reminisce on those times like this: "In the winter we had no chili powder so the only thing we had for a side dish was plain kimchi brined in salt. The Japanese rationed out corn, mixed-grain rice, and the bean scraps left after squeezing soybean oil, and we boiled dried radish greens with salt to make soup. And if only it had just been food! In those times it was hard to even find a decent jacket to wear. We sewed together scraps of fabric, black pieces, red pieces, and the thread would show through, to the point that those who didn't know better thought all meditation practitioners must dress like this. Even as we farmed crops and chopped trees like laborers, it didn't feel difficult because of our joy in practicing."

It must be because of elder nuns like her, who had walked our path first and had dedicated themselves in a time when bhiksuni communities were held in low regard, that our monasteries can stand proudly today and provide an environment for us to cultivate our strength to practice. Because of this I take care to never forget my gratitude to the senior nuns.

Sometimes when we were meditating we would get a little hungry, and the nun in charge of the kitchen would make us sweet *songpyeon* rice cakes out of potato starch. Difficult to find in the south, they were a precious treat.

As the end of the retreat approached, we picked corn fresh from the field and ate it steamed in the iron cauldron, and the taste was really beyond compare. For side dishes we always had mountain greens, of which the best-tasting was ragwort, and in the fall wild grapes and gooseberries were abundant. With a life like this, the monks and nuns who love the mountains and enjoy the happiness of living within them have nothing to want for.

The Innocent Friendship of the Elder Nuns

My students may remember me as someone who served Inhong Sunim loyally, but there were times I acted immaturely toward her as well. Looking back on it now I feel very sorry for it, but back then I think I acted the way I did because I had wanted nothing but to pack my bags and leave to study as soon as I could.

It was the day, in my late twenties and having finished my year as catechist, that I was leaving to find the place I would study next. It was the day before the winter retreat began so my mind was busy. I paid my respects to my vocation master, and right as I started to get up she commanded, "Be the catechist one more year."

Sitting in front of the desk, I hurled a fountain pen outside into the distance and stood up. She must have been taken aback, but she didn't stop me. After lunch, I got on the bus from Eonyang to Daewonsa in Jirisan, and Hyanggok Sunim happened to be on the bus as well.

But as soon as we passed Yangsan, the front wheel of the bus fell off. The passengers screamed, frightened and surprised. Looking outside, on one side was the mountain and below that was a cliff. It was a nerve-wracking moment. He must have been worried too, because Hyanggok Sunim said to me, "You should get back to Seongnamsa now!"

Without any other choice, I returned to Seongnamsa, and as if she had been waiting for me, my vocation master said, "The threshold of the door might be low on the way out, but it is high on the way back in."

Since I had disobeyed her will and left, she was looking to use this opportunity to bend her disciple's spirit. Sunim took the cudgel next to her and struck me with it. Without even knowing it, I burst into tears like a small child and yelled, "Why would you hit me instead of using words?"

With that, I grabbed the bottle of ink on the abbess chamber desk and hurled it at the wall. Cheolma Sunim, who had so far only been watching and laughing to herself nearby, jumped up in surprise. In later days,

Cheolma Sunim would often reenact the incident and embarrass me with my disobedience toward Inhong Sunim all throughout my younger years.

After my appointments as catechist and then prior, I didn't take up the abbess position. I thought I had fulfilled the necessary amount of service toward fostering harmony among the assembly, and more than anything I just wanted to return to my life as a wretched nun and focus on my studies.

My vocation master would give everyone who had completed a term as abbess a decorative folding screen. Beophui Sunim received a screen that had Gyeongheo Sunim's "Song of Seon Meditation" written on it in hangul by Elder Seokju Sunim. Hyeonmuk Sunim, who had spent a lifetime as rector, snapping the bamboo clapper in the meditation hall, and Beopyong Sunim, who had long held the duties of abbess, were each given the "Chapter on the Vows of Samantabhadra," which Seokjeong Sunim had written during his hundred-day prayer.

There was also a folding screen on which Tanheo Sunim, a famous scholar-monk, had written Bodhidharma's *Bloodstream Sermon* when he came to Seongnamsa. When I said to Inhong Sunim that I wanted to have the *Bloodstream Sermon*, she laughed and gave it to me, saying, "Take good care of it." I had already resolved not to be abbess in my head, so I made sure to get my folding screen first. It's still safely stored at Geumganggul today.

My personality is definitive about beginning and ending things, so when I feel something is right I'll decide and act right there and then, and when I feel it's wrong I'll get flaming mad on the spot and never look back. As a result, from the outside there are times that I seem like an extremely volatile person. I am cold to my blood relatives, I don't speak unnecessarily, and when I do speak I'm the type to condense my words down simply.

Maybe because of this, my disciples say that I'm scary, even when I'm smiling. I'm strict by my principles so I know I must come across that way. I've loosened up a little now that I've passed seventy. As I grow old I figure I should also be able to get along and make others feel comfortable, so when we're all driving somewhere in the car I'll sometimes say, "Alright, let's sing some songs," and I'll request a song from Hyeonmuk Sunim, who is a good singer. Occasionally I'll sing too, and my go-to song is "Old Hwangseong."

I wonder if people don't show their true selves when their guard is down. I remember the time when Inhong Sunim was serving as a council member of the Jogye Order of Korean Buddhism. Suok Sunim, abbess of Naewonsa in Cheongseongsan; Beopil Sunim, abbess of Daewonsa in Jirisan; and Inhong Sunim, abbess of Seongnamsa; these three members met at Naewonsa and left for Seoul early in the morning for a Council Assembly.

The way to Naewonsa is sometimes called Little Geumgangsan for its beauty, and the water that flows along its creek is Naewonsa's pride and joy. As they walked along this road less traveled, however, the three of them suddenly began to sing. As their attendant, I was following behind and was smiling as I thought, "They must not even know I'm here," when suddenly Inhong Sunim shouted, "I am the leader," and commanded, "Every five minutes we'll each be the leader." A game of leader began; if the leader orders you to do a Dharma talk you must do a Dharma talk, and if they order you to sing you must sing.

For five minutes the three of them showed all of their talents. As they went around, reciting poetry and singing songs and making speeches, they were the portrait of three friends in their own world, a sight not ordinarily visible.

Figure 6.3. Leaving Gajisan for a change, we went up to Hwaeombeol in Cheon-seongsan where the famous monk from the seventh century, Wonhyo, had preached. Picture with the rector of the meditation hall at Seongnamsa, Hyeonmuk Sunim, and Domun Sunim. Author provided.

Suok Sunim was one of the three great lecturers of the modern bhiksuni world. She brought a great resurrection to Naewonsa in Cheongseongsan, which had become ruined in the war, and as a Jogye councilmember she contributed enormously to the advancement of the order. Every time I saw her, I felt the combined presence of her learning and her virtue, and Naewonsa, where she spent her life, now flies its name high as a center of meditation for bhiksuni.

Beopil Sunim had worked at a bank before she was ordained, a rare occurrence during the Japanese occupation, and went on to rebuild Daewonsa, which had been destroyed during the Korean War. In those times, when those in both the secular and religious worlds were struggling to get by, to achieve such an enormous monastery project would have been an impossible feat without exceptional faith and strength. Beopil Sunim completed the construction of a Pagoda accompanying the Great Buddha Hall, and this is where Seongcheol Keun Sunim had once practiced as a layman. In the spirit of everyone coming together to pitch in, her companions Inhong Sunim and Suok Sunim followed her lead, personally begging alms to aid the construction of Daewonsa.

After that, a meditation hall was constructed in front of the Pagoda, and nuns today from all directions gather there to practice and cultivate. In my midforties I too went there to spend the winter retreat with twenty or so other nuns. Located within a true gift of nature, Yeongbong Peak on Jirisan, the Pagoda was a place that awakened great faith in those who practiced there. Enduring the cold winds of the deep mountain valleys, however, I ended up catching a cold. When I did, Beopil Sunim personally simmered pears in honey for me and made room for me to practice in her own side room. Thanks to her warm and thoughtful care, I was able to safely complete my winter retreat.

I remember another memory from the council meeting. A discussion about the unification between celibate and married monks[4] was running longer than expected, and because it was the rainy summer season my vocation master's hemp clothes got soaking wet. So I told Inhong Sunim, "Leave the clothes with me and go. I'll take care of them."

Hemp clothes are dyed with lumps of oak charcoal, which are soaked in water, dried, then powdered; this dye produces a fine gray color. I didn't have any charcoal powder at the time, so I had no choice but to use ink, and I used too much, turning her hemp clothes black. Even so, my vocation master didn't say a word and wore them for the rest of the conference.

Keun Sunim and many other monks laughed as they saw her clothes in passing, and even Jaun Sunim chuckled and asked, "Disciple Hong, what's wrong with your clothes?" but Inhong Sunim didn't show any discomfort. Accompanying her by her side, I felt nothing if not apologetic.

After the conference, I accompanied my vocation master to Sujeongam in Beopjusa. She had instructions from Jaun Sunim to put together a book of *Bhiksuni Precepts* so we were visiting to get some advice. There too, the monks asked, "Inhong Sunim, why are your clothes like that?" Even then, Inhong Sunim only smiled sunnily.

Returning to Seongnamsa, I laundered her clothes, but no matter how many times I washed them, the black water wouldn't come out. That time when she, usually so unforgiving of mistakes, looked past mine generously, is a memory I can't forget no matter how much time passes. My vocation master was a person who, in good times or bad, would always inspect people's inner hearts first. If she were here now, I wish I could dye her clothes for her once more with that fine charcoal-gray water.

Figure 6.4. The way to Ongnyudong near Seongnamsa. Author provided.

Chapter 7

Haeinsa Monastery

In the Refuge of Wisdom and Compassion

My First and Final Letter from Keun Sunim

In the two or three years after the Simgeomdang *gyeolsa* ended in 1972, many people came to be ordained at Seongnamsa. It was then when I was about thirty-six that I received my first disciple, and over the next twenty years or so I gained twenty-four disciples; counting the disciples of those disciples, my grand-disciples, I have somehow come to be responsible for a lineage almost seventy strong. Most of them had made up their minds to become ordained after hearing a Dharma talk from Seongcheol Keun Sunim. As Keun Sunim's Dharma spread, disciples came swarming in. People ask: "How do all these people come to leave home after hearing Keun Sunim's lectures?" The answer is simple. You must have good roots. One is able to find their path and turn toward it because they planted good roots in a faraway past life, worthy of bearing good fruit. The business of being a nun isn't something that can be forced. Just as a duck must live in the water and a quail must live in the mountains, you follow the path that you've grown familiar with through countless past lives. That's why I don't often advise people to leave home. You must make the choice yourself if you want the strength to leave the life you've been living. This is true resolve.

When I receive a new disciple, I have them perform three thousand prostrations, once when they receive their Dharma name and once when they shave their head, and I have them study under Keun Sunim's guidance.

I had never even dreamt of building a temple myself, but as the number of my disciples grew I no longer had a satisfactory place to practice with them, and I ended up building the hermitage of Geumganggul at Haeinsa. After consulting with Cheonje Sunim, who was at the time the prior at Haeinsa, about building Geumganggul, I didn't show my face to Keun Sunim for three years for fear he would find out. I couldn't go to him because I had broken my promise to live and study hidden away as a wretched nun.

After Geumganggul was built, I received a letter from Keun Sunim, the first and last of my life. It was a harsh rebuke in a letter.

> If one cannot clear their mind in this life,
> It is impossible to swallow even one drop of water.
> You must not do things that hurt your studies.

All things happen for a reason.
So leave all matters up to their causes and conditions,
There is no need for useless concerns.
Things we do for ourselves and others may be kind,
But all contribute to the cycle of life and death.
Under the moonlight, amid the wind of the pine trees and
   kudzu vines,
I wish to observe the untainted meditation of the patriarchs.

Not until after I had received this letter, which he had flung at some nun from Seongnamsa who had come to see him, could I finally show my face in front of him. Keun Sunim by nature never asked about matters already in the past, and in accordance with that he didn't bring up Geumganggul again.

One day, the parents of a disciple who had contributed a great amount of aid toward building Geumganggul said to me, "If our sunim daughter receives and eats out of other people's offerings, wouldn't this become a debt and interfere with her studies? What if she lived on her parents' food and practiced that way?" and expressed their desire to donate three acres of rice paddies to the temple.

When I asked Keun Sunim what he thought about it, he told me, "The opportunity to build merit must be given to many, not just to one person. You can't take everything just because it's given."

After hearing his words, I declined the offering; when they offered another two times even more earnestly, I politely refused. "No more. It is Keun Sunim's word. Offerings must be received from many for merit to be planted."

Keun Sunim often said that money was just like arsenic, and he told us, "The one who spurns money given for free is the bravest and most pure."

Geumganggul inherited its traditions of practice from Seongnamsa word for word. When a postulant comes to Geumganggul, they are made to do a daily 3,000-prostration prayer for one hundred days. This is to strengthen their resolve to practice and become ordained as a disciple of the Buddha.

There are those who ask, "Aren't you really selective about the people who get to come to Geumganggul?" This is not to discriminate between people. Followers of the Buddha must be exceptional among humans; how could we not be selective about their potential? This is to see if they have a clear sense of purpose. When one starts without a goal, vaguely thinking that the life of a practitioner is simply one of frugality, a hundred out of a hundred times they will fall from the middle way.

After a hundred-day prayer you build your own resolve for practice and ordination. If you do a thousand prostrations, your ordained life will be built upon the faith of a thousand prostrations; if you do ten thousand, upon the faith of ten thousand. In the work of a nun, resolve is the firmament; practicing without it is like building a house up among the clouds.

Postulants who have completed the hundred-day prayer use that strength to adapt to monastery life naturally. At first they even fumble with a broom to sweep the courtyard, but as they learn the small tasks in the temple they shake off the habits of secular life and, lowering themselves to the bottom-most position, they begin to build true merit. To cast aside the habits one has held their entire life in a single morning and acclimate to life in the temple household is not an easy thing. However, it is something that can be overcome with the strength built through completing the hundred-day 3,000-prostration prayer.

We open the day at Geumganggul at 3 a.m. with a morning service, and then a recital of the *Surangama Sutra* dharani. Once everyone finishes their respective daily prostrations, at six we have a communal morning meal of porridge. At seven, we meditate in the Great Hall. Students learn the principles and etiquette of monastery life from texts such as the *Admonition for Beginners*, which teach the mindset required of those who enter the Buddhist monastic community.

At ten there is an offering ceremony. Upholding Keun Sunim's discipline, we perform the Heroic March dharani and 108 prostrations, and offer rice upon the Buddha's altar. We often hear the rumor that Geumganggul nuns are bad at prayer chanting, but the ones of us who are good at it are really quite good.

At 1 p.m. there is another meditation session in the Great Hall. If there are matters requiring group labor, we join in. We grow our own vegetables, sowing the seeds, weeding, and harvesting the crop. Dinner is at five. The sun in the high mountains is short so darkness falls quickly on the temple household. Once the 7 p.m. evening service is over it truly is complete silence. From here on everyone has their own time. Some recite sutras in the Great Hall, some chant prayers or perform prostrations. At nine the lights go out. After spending six months or so in this way, one possesses the foundational refinement to be ordained as a respectable sramaneri, a novice nun.

When one receives the sramaneri ordination at Geumganggul, they do a 3,000-prostration prayer for three days without resting.

Now with this body I pursue attainment of the Buddha's body.
I will follow the Buddha's precepts firmly and not transgress
    them.
I only wish that all Buddhas will be a witness for us.
Better to lose my body and life, I will not retreat until the end.

Life at Geumganggul is self-sufficient. In the spring the nuns go out to the field to plant potatoes, beans, and other vegetables, and to pull weeds in the summer. As the end of the summer retreat approaches we plant radishes and cabbages, vegetables for winter kimchi-making. The daikon radishes and cabbages that grow in the autumn fields are more beautiful to me than flowers in a garden.

I'm asked if the role of teacher is difficult, but I don't raise my students, they walk diligently on their own; so I don't have any trouble with them. I tell my disciples simply: "Walk on your own accord!"

A monastery is like a blacksmith's forge. It is a place where one enters a thousand-degree furnace, full of flames that melt cold steel, and is reborn as a strong and resilient practitioner.

As one ages it is natural to have some attendants by your side, but I am unusually detailed in teaching my attendants. I scold them for the smallest mistake, but you mature just as much as you've been corrected. At the very least, if someone has been an attendant by my side I would hope they display their upright character no matter where they go.

From 1976 to 1989, we built the Great Buddha Hall, Geumgang Bojeon, the meditation hall Munsuwon, and the nun's living quarter, Geumganggul. In the Geumgang Bojeon, hundred-day 3,000-prostration prayers, Abira prayers, and Heroic March dharani prayers go on without end. After the morning service, the entire assembly does their daily routines of a thousand or six hundred prostrations. Then, they gather in the Munsuwon to meditate.

When Keun Sunim passed away, all of my disciples assembled in Geumganggul and entered a fierce three-year *gyeolsa*, just as we once did long ago. So intense was their practice that they wouldn't listen even when we told them to take things slower. I had said to those practicing: "Your eyes are sharply open. Thank you for living diligently."

During his lifetime I only heard rebukes from Keun Sunim, but before he passed one of my disciples asked him, "How must we study when Keun Sunim leaves us?" I'm told that he replied, "Receive guidance from your Sunim."

Could there be another way to study? I am only doing the things Keun Sunim taught me to in his lifetime. Practice is not something that can be foiled for lack of a teacher. The nobility of this discipline lies in putting these teachings into practice.

Scenes of Ordination

They say you must have fortune enough to cover the sky and more in order to walk the path of a practitioner. As I've lived I've found no falseness in these words. Once, when I was visiting America, our travel guide asked his sister-in-law walking beside him to ask me why I had become a nun, and this is how I replied: "Please tell him that I became a nun because I loved myself so much, and viewed myself as precious." You cannot become ordained without loving yourself, the main character, of whom there is only one in the entire universe. I chose this path because I thought attaining eternal freedom was the greatest way to value myself, and in a lifetime I've lived without a single moment of regret.

Those who enter the monastery dream of eternal freedom from life and death, and leave their homes bearing the loftiest of aspirations. However, back then as well as now, leaving home doesn't seem to be the easiest thing. Even when my disciples have made up their own mind firmly, their homes and families, especially the mothers, now and again throw up a fuss about bringing their child home.

There was an instance where Beopjeong Sunim, while he was at Bongeunsa Daraeheon, told one female school teacher who had come to see him with the wish to become a nun, "If you go to Seongnamsa, Bulpil Sunim will be there, so go visit her," and sent her to me. When I inspected her I saw she had the desire to be ordained, a clear temperament, and she seemed to be quite confident as well. Hearing the story of her life I thought, "She'd be good at being a nun," and I accepted her as a postulant.

She was staying at the temple performing a hundred-day 600-prostration prayer, when one day around dinnertime her mother showed up and loudly announced she would be taking her daughter away.

"This is a place of practice, so just take your daughter and don't make so much noise. I didn't call her here, she came of her own will, so take her away quietly."

She seemed a little shocked that I simply relented and didn't argue about whether she could go or not. She had always been very opposed to her daughter becoming a nun, to the point that even Beopjeong Sunim had thrown up his hands on the matter, so I figured it was useless to make a fuss about not allowing it. If one is destined to be at the temple they'll be there no matter what anyone says, and if they're not then there's nothing even the Buddha can do about it. Do not grasp at those who leave and do not turn away those who come, don't they say?

Sometimes when the parents come they drag the children away kicking and screaming, and sometimes even beat them. Thankfully, however, that mother listened to reason. She had a deep preconceived notion of religion as being exclusionary, but in the end, she left with prayer beads hung around her neck and having embraced Buddhism.

No parent in the world can win over a child who is not simply trying to satisfy a curiosity about living quietly in a temple for a while, but who has made the resolution to devote their whole life to the path of a monastic. I've even seen a mother and father who followed their child wherever she went, plotting to kidnap her, but when she would not change her mind after several attempts, they asked her to at least live at Seongnamsa near her hometown, so they could see her often.

Once, a dignified-looking grandfather came to Geumganggul and demanded I hand over his granddaughter: "If you do not hand her over I will report you to the Committee for National Security for crimes of abduction."

At the time the institution known as the Special Committee for National Security Measures held Korea by the neck. Remembering my own grandfather, who concealed tears when his granddaughter left home, and understanding his feelings about a granddaughter who had become a nun as soon as she finished school, I spoke to him quietly.

"Don't ask the Committee for National Security, ask your granddaughter first. Persuade her to come with you."

Of course, his granddaughter said she would not go back, and her grandfather left alone.

"You better study hard so you don't get taken by the Committee for National Security."

My disciple and I laughed a great deal together over her grandfather's national security proclamation.

Before you say anything, there have also been parents who nobly accepted the news of their child leaving home. The father of Seonho Sunim, who had left home after practicing medicine as a pediatrician, was a doctor at a university hospital and a professor, and the most gentlemanly person of all the parents I had met. When his doctor daughter was ordained, he came to me and said, "She studied in medical school as she wanted, graduated and worked as a doctor, and now that she says she will walk the path she wants to, I want to support her. I think I've done everything I can as a parent."

When my disciple Domyeong, who majored in physics, graduated and announced her desire to leave home, her mother disapproved, so she went to Keun Sunim and said: "My mother says I could just believe in the Buddha's Dharma in this life, why do I have to become a nun?"

Keun Sunim replied in this way: "Then why are there different majors in college? You can't pursue this road if you live in this material world. If you want to follow the Path, you have to shave your head!"

Hearing just those words, Domyeong's doubts fell away and she left home. During her postulancy, while she was visiting Baengnyeonam, Keun Sunim asked Domyeong, who had left home without telling her father, "What does your father say?"

"He still thinks I'm praying at the temple."

"Then tell him you'll be praying for sixty years."

Domyeong's parents went on to support their daughter's life as a nun wholeheartedly.

There are also instances of parents accepting their child's wish and bringing them to the temple themselves. My disciple Jigwang's parents accepted the news with glad hearts and escorted her directly to me. Jigwang's father was the chairman of the board of a high school in Changwon and, having gained resolve after hearing a Dharma lecture from Keun Sunim, was able to embrace his daughter's leaving home enthusiastically. Jigwang's younger brother had been ordained as well, so both his son and now his daughter had become disciples of the Buddha. Not only that, Jigwang's aunts on both her father's and mother's side, as well as her uncle on her mother's side had all been ordained, so with five nuns all from the same family, one could say the whole household made up its own temple.

Daean and Daeseong were an instance where two friends entered the Sangha under the eye of Keun Sunim together. They were in the same class at Busan Girl's High School and Sungkyunkwan University; Daean became my disciple, while Daeseong was Beopyong Sunim's. Another time, a mother and her only daughter became nuns together. In the case of my first disciple, Doryung, all three sisters became nuns.

All the disciples who have built resolve and entered the Sangha under Keun Sunim's teachings live dignified lives wherever they go, studying diligently and earning the respect of devotees. Among them, several have already passed sixty years old. This is what I told them as they entered the Sangha: "Don't go anywhere just because someone else is going too. You have to build the strength to follow your path by your own will. The goal of leaving home lies in freedom from birth and death. Hold only *hwadu* in your mind and practice diligently!"

At some point I've started saying the exact words Keun Sunim told to me: "Don't let go of your first intentions and practice diligently until you die. This kind of study is one you do in hiding. If you wanted to live showing your face, you should have stayed in the secular world; why come here into the mountains? Never step a single foot out."

When I look at them now, my disciples all seem like fools. They are constantly losing battles to others. Sometimes I wonder if I have taught them poorly. They say that when someone in the seminaries seems a little bit strange, people ask, "Are they from Geumganggul?" Living so strictly by the precepts and detached from the outside world, their personalities must seem conservative and frustrating. But a monastic cannot be respected without committing to practice, so even if they are a little hard to deal with, I want them more than anything to become practitioners who cultivate well.

The only thing I want to say is this: "For enlightenment, sacrifice this life. As you undertake monastic practice, cut off the matters of the mundane world, take honest poverty as your foundation, and respect all others like the Buddha himself. You must practice with all your effort in order to attain eternal freedom from birth and death."

No One Ever Died Doing Prostrations

There are several people who call me the champion of assigning prostrations. I think I must hear that sort of thing because of my tendency to request prostration practice from the people I know, irrespective of their rank or our relationship.

The devotion and strength of your vow must be the foundation of your practice if you want to achieve exceptional wisdom. Devotion is the belief that you are a Buddha possessing infinite ability. And your vow is your promise to use the power you gain from practice to benefit the sentient beings of the world. You must attain both of these to obtain exceptional wisdom in prostration practice as well, and you must gain wisdom to apply it to your life and live without regrets.

Keun Sunim taught both of these values by assigning 3,000-prostration prayers, not only to monastics but to lay devotees, and the number of people who have changed their fate with the strength gained from this wisdom is incomprehensibly great. The place where Keun Sunim first directed devotees to do prostrations was at Anjeongsa Cheonjegul, in the early 1950s. For decades since, prostrations have become a staple of practice at Baengnyeonam, and even now, twenty years after Keun Sunim's passing, the footsteps of those who come to practice at the temple through 3,000- or 10,000-prostration prayers at Baengnyeonam have not ceased.

"No one's ever died from doing prostrations. Everyone must do prostrations in repentance, no matter who they are."

These are words many have heard from Keun Sunim. Keun Sunim told everyone who did prostrations to repent for the sentient beings of the world.

While many of my disciples have passed sixty years old, six hundred daily prostrations is still a given, with some performing one thousand, even three thousand a day. I have several disciples who have done one thousand prostrations every day since the day they first became nuns, decades ago. I don't know about other matters, but on the field of prostration prayers at least I wonder if Geumganggul might be the best.

Those who left home after hearing Keun Sunim's Dharma talks have a different depth of resolve, and they build their faith through prostration. Just as streams flowing from different places will all become the same salty water when they reach the sea, anybody who does prostrations gains awareness in their reason and clarity in their goals.

Of all the prayers prostration is the greatest one. When you bow you see every flaw you have from the ground up in complete detail, so repentance is unavoidable. And as your knees, your head, and your heart touch the ground you gain infinite strength and wisdom.

All have their own hurdles, 108, 1,080, 3,000, 10,000 prostrations. Just because they are the legs of a nun doesn't mean they're made of steel. You overcome it because it is a promise with yourself and a promise with the Buddha. When you do ten thousand, three thousand fly by, and then around seven thousand is when you start saying you're going to die. Even so, you must keep going. After a while, suddenly you've reached the goal.

One disciple was doing a 3,000-prostration prayer with her sister at Baengnyeonam before she became a nun when Keun Sunim walked up to them and asked, "Do you all know what the biggest disease in this world is?"

"It's cancer."

"Nope."

"It's mental illness."

"Not that either."

"Then what is it?"

"The laziness bug is the biggest disease."

He was quite right. All crimes and failures are born from laziness. The second you think *I'll do it*, you need to do it right away; as soon as you think *I should get up*, you have to get up. Everything goes smoothly when you don't put things off. When you rest today to do it tomorrow, you're losing to yourself. If you can just gain control over that, then you can do three thousand, even ten thousand prostrations.

Keun Sunim also asked that we do prostrations long-term. One of my disciples once asked him this: "If you did a lot of prostrations all at once and dissolved all your karmic hindrances, wouldn't you be able to study better from then on?"

"That's not how it works. Sticking with it all your life is what's important, not doing ten thousand a day for a hundred days and leaving it at that."

There was a time I too did 108 prostrations. When I first started my legs would tremble. The prostrations that began like that became three thousand, ten thousand over time. As I did them, I learned that the difference in devotion between a thousand prostrations and ten thousand is the difference between heaven and earth. As you practice, you tire, even become malnourished because you don't eat well. Even when you're that ill, you still go to the Dharma Hall and push through three thousand prostrations. When bowing, you must press your forehead completely against the floor, and when you bow while calling the name of the Buddha you can receive *sugi*, an assurance of enlightenment from the Buddha.

Everything in this world is created from the self. If I make up my mind and just do it, everything is possible. After three thousand, ten thousand prostrations you gain confidence, and from there you earn the necessary calluses to attain wisdom.

When Keun Sunim first assigned three thousand prostrations to anyone he would have you do them all at once, without moving from the spot right where you stood. He had you do them all right then without having the chance to drink any water or sit down or go to the bathroom or anything else. That was how much care he must have wanted us to put into them.

Figure 7.1. At Baengnyeonam of Haeinsa, where Keun Sunim lived. It is the place where many devotees came to meet Keun Sunim and perform three thousand prostrations. Author provided.

Chapter 8

Eternal Moments

The Ringing Bells of Nirvana

It was the late fall of 1993, the Gayasan forest ablaze in fall colors, just before the light of late autumn had reached the windowsill. Keun Sunim passed into Nirvana at the Haeinsa Toeseoldang, on November 4th.

> Deceiving people all my life,
> My sins outweigh Mount Sumeru.
> Falling into hell alive, my grief divides into ten thousand pieces.
> Spouting forth a crimson wheel, it hangs upon the blue mountain.

"Practice hard" is what he said before leaving this death poem.

One of the monks watching over him by his side, Wonyung Sunim, asked, "When Sunim leaves, on whom should we rely?" He replied, "The *Seonmun jeongno* [Seongcheol Sunim's work, *The Orthodox Path of Seon*]."[1]

Fifty-eight years ordained, of secular age eighty-two. With the tolling of the Nirvana bell, Gayasan Haeinsa fell into a deep silence. His funeral was November 10, 1993.

After Keun Sunim's death, mourners began to gather before the funeral altar had even been built. At first it was the hikers who had come to climb Gayasan, and as time passed the devotees in the area began to gather. In the afternoon, obituaries and articles began to blanket the newspapers. That night and the next day, many reporters arrived.

Monks and nuns from all over the country came to mourn and pay their sincere respects to the departed Keun Sunim. The monks of his practice community recited the *Diamond Sutra* in Gunghyeondang, where his funeral portrait was placed. The grieving hearts of the monks, nuns, and devotees who had come to pay condolences filled Haeinsa to the brim.

In the morning, a quiet rain began to fall. Despite the grim weather devotees continued to gather to remember Keun Sunim's passing.

At 11 a.m., in the front courtyard of the pavilion of Gugwangru, the sending-off ceremony began with five chimes of the great bell and lasted two hours. It had come time for Keun Sunim to leave through the mountain gate that had been his refuge for fifty-eight years. Sunim's body was raised on a litter covered with yellow chrysanthemums, and the gathered mourners followed behind as it was borne to the funeral pyre.

A great flag and Keun Sunim's funeral portrait led the procession, and behind them followed other great masters, monks, nuns, and devotees, carrying over a thousand banners of mourning. The devotees who filled the mountain path from end to end grieved and wept with one voice. The people formed a great ocean, flowing through the trees and over the hills.

In the middle of the cremation site, the funeral platform was fashioned to resemble an enormous lotus flower. The bhiksunis, pouring all of their devotion and sincerity into their work, had adorned the pyre in paper lotus petals.

The body was pushed into the entrance of the lotus pyre, and Keun Sunim's head disciples, Cheonje Sunim and Wontaek Sunim, were the last to take up pieces of kindling and block the opening.

Once the monks' chanting ceremony had concluded, representative monks from the Jogye Order and from Keun Sunim's peers lit cotton torches. Together, with one motion on the shout of "Alight!" they placed the flames within the lotus pyre. And at the same time, the monks who were watching over the cremation called out together.

"Sunim! Fire is entering your house. Come outside."

"Sunim! Fire is entering your house. Come outside."

"Sunim! Fire is entering your house. Come outside."

The flowering sparks of flame that flew up to the sky from Keun Sunim's lotus pyre let out a red light that hung upon the blue mountain. It was just as in the death poem that Keun Sunim had left behind in his last moment.

Keun Sunim's sending-off ceremony, his procession to the funeral pyre, the sound of chanting beginning to disappear, and the beautiful changing colors of fall seeming to have lost their light; in the days following, all the leaves in the mountain came falling down.

I have borrowed these words from Wontaek Sunim's *Story of Seongcheol Sunim's Attendant* [*Sibong Ilgi*]. This is because I was not able to attend Keun Sunim's funeral ceremony or his cremation. After Keun Sunim passed I began to see articles speculating about me, his daughter, and about my name—*Bulpil*, unnecessary—and so I did not show my face once until the ceremony was over. I was the one who had to be the closest to Keun Sunim, but also the furthest away.

Climbing up over Geumganggul and past two mountain ridges, I could see Keun Sunim's lotus pyre. As I watched the flame, Keun Sunim's final presence, I raised not three but nine prostrations toward him. Nine bows promising, past, present, and future, three ages together, that we would meet again.

"I served you poorly in this life, so I will meet you again in the next."

Keun Sunim turned to me and said this shortly before he passed, "Once I'm gone, you think you're ever gonna meet someone like me again?"

Those words approached me from deep within my heart, surrounding me like the blue flames rising from the burning lotus pyre. Thinking of the events of just that one day makes my heart rip open and my innards come to pieces, but faced with the thought of that karmic link, stretching through thousands of lifetimes, a single sigh could become a wind, and a tear could become an ocean; and still there would be sighs and tears left.

"I will open my mind's eye in the ocean of life and death, and meet you again as a being of eternal freedom. Sunim, I want to see you. Where are you?"

As the countless grieved during the seven-day mourning period, seven times there were miraculous occurrences of light in the mountain behind Toeseoldang and Baengnyeonam, shocking and moving the assembled masses. Thirty thousand people had gathered at Keun Sunim's funeral pyre, creating a human sea that stretched out thirty *li*, a solemnly majestic sight that could not be described in words.

After the cremation, around a hundred pieces of sacred relics were gathered, and as they were distributed during a Dharma sermon during the forty-nine-day ceremony, over one million devotees, eclipsing religion itself, gathered to admire the sight, a rarest of rare moments in Buddhist history.

My Resolve Will Not Waver

After Keun Sunim's passing many people asked, "What kind of person was he?"

Whenever I get this sort of question I think of the resolve prayer Keun Sunim wrote in his younger days. Of the many writings Keun Sunim penned during his life, I believe this prayer is the one that depicts best how Keun Sunim lived his life. I keep it hanging in the living quarters of Simgeomdang and read it again from time to time.

Having written down these principles, Keun Sunim lived his whole life by them, never straying from them for a moment. He was a man who held an iron resolve to cultivate his mind and governed himself upon a razor's edge. There are no words that can take his place.

Keun Sunim was rigorous with the promises he made to himself. When he drew a line, the sky could fall and it would not waver. That meticulous dedication in keeping his oath to himself must have been what allowed him to keep such discipline for a lifetime.

During his brief stay at Geumganggul, a person who had devoted himself to Keun Sunim as if he were his own father came by to visit him. Keun Sunim was out doing walking meditation at that moment, so I went to him and asked, "Even if you are outside, it would be good if you received his greeting."

Keun Sunim shouted over at me in response, "You must keep the promises you make with yourself!"

It was during the time he had resolved not to meet with anyone.

He's so thorough that he makes no exceptions for anyone, I thought to myself.

Within his scolding I saw both punishment and lesson.

It was when Keun Sunim was the head of the Jogye Order and spiritual master of Haeinsa. When his head disciple Cheonje Sunim showed intent of becoming the abbot of Haeinsa, he asked him, "I am the spiritual master and you are my disciple. If I were to make my own disciple the abbot, would the assembly ever listen to me? Do you have to become abbot?" Faced with those words, Cheonje Sunim was said to have folded any dreams of becoming abbot outright. One can catch a glimpse of Keun Sunim's rigor in a teaching written in the practice notes Cheonje Sunim took during his ten years as a postulant.

The hardest thing is to pretend you don't know when you do.
The bravest thing is to lose when you are right.
The most difficult thing to learn is to take on the faults of others.
The mightiest person in the world is the one who respects
every other.

Even when he took his meals, he would eat just one piece of dried seaweed, one piece of carrot, and one bowl of rice. He would teach his attendants, "Even beans can be bigger or smaller, so weigh each of them before you eat." He observed a no-salt diet his entire life, without a single exception.

Once, when I had a new prayer cushion made for him, he scolded me, "My room is so small, what else do you want to put in it?" I ended up taking it back down the mountain. When he had gotten to be quite old, I brought him a nice light blanket and again got a telling off: "Must I sleep under a silk blanket like this? Take it away!" The piercing gaze of his refusal is something I can't forget.

He didn't even own a notebook to write memos in. He wrote notes on the back of the pages from a daily calendar of an Oriental medicine center. Even for longer writings he would only occasionally use lined paper; usually he would just write on calendar pages or on a scrap of blank paper.

His trash, too, he wouldn't just throw away. Once he used a Q-tip he would save it and use it again until he couldn't possibly anymore, and he organized everything before it went into the trash can. Whenever I think of Keun Sunim I can't help but look at my own life and wonder if I'm living it right.

One time I went up the mountain, he was in the middle of scolding an attendant. He told me it was because he threw away a toothpick he had been using, so I tried to stand up for him.

"Isn't it dirty to use one you've already used?"

"What? Why do you wash your spoon and eat with it again? What's different between this and that?"

He had been whittling down that little toothpick to use again and again, until it was so small he couldn't even pick it up. When I went on my first sacred pilgrimage to India and brought him back an ivory statue of the Buddha, he wouldn't accept it, saying, "You're merciless. Isn't this Buddha made of elephant bones?" He must have been the most uncompromising person in the world, and that's probably why he studied so fiercely as well. I heard that in his youth, once he went into meditation he would stay there for so long that his cushion would be moldy by the time he finished.

He had forgotten what lying down was, until it was more difficult for him than sitting. One time, while I was at an exhibition of Kim Hoseok's portraits of Keun Sunim, I saw one portrait of him laying down. I asked, "Do you think that drawing is correct, when he's spent his whole life sitting up?" and I made them take it down.

An incident where he saw a devotee throwing away a watermelon rind with some red flesh still on it and made her pick it up and eat it again became a popular story in town. Monk, nun, or layperson, he was that strict. When female devotees on their first visit to the monastery would come dangling with earrings and necklaces, he would berate them, saying, "Are you trying to seduce a monk?" From then on, only those wearing gray robes were allowed to walk through Baengnyeonam.

Wanting to one day own a piece of writing in his own hand, I pleaded with him, "Give me one too"; but he refused, telling me, "You shouldn't have what others don't." So today I don't own anything in his handwriting that he wrote with me in mind.

When his library Janggyeonggak, which housed a large collection of his scriptures, had to be torn down and rebuilt, Keun Sunim came to stay at Geumganggul for the first time. He had never even passed by, in the ten years since Geumganggul was built. Though there wasn't any fitting place for him to stay there, more than anything it had been the moving of his treasured book collection that made him visit for a while.

He stayed there for about six months before returning to Toeseoldang. Looking back, the only time I was together with Keun Sunim in one place since the day I was born was just those few months. I say we were together, but he stayed in Munsuwon, which is the meditation hall at Geumganggul, with four attendant monks, just as he did at Baengnyeonam, and I could not go there unless Keun Sunim asked for me.

A Place Outside Time and Space, Geoboesa

Keun Sunim's family home had long since fallen apart, with only the land being preserved, but September 9, 1996, three years after his passing, there was a ground-breaking ceremony for a restoration of his home, grandly celebrated in the middle of a crowd of monks, devotees, and residents of the county.

Wontaek Sunim undertook the task of building Keun Sunim's relic tower at Haeinsa, and I took on the project of restoring his birth home, since it was my birth home as well. Having taken on this piece of home-work, I traveled with some Seongnamsa nuns to the birth site of the great monk Yujeong in Miryang near Seongnamsa. Venerable Yujeong's birth site had been restored the year before, but because it was maintained by the county and had no groundskeeper who lived on-site, there were some spots here and there that left something to be desired. With my restoration task in mind, I paid close attention to these small details.

Looking around the birth homes of the writers Yunseondo and Jeongcheol, both famous historic sites, I felt my shoulders grow heavy. Even after many years the sites were well organized and preserved in good shape. There were definitely lessons to be learned from these historic sites with such storied pasts.

When we visited his birth site, the original house had of course crumbled, but the beautiful forest that had stood around the Gyeongho Lake had been cleared to the lakebed in the Nam River Dam construction. The mountains that faced the house on either side, which would bloom with azaleas in the spring, were now unrecognizable because of a newly opened highway tunnel. It was just like an old saying: mulberry fields had transformed into an ocean. It had been decades since I had left my own home, so what could I have to say?

Coming to this place that was Keun Sunim's birthplace and my own, there was nearly no one in the area who was familiar with the Dharma. Reminded of the saying that a beacon does not shine on its own base, I felt deeply ashamed. As I thought ahead, standing in that place with no home and no monastery, there seemed to be much to do indeed.

First things first, restoring the site was the most urgent task. Some passerby, following who knows what kind of rumor, saw me standing in the work site and asked me, "They said that Seongcheol Sunim's daughter Bulpil Sunim is here. Where is she?" I told him, "She's at Haeinsa."

I slept in a forty-square-meter shipping container and worked in the open field, with no trees to shade me from the sun. Layman Gubong sent over many white pines and other trees that Keun Sunim favored. Planting trees in that wide empty nothing was quite a big undertaking. The one and a half acres of land that my grandfather left in my name took thousands of trucks worth of gravel and sand to fill.

Once I've started something, I'm the kind of person who finishes it, no matter what anyone says. When I'm doing construction, all I can see is stones; when I'm landscaping, I only see trees. When we began building the stone fence around the site, I even visited the Huiwon Garden, which I had heard has the best stone fences in Korea.

Work just needs to get done. My natural work pace is like an express train. Whatever it is I've decided on, I like to get it done right away and wash my hands of it, so the restoration project was completed within three years. One monk who came to look around greeted me by saying,

"It's incredible, you've finished something in three years that couldn't have been accomplished in ten!"

The birth home site looks just like its old self, with the women's quarters in the center and the men's quarters to the east. There is a historic exhibit on the west side, and toward the front in the center is a tall, pointed gate that links the long stone fence on either side. Taking the pen name of my grandfather, we named the central quarters "Yuleun Gogeo" and the men's house "Yuleunjae."

In Buddhism, the word *geop* [Sk. *kalpa*]refers to a very long, long time. One *geop* is the time it would take for a celestial woman, who comes down from the heavens once every hundred years, to wear a boulder sixteen kilometers wide down to nothing by brushing against it with the tip of her garment. How long such a time would be is hard to imagine. *Geoboe* [beyond a *geop*] means that something is outside of that very long, long time and so represents an absolute world, which transcends time and space.

At Geoboesa, the Dharma Hall houses the likeness of the Buddha in the center and Keun Sunim's portrait to the west; in the front courtyard there is a statue of Keun Sunim. To the east there is the meditation hall,

Figure 8.1. A view of Geoboesa. Author provided.

Sanggeumdang, the living quarters, Jeongodang, and at the entrance we built a raised pavilion, Byeokhaeru.

What I felt all throughout the building of the birth home and Geoboesa was that the construction flowed smoothly along like water through the power of Keun Sunim's achievements and merit. Every time the work met a setback or an issue, the people who helped us through were always those who had respected and followed Keun Sunim while he was alive.

Layman Gubong had always served Keun Sunim like his own parent. After becoming close with Keun Sunim while he was holding a forty-nine-day ceremony for his father at Baengnyeonam, he and his wife Laywoman Jeonghaengin performed five hundred prostrations and recited the Heroic March dharani every day for thirty-two years without exception. Even now, over seventy years old, they still do 108 prostrations a day.

After hearing that Baengnyeonam was too cold for an old man to live, Layman Gubong arranged a quiet dwelling at the hermitage of Hwaseungwon in Busan where Keun Sunim could live undisturbed. Keun Sunim named this place Geoboesa, and every year he would go down to stay there in November, returning to Baengnyeonam in May. The temple now named Geoboe takes its name from that dwelling.

Around a month before all the construction was finished, we invited cultural ministers and professors from Sancheong, Hamyang, Jinju, and Hapcheon for a spiritual ceremony. Some one hundred Confucian scholars were present as well, and they praised me saying, "Now that Bulpil Sunim has been pious to her grandfather and pious to Seongcheol Sunim, she's more excellent than Father Kim Daegeon!"[2]

Some people ask how a person who meditates all the time has so many opinions about building houses, but it's not something I ever learned. I work by intuition, so if something seems good I just push forward with it. My vocation master picked me as the worst worker among her disciples, but when she came to see Geumganggul once it was finished, she seemed quite surprised! When we repaired Simgeomdang, too, she said, "Anyone can prune a tree, but only Bulpil can do it so neatly!"

When Keun Sunim's old belongings started being brought into Geoboesa, I decided, *This is not my place to live.* Thinking that Keun Sunim's disciple should be the one to watch over the temple, I called Wontaek Sunim right away and asked him to take over before the opening, but he declined, saying, "How can I accept when you've worked so hard to build it?" He refused three more times, so I said, "Then are you going to leave Geoboesa to become the temple of Keun Sunim's daughter?" to which he finally had nothing left to say.

It was a spring day, March 30, 2001.

We invited the head of the Jogye Order, as well as monks, nuns, and laypeople from the entire Buddhist community, and other dignitaries, for the opening ceremony, when suddenly out of nowhere a heavy snow began to fall, transforming the surrounding landscape into a snowy vista in the blink of an eye. The attending dignitaries and monks were in for quite a bit of inconvenience with the blizzard and the sudden cold. Some said the snow was an auspicious sign that showed the divine blessing of the ceremony, while one of the dignitaries said, "Keun Sunim must have sent the snow as a scolding, because we're stirring things up too much by restoring his birth home and erecting a statue of him." And when the ceremony ended and the weather cleared, they said, "Keun Sunim's anger must have cooled."

I give my thanks to all of the area residents, Sancheong County, Governor Yeongsun Kwon, and Jaegun Lee, for their cooperation and help in completing the birth home construction, and I thank the supporters who dedicated their sincere care to this project.

I wrote these words when I returned to Geumganggul after the dedication ceremony for the birth home site and Geoboesa. From the day of the ceremony onward I completely removed myself from any matters relating to Geoboesa, and these days I don't even think of it as something I was responsible for. But the frequency with which I've been asked, "Sunim, why have you become so old?" since then probably owes to the trouble I went through during that time.

Wontaek Sunim erected a stupa to house Keun Sunim's relics at Haeinsa. Inhong Sunim, who was my vocation master while she lived, spoke thusly about Wontaek Sunim: "He is a devoted disciple who never once left Keun Sunim's side and served him well in life and after death with the faith and dedication he held for him. He is a person who was born to serve Keun Sunim."

I'm sure she wasn't the only one to think so. After graduating in international relations from Yonsei University, he was ordained at twenty-eight with Keun Sunim as his vocation master and served at his side for twenty years. Even after Keun Sunim's death, he has continued to devote himself for another twenty years by publishing books, building a relic stupa, and founding the Baengnyeon Cultural Foundation, so to describe him as a person born for Keun Sunim is true a hundred times over.

There was one time I went up to Baengnyeonam with a disciple. There wasn't a good place for us to wait around until Keun Sunim gave us permission to visit, so we were in Wontaek Sunim's room. It was while he was living as Keun Sunim's attendant and organizing his manuscripts, so it was quite messy. I told my disciple, "Try neatening it up a little," and I had her clean up the room. But later when Wontaek Sunim saw what we had done, he told me, "My room has order within disorder." At that moment it occurred to me that though he might seem mild on the outside, he was a very scary person on the inside.

When Wontaek Sunim became the financial manager at Haeinsa, Keun Sunim told him, "Your life needs to be just like your room." It must have been a request for him to do things differently from the others, to *live by the order you create.* Then he simply said, "Don't ever use the big temple's money, just take Baengnyeonam's money for what you need."

It is probably because Wontaek Sunim performed practice through organizing Keun Sunim's manuscripts, listening to lecture tapes until his ears grew numb, that he was able to write his autobiography, *Story of Seongcheol Sunim's Attendant*, so beautifully. If he hadn't possessed such self-discipline, he couldn't have been able to so vividly depict Keun Sunim's deep inner nature. Even today, Wontaek Sunim sends his respect and reminiscence for his teacher in these words: "I said that I served him with my whole heart, but looking back, it feels like I saw Keun Sunim but I still did not see him, met him but still did not meet him."

Wontaek Sunim, who for long years endured countless scoldings from Keun Sunim, even at this moment is running around busily day and night to prepare for the one hundredth anniversary of Keun Sunim's birth. How could words express that utmost devotion and care?

March 1997, a Blossoming Spring Day

Watching Keun Sunim's funeral, I made up my mind to leave everything behind to practice in the deep mountains and returned to the hall of Simgeomdang at Seongnamsa. Over twenty years had passed since the times of intensive practice with the senior nuns and my companions in my youth, but Simgeomdang looked the same as it had then.

When I told Inhong Sunim, who was now approaching ninety years of age, that I would be practicing at Simgeomdang, she welcomed me with these words: "You might not be the Tiger of Gayasan, but you can be the Tiger of Gajisan. Practice well."[3]

Since then I've spent my winter and summer retreat every year at Simgeomdang. Every retreat period I'd drop by her living quarters and greet my teacher.

"Sunim, do you still have *hwadu*?"

When my teacher was feeling energetic and in good spirits, she would smile and give me a thumbs-up, but when she was tired or in pain, she would ask, "Do I look like I don't have *hwadu*?"

In 1996, the last day of the lunar year, she looked especially out of sorts.

"Life and death are one and the same, so I'd like to go when my mind and body are comfortable."

When I heard those words, I called Beophui Sunim, Hyunmuk Sunim, Beobyong Sunim, and Domun Sunim. Hyejeong Sunim, the abbess, also received word and came. When we had all gathered, my teacher said, "Get ready. I've lived a long time."

She had felt that her karmic link to the world was reaching its end. All of us, even Beophui Sunim, the pious disciple who had followed Inhong Sunim like a shadow ever since she became a nun at Hongjesa, could do nothing but silently look on.

Beophui Sunim, with a pleading heart, implored, "Sunim, when today is over you'll be ninety. Go in the springtime, when it is flowering and warm." Just as we always did, we all sang the popular song "Old Hwangseong" to cheer our teacher up. Sunim laughed and waved her hands happily.

The tiger-nun, who used to prowl every corner of the monastery and hand out admonishments in a thundering voice, now gone without a trace, she looked as innocent and happy as a young child. All attachments to the self had fallen away. She carefully looked around at each of us.

When we asked, "What do we do when you go, Sunim?" she replied, "Come together as a monastery and protect Seongnamsa well."

"What does a practitioner have besides *hwadu*? Even when you die you must go with your *hwadu*."

When my teacher was seventy-two, she went up to Sangmujuam deep in Jirisan with only a single attendant, practicing in that cold and barren place with a final resolve. Living in her quarters at Seongnamsa, she never missed the morning service, and even once she passed eighty she always did 108 prostrations at the evening service. During the intensive practice she carried the bamboo clapper, reprimanded us like a tiger to stay awake, and performed 3,000-prostration practice with us even past the age of seventy. Her whole life she put into action her motto, "Whenever you are lying down comfortably, think of the sentient beings who suffer the pain of hell."

Even in her old age, my teacher was always listening to Keun Sunim's Dharma talks. On her bookshelf she kept a collection of his lectures and tape recordings, and she especially enjoyed listening to his lectures on the *Zhengdaoge* and the *Platform Sutra by the Sixth Patriarch*.

"Don't live on your own, live together and practice in a community." This was what my teacher would always say.

It was a flowering spring day the following year, March 8, 1997, of the lunar calendar. Watched over by us, her disciples, Sunim quietly entered into Nirvana. Her secular age was ninety, Dharma age fifty-six.

> I should walk the path where the Buddhas of the past, present,
>   and future have gone.
> Life in Samsara for ninety years is nothing but an illusory dream.
> In that place where a lonely boat departs,
> Only the round moon shines brightly in the sky.

It has been fifteen years since my vocation master passed, leaving behind this death poem. My teacher! Who was stricter on herself, more exacting to her practice and principles than anybody. Who, in a time when nuns struggled to have a presence, raised up their stature, laboring tirelessly to instill in them the mindset of the practitioner, and dedicated herself to educate future generations. She who always lived as a humble practitioner with no attachments, whose only bequeathals to us were a statue of the Buddha and her admonitions, and whose only possession was the rosary that hung around her neck.

I picture her face in her favorite teacup. Now that she has gone, her only image is a photo on a piece of paper.

"Shouldn't you practice hard and at least become the Tiger of Gajisan?" I miss that admonishment and spirit, as stern and rigorous as a column of ice. "Come together as a monastery and protect Seongnamsa well." Her last words hover in my ears.

When the mountains and springs regained their life and the brightly budding green leaves brought the news of spring to Gajisan, ten years after her passing, her biography, *Leaving the Path to Find the Path*, which held intact the complete story of my teacher's life, was published. I miss her.

It has been a long time since my teacher passed away, but Seongnamsa still carries on its renown as a refuge for practice and meditation. The leaders of Seongnamsa, meditation hall master Beophui Sunim, rector Hyunmuk Sunim, former abbesses Beobyong and Domun Sunim, and current abbess Dosu Sunim, and many others live together in harmony, always reflecting on themselves as practitioners and attentively upholding the will of the assembly. In Simgeomdang, Jeongsuwon, and Geumdang, bright-eyed postulants have gathered from every direction, and during the retreats they continue a practice reminiscent of the *gyeolsa*.

Not a single member is absent at the dawn service, which bolsters the determination of every practitioner present, and at meal times the whole assembly gathers to continue the tradition of eating together. Upholding Inhong Sunim's teaching, "If you do not practice, you are not a practitioner," Geumdang has become a place for *gyeolsa* year-round, and the assembly lives diligently in order to continue the legacy of the Buddha's wisdom.

Since she opened the monastery for the education of the next generation of nuns in 1957, the disciples and grand-disciples, and even great-grand-disciples who have become nuns at Seongnamsa are more than three hundred, and the wandering nuns who have practiced in Simgeomdang, Jeongsuwon, and Geumdang number over 1,500. And my vocation master, who since the founding of Seongnamsa had completed the greatest temple construction and fostered the greatest number of students of any bhiksuni, has now become part of Korean Buddhism's history.

From Eternity to Eternity

I like the winter mountains.

When the sun rises in the morning and the wind blows, the tree trunks rattle and the whole earth seems to shake. I like that cold winter sunlight, which pierces through to the deepest parts of my heart as it filters through the bamboo thickets that shelter the base of the mountain.

Drinking a cup of tea in the morning and looking out my window, the red sun rises in the east and a male pheasant, proudly showing off his presence, rests in the grass for half an hour or so, as if he is meditating. The mountain magpies and pigeons follow him in a line to enjoy the fresh morning on the lawn.

The ever-peaceful Simgeomdang. The footsteps of those from the outside world do not reach here, so it feels like a place outside of space and time. In this place, with determined spirits, we held the three-year *gyeolsa* and practiced intensively for a hundred days. Where are the nuns who practiced with me in those days? There are some who I will never see again, and some who are still alive.

"Sitting until they attain enlightenment, the one who dies on the meditation cushion is the happiest." Keun Sunim would say this often. As long as my health permits me to walk, I will spend my retreats at Simgeomdang, and I would like to finish things quietly, here.

Last year, during the winter retreat, I received word of Myoeom Sunim's passing. Visiting Bongnyeongsa, where she stayed, I offered a cup of tea on the altar of the Dharma Hall where her casket was housed, and before I knew it, as I turned away, tears began to fall from my eyes. When I had visited her in the hospital a month before she passed away, she had greeted us happily. She was in such good spirits, saying she would come to visit Seongnamsa in the spring, and now she has returned to a single fistful of earth.

That day, as I returned to Simgeomdang, the days of my life from the moment I first met her when I was thirteen years old passed before my eyes like a panorama.

I ask myself, "In this life, which stretches from eternity to eternity, have you been unashamed and true to your practice?"

While they were living, Cheongdam Sunim, Jaun Sunim, and other elder monks would often look at me and say, "How good would it have been if you were a boy?" Even Elder Jeonghaeng Sunim, whom I would visit at Samseonam in Haeinsa, would forever lament, "Wouldn't it have been great if you were a man?" Just as they said, what would have been different if I were a man? When I think of the different paths in my life it's certain that I was a bhiksu in my past life. So then why did I become a bhiksuni?

When I was younger, in my thirties, I once told Keun Sunim this as we were standing in the Toeseoldang garden, looking out onto faraway Namsan: "In my next life I'll be reborn as a great man and become the spiritual master of Haeinsa."

Figure 8.2. Having left home at twenty, I am now in my seventies. Photo by Kim Minsook.

"It takes more than ordinary practice to become the spiritual master of a monastery."

I have lived my life always holding those words, which encouraged rather than rebuked me, close to my heart. The rest of my life, the rest of my time here, and with all the desperate effort of my lives to come, I will walk the path toward eternal freedom.

Epilogue

A Dedication Poem for Keun Sunim

"Let's look at ourselves properly." These were the words Keun Sunim was most fond of in his lifetime. I wanted to erect a plaque with a poem for him before he died, but I wasn't able to. Perhaps I can finally commemorate him by placing this writing at the close of this book.

When Keun Sunim was elected to become the seventh patriarch of the Korean Buddhist Jogye Order in 1981, he published a Dharma speech in Korean hangul for Buddha's Birthday. Since then, the Dharma writings released by the patriarch at the beginning or end of every new year have been in Korean, not Chinese characters. "Let's Look at Ourselves Properly" is Keun Sunim's Dharma writing from the Buddha's Birthday in 1982.

What more is there to do besides facing your own self-nature head-on? To those who read this book, I wish to send this final message in Keun Sunim's words.

Let's look at ourselves properly.
You have already been saved.
You have always been a Buddha.
You are always overflowing with happiness and majesty. Paradise
    and heaven are merely the sleeping babbles of a dreamer.
Let's look at ourselves properly.
You eclipse time and space, and are eternal and infinite. While
    the sky may crumble and the earth disappear, you are per-
    petual and unchanging. With form or without, all things
    in the universe are you. So the shining stars, the dancing
    butterflies, all these things are you.
Let's look at ourselves properly.

Every truth is held within you. To seek yourself outside of
  yourself would be to seek water outside of the sea.
Let's look at ourselves properly.
You are eternal and have no end. Those who do not know
  themselves worry about the end of the world and wander
  lost in fear.
Let's look at ourselves properly.
  . . .
The Buddha did not come to save this world; he came to teach
  us that this world has already been saved.
We are truly happy to live within this great truth.
Let us all celebrate for many years to come.

Notes

Epigraph

1. All notes are by the translator. *Sunim* (or Seunim) is the honorific title for both monks and nuns in Korea. Keun Sunim, a special honorific reserved for esteemed or elder sunims, here unspecified, refers to Seongcheol Keun Sunim, a legendary patriarch of Korean Buddhism and the author's father.

Author's Preface

1. Geumganggul is the name of the temple where the author lives, literally, "Hermitage of Diamond," that is, unbreakable wisdom.

Chapter 1. Karmic Connection: Where Will We Meet Again, and as What?

1. Traditional Korean buildings with tiled roofs, commonly used in Buddhist temples.

2. These two texts set the foundation for Confucian primary school learning and classical Chinese literacy (the written lingua franca of East Asia) during the Joseon dynasty (1392–1897). (Neo-)Confucianism was the state religion and guiding ideology during the Joseon dynasty, resulting in the suppression of Buddhism to remote temples deep in Korea's mountains.

3. A person's age is considered to be one at birth in Korea to account for time in the womb. Although the original text refers to her age as six, this would be five for readers outside Korea.

4. *Keun* is an adjective meaning "large" or "great." Keun Sunim (Master Sunim) here refers to Seongcheol Sunim, Bulpil Sunim's (the author's) father and

teacher. The author addresses him as Keun Sunim throughout the work, which the translation has respected.

5. Gyeongheo (1846–1912) was a modern Seon master. He has been credited with trying to revive the tradition of the *hwadu* observance method—the meditation method described in this work—that had been passed down through the Joseon dynasty.

6. In Korean, the suffix *-sa* refers to a monastery, while the suffix *-am* generally refers to a hermitage—a smaller, more isolated temple adjoining a large temple. The suffix *-san* refers to a mountain. These suffixes have been included without translation for the most part to reduce redundancy.

7. Lee Eun-Sang (1903–1982) was a noted modern Korean poet.

8. Refers to Yujeong (honorific name Samyeongdang, 1544–1610), a Buddhist monk during the Joseon dynasty. He is famous for his heroic deeds during the Japanese invasion of 1592 and for being sent by royal decree to Japan to negotiate the retrieval of Korean captives when the war ended in 1604. Songun is his pen name.

9. Vinaya are the rules and regulations that a monk or nun swears to abide by in monastic life; a Vinaya master oversees the ordination ceremony when one enters nunhood.

10. The Bongamsa Pact, a practice community founded by Seongcheol Sunim and others in 1947, was a significant event in Korean Buddhist history that attempted to revive the traditional regulations of the Korean monastery system and to restore the essence of the Korean Seon Buddhism lineage, which had been affected by the Japanese colonial era.

11. According to the Buddhist theory of reincarnation, anybody in one's countless past lives could have been one's mother, father, or any other relation.

12. The Han River Bridge was detonated while four thousand refugees were crossing it, killing eight hundred. Destroying the bridge also trapped many South Korean military units north of the Han River. Being the only bridge that spanned the Han River in Seoul at the time, its destruction was a severe blow to the throngs of refugees attempting to flee south to avoid the fighting.

Chapter 2. Entering the Monastery:
Eternal Happiness and Temporal Happiness

1. Wonhyo (617–686) was a monk regarded as the greatest scholar and most prolific writer in the Korean Buddhist tradition.

2. Chinese *huatou* (話頭), Korean *hwadu*. Similar to Japanese koan. The *hwadu* is a short phrase about a paradoxical and illogical subject that is used as a subject of meditation to focus the mind; its use is common in the teachings of Chinese Chan Buddhism, Korean Seon, and Japanese Rinzai Zen.

3. Nanquan Puyuan (J. Nansen Fugan) (ca. 749–ca. 835) was a Chinese Chan Buddhist master in China during the Tang dynasty, who features in a number of koan (公案) collections. He was the student and Dharma successor of Master Mazu Daoyi (709–788).

4. The concentration of mental effort on paradoxical and illogical subjects called *hwadu* (critical phrase) and this investigation of the meaning in Chan/Seon/Zen practice helps to generate questions or "doubt," which is the force that drives this type of practice forward. Classical Chan texts consist of dialogues between masters and disciples surrounding the phrase, which is unique to Chan Buddhism. This use of *hwadu* meditation remains the principal type of meditation practiced in contemporary Korean Seon Buddhism. See Robert Buswell, *The Zen Monastic Experience* (Princeton: Princeton University Press, 1992), especially 149–160.

5. This Hundred-Day Dharma talk is one of the central summaries of Seongcheol Sunim's teachings. It was published later and excited the public with a new, relevant Buddhism for a fast-modernizing Korea that synthesized modern science, Buddhism, and current affairs.

6. Deeply patriarchal, Confucianism stressed primogeniture—the eldest son was the next head of household, inherited property, and was expected to take care of his parents in old age—and the importance of restraint in showing emotion.

7. The root of the white bellflower, related to ginseng, is popular for its medicinal properties.

8. The sixtieth birthday, or *hwangap*, has special importance in Korea as one of the two most important birthdays, along with the first birthday, and the celebration is traditionally thrown by the eldest son.

9. *Samguk Yusa* is a collection of historical accounts, legends, and folktales of the Three Kingdoms of Korea (Goguryeo, Baekje, and Silla), composed by the monk Ilyeon (1206–1289) during the Goryeo dynasty.

10. See note 2 in chapter 1.

11. Yeongga is the Korean pronunciation of the Chinese Yongjia.

12. Han Yongun (1879–1944) was a writer, poet, revolutionary thinker, and Buddhist monk of twentieth-century Korea during Japanese colonial rule. His aforementioned essay on the book *Tale of the Vegetable Roots*, a book of spiritual wisdom applied to everyday affairs by Hong Yingming (1572–1620), was very popular among Korean intellectuals at that time.

13. A famous koan attributed to Zhaozhou (778–897, J. Jōshū), a Chinese Zen master. When asked if a dog has Buddha-nature or not? Zhaozhou famously answers, "Wu" (*Mu* in Korean and Japanese, meaning "no" or "not"). A central tenet of Mahayana Buddhism is that all beings have the capacity to become Buddha, and his negation, implied to mean "nothingness," sets up the paradoxical doubt necessary for the *hwadu*.

14. Dahui Zonggao (1089–1163) was a Chinese Song dynasty Chan monk. His method of Chan practice called the *huatou* method had a profound influence

on Korean Seon Buddhism as the model method of meditation practice. *Hwadu* is the Korean pronunciation of *huatou*.

15. Kim Beomnin (1899–1964) was a former Buddhist monk who became active in the Korean Provisional Government in Shanghai and in the movement for independence from Japan. After the liberation of 1945, he became the minister of education and a congressman.

16. Choe Beomsul (1904–1979) was a former Buddhist monk of modern Korea who later disrobed, famous for his knowledge on ancient history and classical literature. Pen name Hyodang. He is also known for his teachings on Korean tea traditions.

17. Dongsan (1890–1964) was a renowned Seon master of modern Korea who served as the headmaster of Beomeosa in Busan.

18. A famously beautiful mountain located in what is now North Korea; it is approximately four hundred kilometers (250 miles) as the crow flies from the family home at Mukgokri, requiring travel through rugged mountains the entire way.

19. Meaning "Flower of Transcendence."

20. We wish to extend our sincerest gratitude to Clare You for helping us edit the poem.

21. Li Taibo (701–762), a poet of Tang dynasty China famous for his many poems about the moon.

22. The cycle of suffering through death and rebirth in which the material world is bound.

Chapter 3. Handwritten Sermon Notes:
You Are Inherently Buddha, Yet You Don't Know It

1. After the liberation from Japan after World War II, and especially after the Korean War ended in 1953, celibate monks sought to reassert what they perceived to be the indigenous lifeways of Korean Buddhism and to remove all traces of Japanese influence. The celibate monks launched a vigorous campaign against the married monks who had dominated the ecclesiastical hierarchy during the Japanese colonial period. See Buswell, *Zen Monastic Experience*, 30. The movement ranged from street demonstrations to court battles and sometimes physical confrontation.

2. Lord Mengchang (d. 279 BC) was a general and nobleman during the Warring States era of China, famous for supporting thousands of retainers.

3. The entire Buddhist scriptural canon.

4. *Sarira*, pearl or crystal-like objects purportedly found among the cremated ashes of Buddhist masters and venerated as relics.

5. Master Yongming (904–975) was a noted monk of the Fayan lineage in the Song dynasty.

Chapter 4. Life as a Postulant:
The Bushy-Haired Postulants' First Charge toward Enlightenment

1. Cheongnyangsa is a branch temple of nearby Haeinsa. Abandoned for a long time, it was refurbished several decades ago by Seongcheol Sunim's disciple monks. Though it appears that nuns lived there during the time the author started her serious meditation as a postulant, it is now a monks' temple.

2. See note 1 in chapter 3.

3. Because of logistical and legal reasons (e.g., laws against begging and vagrancy), these twelve austerities are not followed to the letter in modern practice; the spirit of the practice remains.

4. Simgeomdang is the name of a meditation hall, literally, "the hall of Searching for the Sword," where the sword represents the cutting away of ignorance.

5. The following meditation on "One Thing" is from Keun Sunim's Dharma notes.

6. Ilta (1929–1999) is a monk in modern Korea famous for his ardent ascetic practice and for his expertise in Vinaya. He is known for his practice of immolating his fingers.

7. This is a practice defined in the Vinaya, the monastic code of conduct laid out in early Buddhism. Nuns must live near monks, and monks are obligated to come teach the nuns every two weeks.

8. Early Buddhism, such as Vipassana practice, ends this hierarchy at the stage of "continuous awareness at all times." Chan/Zen/Seon, a later Buddhist development, introduced and emphasized the "ultimate mysterious enlightenment," which is only attained through Dharma transmission from an enlightened Seon master. This stage is seen as the perfection of enlightenment.

9. Yeongga is the Korean pronunciation of the Chinese Yongjia.

10. Maha Kasyapa (Sk. Mahākāśyapa) and Bhadra Kapilani (Sk. Bhadra-Kapilānī, P. Bhadda Kapilani) were married but agreed to a life of celibacy because of their shared pursuit of the Dharma. They later became ordained together and both became leading disciples of the Buddha. In Korean pronunciation, Bhadra Kapilani is referred to as "Myohyeonni" (a nun of extraordinary virtue), the suffix -ni meaning "bhiksuni."

Chapter 5. Seongnamsa Monastery:
The Tiger of Gajisan Becomes My Vocation Master

1. Hanshan (618–907) and Shide (J. Kanzan and Jittoku) are a commonly portrayed pair in Chan/Seon Buddhism.

2. A Joseon dynasty scholar who was executed after participating in an attempt to dethrone Emperor Sejo and restore his predecessor, Danjong.

3. These eight rules are contained in the Vinaya and are given to candidates at the time of full bhiksuni ordination; the list includes instructions for the nuns to bow to monks no matter how novice the monk or how senior the nun; to not point out the shortcomings of monks; to not dispute with them; and so on. Modern scholars largely contend that these misogynistic rules were written not by the Sakyamuni (Sk. Śākyamuni) Buddha but were included later by conservative monks.

4. A round, handheld wooden bell used to accompany chanting.

Chapter 6. Practice: In Search of the Path to Eternal Freedom

1. Literal meaning, "first turning of the Dharma wheel." Here the author alludes to the Buddha's first sermon; in a way it was a revelation of what he had awoken to during his ten-year intensive retreat. The author suggests that her father had attained enlightenment during the time and this was the First Sermon after that.

2. Go (Kr. *baduk*) is a traditional strategy board game in which players capture territory on a board using black and white stones.

3. The monastic code of conduct prohibits singing.

4. See note 1 in chapter 3.

Chapter 8. Eternal Moments

1. *Seonmun jeongno* is a masterpiece by Seongcheol Sunim, published in 1981. An English translation is available: *The Orthodox Path of Seon* translated by Juhn Young Ahn. Seoul: Jogye Order of Korean Buddhism, 2022.

2. Kim Daegeon (1822–1846) was the first Catholic priest of Korea, who was martyred in 1846 due to anti-foreign policies at the time.

3. Keun Sunim was known as the "Tiger of Gayasan," while Inhong Sunim was called the "Tiger of Gajisan" after the mountains where their home temples were located.

Index

Printed in the USA
CPSIA information can be obtained
at www.ICGtesting.com
JSHW020931021224
74551JS00005BA/232

9 798855 800418